More than a Monologue

Volume II

CATHOLIC PRACTICE IN NORTH AMERICA

SERIES CO-EDITORS:

Angela Alaimo O'Donnell, Associate Director of the Francis and
    Ann Curran Center for American Catholic Studies, Fordham
    University
John C. Seitz, Assistant Professor, Theology Department, Fordham
    University

This series aims to contribute to the growing field of Catholic
studies through the publication of books devoted to the historical
and cultural study of Catholic practice in North America, from
the colonial period to the present. As the term "practice" suggests,
the series springs from a pressing need in the study of American
Catholicism for empirical investigations and creative explorations
and analyses of the contours of Catholic experience. In seeking to
provide more comprehensive maps of Catholic practice, this series
is committed to publishing works from diverse American locales,
including urban, suburban, and rural settings; ethnic, post-ethnic,
and transnational contexts; private and public sites; and seats of
power as well as the margins.

SERIES ADVISORY BOARD:

Emma Anderson, Ottawa University
Paul Contino, Pepperdine University
Kathleen Sprows Cummings, University of Notre Dame
James T. Fisher, Fordham University
Paul Mariani, Boston College
Thomas A. Tweed, University of Texas at Austin

More than
a Monologue

SEXUAL DIVERSITY AND THE CATHOLIC CHURCH

Volume II: Inquiry, Thought, and Expression

*Edited by J. Patrick Hornbeck II
and Michael A. Norko*

FORDHAM UNIVERSITY PRESS
New York   2014

Fordham University Press has no responsibility for the persistence or accuracy of URLs for external or third-party Internet websites referred to in this publication and does not guarantee that any content on such websites is, or will remain, accurate or appropriate.

Fordham University Press also publishes its books in a variety of electronic formats. Some content that appears in print may not be available in electronic books.

Library of Congress Cataloging-in-Publication Data is available from the publisher.

Printed in the United States of America

16 15 14   5 4 3 2 1

First edition

To
Susann and Patrick (J.P.H.)
and
Debra (M.A.N.)

Contents

Acknowledgments

This volume draws upon the tireless and generous work of scores of faculty members, advisors, administrators, staff, students, and volunteers from the four institutions that hosted the events of the More than a Monologue series of conferences: Fordham University, Union Theological Seminary, Yale Divinity School, and Fairfield University. To each of them we are enormously grateful, though they are too numerous to thank all of them by name. We do, however, especially recognize the leadership of Kelby Harrison at Union Theological Seminary and Paul Lakeland at Fairfield University in the planning efforts. We also extend our gratitude to all those who accepted invitations to speak at the four conferences for their witness and their presence in faith and spirit. To our communications consultants, Geoffrey Knox and Roberta Sklar, whose experienced advice advanced the success of all our endeavors, we express our profound thanks.

We have incurred an additional set of debts in the production of this volume. In particular, we extend our warmest appreciation to Amanda Alexander, our editorial assistant, for her stalwart contributions to the many tasks of editing and organizing the essays in this book, especially at its most chaotic moments. Terrence Tilley and the Fordham Department of Theology have provided invaluable intellectual and logistical assistance and support, for which we are most grateful. We have enjoyed the financial support of Fordham University's Office of Research for the production of this book and of the Arcus Foundation for the entire series of conferences, without which our reach would have exceeded our grasp. At Fordham University Press, we are indebted especially to Fredric Nachbaur for his constant encouragement and direction, as well as to all his colleagues and the members of the Press's editorial board. We also wish to acknowledge the profound assistance of the anonymous readers who offered insights and suggestions about this book.

Finally, we would have nothing to contribute without the scholarship, perseverance, and bounty of each of our authors, to whom we send our deepest thanks and congratulations. Among them we extend special thanks to Paul Lakeland for his guidance, wisdom, and encouragement not only of this volume but of the entire More than a Monologue project. To all those who have encouraged and supported our efforts, we acknowledge our many and rich blessings.

Furthermore, it is to be hoped that more of the laity will receive adequate theological formation and that some among them will dedicate themselves professionally to these studies and contribute to their advancement. But for the proper exercise of this role, the faithful, both clerical and lay, should be accorded a lawful freedom of inquiry, of thought, and of expression, tempered by humility and courage in whatever branch of study they have specialized.

—*Gaudium et Spes*, no. 62

Introduction

J. PATRICK HORNBECK II

Fordham University

MICHAEL A. NORKO

Yale University School of Medicine

This volume and its companion (subtitled *Voices of Our Times*[1]) represent an effort to memorialize and broaden the discussions begun in the scholarly presentations that comprised one focus of the More than a Monologue series of conferences that were held in the autumn of 2011.[2] The subtitle of this volume, *Inquiry, Thought, and Expression*, recognizes that these essays are presented in solidarity with the wisdom promulgated by the Second Vatican Council in *Gaudium et Spes* (the Pastoral Constitution of the Church in the Modern World).[3] The Council expressed its hope for the Catholic Church that the laity would pursue theological training and that they, along with the clergy, would contribute to the advancement of theological discourse. In order to do so, the Council affirmed that both clergy and laity "should be accorded a lawful freedom of inquiry, of thought, and of expression, tempered by humility and courage in whatever branch of study they have specialized."[4] These essays, which flow from many of the presentations from the conference series, constitute a faithful articulation of that ideal. The scholars represented here analyze difficult and challenging questions about sexual diversity and offer their thoughts and reflections as a way of moving the discourse forward. The Council intended theological discussions not to remain static but to respond dynamically to the "signs of our times"[5] in a rapidly changing world: "Theological research, while it deepens knowledge of revealed truth, should not lose contact with its own times, so that experts in various fields may be led to a deeper knowledge of the faith."[6]

The More than a Monologue conference series was a deliberate attempt by two Roman Catholic universities and two nondenominational divinity schools in New York and Connecticut to engage in open conversations about sexual diversity and the Catholic Church. The series was meant to represent *more* than the most often heard monologic voice, that of the institutional church, on the subject of lesbian, gay, bisexual, transgender, and queer (LGBTQ) issues and persons both within and outside of the church. It was hoped that the conferences also would be *more* than the monologic, but less often widely heard, voices of response and critique to institutional positions on LGBTQ matters. These volumes are an extension of that hope—a hope of and for the church that has undergirded the entire project.

The first conference was held at Fordham University, entitled "Learning to Listen: Voices of Sexual Diversity and the Catholic Church." The organizers believed that it was important to begin the More than a Monologue series with a day dedicated to active listening to a range of voices touched by questions of sexual diversity. Without listening, of course, dialogue is simply not possible. But in the introduction they wrote for the conference program, the organizers also highlighted the importance to Catholic faith of "the habit of attentive, capacious and responsive listening," a subject they described as having been "underscored" by Pope Benedict XVI in *Caritas in veritate*.[7] The Fordham conference set a tone of respectful and compassionate listening as a foundation for the consideration of personal narrative and the intricacies of human experience; these considerations were seen as fundamental to fruitful contemplation of sexual diversity in the context of the church. The essays by Michael Sepidoza Campos and Kelby Harrison in this volume were drawn from this conference.

The conference at Union Theological Seminary next addressed the topic of "Pro-Queer Life: Youth Suicide Crisis, Catholic Education, and the Souls of LGBTQ People." This event was an effort to focus attention on the suffering of LGBTQ people within society as a result of exclusion, bullying, and homophobia, including the significant problem of suicide by LGBTQ youth and young adults,[8] as well as on the role that educational institutions play or should play in mitigating or even reversing these dehumanizing effects and promoting genuine human flourishing. As the largest provider of private education in the United States,[9] the Catholic Church is well situated to influence the cultural, intellectual, spiritual, and moral development of young people. Speakers at the conference argued that this potential influence should include serious efforts to reverse the bullying and mistreatment of students on the basis of sexual orientation or gender expression. In their 1997 pastoral letter "Always Our Children," the U.S. bishops wrote, "It is the Church's responsibility to believe and teach this truth" that "[e]very person has an inherent dignity because he or she is created in God's image."[10] In many places, Catholic educational institutions get this right, in other places they need to do more, and in some places institutions may be complicit in the wounding of young LGBTQ persons. It was the goal of this conference to raise awareness of these realities and begin discussions that would lead to a more universally pastoral and life-giving approach in Catholic educational institutions and thus to a Christian model for the wider culture. The essays in this volume by Patrick S. Cheng and Fredrick S. Roden were derived from presentations at this conference.

The conference at Yale Divinity School was designed to explore the range of diverse Catholic viewpoints on same-sex marriage or marriage equality, as many prefer to label the topic. The conference title, "Same-Sex Marriage and the Catholic Church: Voices from Law, Religion, and the Pews," was meant to capture and present multiple sources of the diversity of Catholic thought as a response to the Connecticut bishops' apparent assertion of unanimity among all of the Catholic faithful in the state in condemning the Connecticut Supreme Court decision legalizing same-sex marriage in 2008.[11] Constitutional law scholars explored the legal terrain of arguments about same-sex marriage in the context of civil rights and religious freedom, especially within pluralistic societies. Religious scholars engaged discussions of same-sex marriage from the vantage points of ethics and theology, demonstrating again the multiplicity of Catholic thought on this topic. Completing the day were presentations of personal narratives, pastoral witness, and the challenges of campus and parish ministry to and with LGBTQ persons as examples of the lived experiences of lay Catholics. The essays in this volume drawn from the Yale conference are those of Michael John Perry, Patricia Beattie Jung, Joan Martin, and Lisa Sowle Cahill.

The concluding conference of the series was held at Fairfield University, on the topic of "The Care of Souls: Sexual Diversity, Celibacy, and Ministry." This was an effort to focus specifically on LGBTQ persons who are engaged in ministry in the church, both lay and ordained, to examine the challenges they encounter in those roles as well as the ways in which they are gifts to the church and of the church to the wider community. Speakers described the tensions between ministerial realities and the official positions of the institutional church—for seminarians, priests, and other ministers themselves, as well as for the people to whom they minister. But the conference also presented a description of the power and fruitfulness of support in religious community life, at least for lesbian nuns—a subject seldom explored in previous public discussions. In contradistinction to this was an examination of the perils of power as a basis for interaction in ecclesial relationships among an exclusively male ordained ministry. Essays in this volume by Mark D. Jordan, Elizabeth Dreyer, Jeannine Gramick, Jamie L. Manson, and Gerard Jacobitz were drawn from this conference.

Together, the four conferences were designed to provide a public forum for the Catholic apostolate and the wider public to enter into open discussions about sexual diversity and the church. Vatican II espoused a church that was open to such conversation and indeed required it. As the Council Fathers acknowledged in *Gaudium et Spes*, there are "treasures hidden in the various forms of human culture, by . . . which the nature of man himself is more clearly revealed and new roads to truth are opened." To promote the exchange between the church and the

> diverse cultures of people . . . the Church requires the special help of those who live in the world, are versed in different institutions and specialties, and grasp their innermost significance in the eyes of both believers and unbelievers. With the help of the Holy Spirit, it is the task of the entire People of God, especially pastors and theologians, to hear, distinguish and interpret the many voices of our times, and to judge them in the light of the divine word, so that revealed truth can always be more deeply penetrated, better understood and set forth to greater advantage.[12]

In the first volume, subtitled *Voices of Our Times* in honor of this important insight from Vatican II, contributors reflect on their personal and professional experiences of Catholic responses to and engagements with sexual diversity. They thus lift up for public hearing a chorus of contemporary voices—some of hope, others of fear, some of joy, others of suffering. Since the experience of the faithful represents an important locus for theological reflection, these contributions constitute a series of windows into the ways in which American Catholics live with, without, and despite their church's teachings on sexual diversity. The present, second volume aims to continue the conversation begun in *Voices of Our Times* by bringing together academic writings by theologians, ethicists, legal scholars, literary critics, and advocates.

Before turning to their essays, however, and before considering how their findings might contribute to the advance of contemporary Catholic thought, it will be useful for us to review briefly the historical development of official Catholic statements about LGBTQ issues as well as the development of theological responses to those teachings.

The Historical Development of Catholic Thought on LGBTQ Persons and Issues

As we have indicated, the writers whose essays appear in this volume are the latest to intervene in nearly four decades of academic, pastoral, and popular conversations about sexual diversity and the Roman Catholic Church. Before we turn to our authors' contributions, therefore, it seems appropriate for us to reflect briefly on the recent history and present state of Catholic discourse about sexuality in general, homosexuality in particular, and the complex and intertwined relationships among ideas about sexual activity, marriage, ministry, and anthropology.[13]

The overarching title of the conference series that gave birth to this volume both referred to a "monologue" and offered the hope that those who spoke at its constituent events might, in so doing, be able to "change the conversation about sexual diversity and the Catholic Church."[14] Significantly, conference organizers deliberately left open the question of whose was the monologue that needed change. As we hope to demonstrate, the history of intra-Catholic discussions about sexual diversity suggests that such conversations have taken the form not exclusively of the monologue of the ecclesiastical Magisterium but rather—if it is possible to mix the two metaphors—of multiple monological ships, some carrying heavier and some carrying lighter freight in the church and in the public square, and most often passing in the night.

Perhaps nowhere can the multiplicity of contemporary Catholic views on sexual diversity be more clearly seen than in the language that writers use to describe themselves, those who disagree with them, church teachings, sexual acts, and even the very persons about whose lives and loves they are writing. Is homosexuality a "problem," as it is called not only in some

Vatican documents but also in the writings of some moral theologians who do not seek to condemn all same-sex sexual activity?[15] Or is it the case that "homosexual affections can be as selfless as heterosexual affection" and that debates about same-sex marriage have "created a wonderful opportunity for all Christians, whether gay or straight, to think about why they celebrate marriage"?[16] Should those in same-sex relationships and those who engage in same-sex sexual activity be called "gay" or "lesbian," as many such persons choose to describe themselves, and should they be thought of as possessing a distinctive sexual orientation, or are terms like these so bound up with particular social and political agendas that ostensibly more neutral terms like "homosexual person" and "same-sex attraction" should be used instead?[17] Are these latter terms too reminiscent of earlier, now mostly discarded, clinical ideas that labeled sexually diverse persons "deviants" and "inverts"?[18] Is discrimination against such persons simply a matter of individual, isolated acts of prejudice, or are such acts part of a broader system of privilege that some have called heterosexism?[19]

Many more questions like these could be asked, but all of them point to one of the primary difficulties that Catholics encounter when they attempt to engage in conversations about sexual diversity. Even the most basic terms of discussion—words like "orientation," "gay," "marriage," even "intercourse"—can be taken to denote a speaker's theological, political, and cultural positions before she or he has finished speaking.[20] Neutral terminological ground often seems impossible to find, as illustrated perhaps most prominently by the continued use on the part of some church officials of the traditional moral-theological language of "objective disorder," in opposition to the continued repudiation of such language on the part of some theologians, ethicists, and pastoral ministers, who view it as "powerfully stigmatizing and dehumanizing."[21] No attempt to describe Catholic responses to sexual diversity can afford to pass over in silence these terminological battlefields.

Nevertheless, to focus exclusively on linguistic differences would be to minimize other elements of Catholicism's highly contested discourses about sexual diversity. If the terms used by different parties to these conversations are widely divergent, even more so are the theological and ethical propositions that they endorse or reject. Key sources for such propositions are the ten major documents on sexuality, same-sex relationships, and marriage that Vatican offices and the United States Conference of Catholic

Bishops have promulgated over the past four decades.[22] Four of these, in 1975, 1986, 1992, and 2003, were issued in the name of the Vatican's Congregation for the Doctrine of the Faith (CDF), the body charged to "promote and safeguard" the church's teachings; an additional two documents, including one, in 2005, that prohibited the admission of men with "deep-seated homosexual tendencies" to the seminary or religious life, came from the Congregation for Catholic Education; and yet another document, from the Pontifical Council for the Family, contained the church's pastoral and legislative responses to what the council called "de facto" unions, both same and opposite sex.[23] In addition, the U.S. bishops have recently issued three documents on matters related to sexuality and marriage; one of them, the 1997 pastoral letter "Always Our Children," continues to be cited frequently and approvingly by some of those who disagree with the church's teachings.[24] Many of the essays in this volume engage at length with official documents such as these, analyzing both their content and their rhetoric.

Yet while these documents contain the positions of the church hierarchy on a range of questions related to sexual diversity, and while they have often served as lightning rods for criticism and contestation, it would not be accurate to describe the history of Catholic discourse on this topic solely as a history of official pronouncements followed by unofficial responses. Before the CDF issued its first document describing "homosexual acts" as "intrinsically disordered," the then-Jesuit priest John McNeill had published a series of articles in the *Homiletic and Pastoral Review* in which he argued that "a homosexual can . . . be morally justified in seeking out ethically responsible expressions of his sexuality."[25] Two years later, in 1972, the moral theologian Charles Curran acknowledged that he and many of his fellow ethicists were uncertain how to characterize homosexuality: "Is it illness, a totally neutral phenomenon, or something created by the prejudices of society?" His response was that although same-sex sexual activity is not itself a good, it can, under certain circumstances, be an acceptable choice for those who are oriented toward persons of the same sex.[26] Possibly in response to writers like McNeill and Curran, the CDF declared in its 1975 document that "at the present time there are those who . . . have begun to judge indulgently, and even to excuse completely, homosexual relations between certain people."[27]

Thus the history of Catholic discussions about sexual diversity comprises neither a single monologue nor genuine dialogue. Formal ecclesial statements have both reacted against and prompted reactions from theologians, pastoral workers, and others. But, as we have already seen, those who are writing and responding are not always able to understand one another's words in a spirit of what the Jesuit ethicist David Hollenbach calls intellectual solidarity, which he defines as "an orientation of mind that regards differences among traditions as stimuli to intellectual engagement across religious and cultural boundaries." He notes that "this receptive orientation expects to be able to learn something valuable by listening to people who hold understandings of the good life different from one's own."[28] Indeed, some have argued that the differences in power between the institutional church and historically marginalized gay and lesbian persons are so great that notions like "intellectual solidarity" risk giving too much moral credence to official statements whose rhetoric, these commentators have suggested, inevitably creates a biased and uneven field for discourse.[29]

Understanding that we do not have space to describe every issue that has been contested nor every perspective that has been advanced, in the remainder of this section we aim to trace the contours of recent conversations among Catholics about three key dimensions of sexual diversity. First, we survey a spectrum of views about *sexual activity* between persons of the same biological sex found in recent writings in Christian ethics and moral theology, considering briefly both the sources and the anthropological presuppositions of these positions. Next, we rehearse several arguments about the *nature and purpose of marriage* that have led Catholics to take a range of positions on the question of civil marriage for same-sex couples. Finally, we describe the variety of roles that the figure of the *gay Catholic priest* has played in recent debates. These three topics correspond with the foci around which the majority of essays in this volume revolve: theology, law, and ministry.

It might seem that the central ethical question bound up in most debates about sexual diversity is a highly specific one—is it morally just and/or in accord with the divine will for two persons of the same biological sex to engage in mutually consensual sexual activities? Yet this question cannot be asked in isolation. Catholic writers across the theological and political spectrum agree that the church's official position on same-sex sexual activity both rests upon and possesses significant ramifications for a host of related teachings on matters such as contraception, gender roles, clerical celibacy, ecclesiastical authority, and ultimately theological anthropology—that is, how one theologically conceives of the human person. Mark Jordan has traced the far-reaching effects that a change in the church's teachings about homosexuality would all but inevitably have; it is for the same reason that, from substantially different vantage points, James Hanigan once called homosexuality the "test-case for Christian sexual ethics" and Anthony Giampietro has observed that "a shift to allow same-sex couples to participate in the institution of marriage would require a shift in how sexual activity is viewed in general."[30]

Several writers have proposed typologies that seek to describe the major stances about same-sex sexual activity taken by Christian ethicists over the past several decades. Patricia Beattie Jung and Ralph F. Smith, for instance, suggest that ethicists and moral theologians have treated homosexuality in one of five ways: as freely chosen and simply immoral, as a form of mental disorder akin to alcoholism, as a severe disability akin to blindness, as a more limited disability akin to colorblindness, and as a naturally occurring variation akin to left-handedness. Jung and Smith themselves adopt the last of these positions, observing that "this fifth position on homosexuality is not heterosexist, and it provides a contrast with the heterosexist dimensions of the other points of view."[31] Taking another tack, the Catholic social critic Andrew Sullivan has divided commentators about homosexuality into four categories: "prohibitionists," "liberationists," "conservatives," and "liberals." For Sullivan, these categories transcend the standard left-right continuum of most U.S. political discourse; thus a person he labels "conservative" is "a variety of liberal: someone who essentially shares the premises of the liberal state, its guarantee of liberty, of pluralism, of freedom of speech and action, but who still believes politics is an arena in which it is necessary to affirm certain cultural, social, and moral values over others." Sullivan's "conservatives" differ from "prohibitionists," who would enact penalties for homosexual conduct, from "liberationists," for whom "homosexuality" and "heterosexuality" are social constructs, and from "liberals," for whom the rights of individuals are paramount.[32]

Sexual activity. While others have developed extensive bibliographies of Christian and Catholic ethical writing on same-sex relations, here we wish to focus specifically on two elements of the conversation as it currently exists.[33] First, in the wake of Pope John Paul II's prolific writings on love, the family, and the body—that is, what the late pope called "the theology of the body"—recent official Catholic discourse has made much of the notion of "complementarity" of the sexes in order to justify prohibitions on same-sex sexual activity and same-sex marriage.[34] Yet as David Matzko McCarthy has observed, complementarity, "at least its current use, is an innovation in understanding the conjugal union. A document as late as Vatican II's Pastoral Constitution on the Church in the Modern World, *Gaudium et Spes*, makes no mention of it."[35] This notwithstanding, in the opening decade of the twenty-first century, the notion of complementarity has come to serve as a sort of keystone for writers across the theological spectrum. For revisionists such as Todd A. Salzman and Michael G. Lawler, "a 'reconstructed complementarity,'" that is, one capable of taking into account differences in sexual orientation as well as genital anatomy, "can serve as a foundational ethical principle."[36] For "new natural lawyers" like Patrick Lee and Robert P. George, biological complementarity remains the sine qua non for morally good sexual activity and indeed is required for a particular sexual act even to merit the name "intercourse."[37] Second, tied up with the question of what kinds of complementarity are ethically appropriate is the question of what sources theologians and ethicists should attend to in reaching their conclusions. The debate between Salzman and Lawler, on the one hand, and Lee and George, on the other, illustrates this point as well. Whereas Salzman and Lawler quote the Catholic ethicist Margaret Farley to the effect that there are "clear and profound testimonies to the life-enhancing possibilities of same-sex relations and the integrating possibilities of sexual activity within these relations," Lee and George argue that while "polyamorists, polygamists . . . and even many adulterers and unmarried teens report positive feelings about their sexual acts . . . such personal testimony fails to show that such acts truly embody a personal communion or are morally good."[38] When there is so little consensus about the status of human experience (and of testimonies to it) as a source for theological or ethical judgments, it is unsurprising that these and other authors end up speaking past one another.[39]

Marriage. Perhaps nowhere in the conversation about sexual diversity have disagreements become more firmly entrenched than with regard to the question of civil—or even sacramental, as Paul Lakeland advocates in the Afterword to this volume—marriage for same-sex couples. In 1995, the

Netherlands became the first of now eleven countries to extend marriage to same-sex couples; beginning with Massachusetts in 2003, nine U.S. states and the District of Columbia have done the same. As in so many cases, much of this debate turns on questions of first principles. What, for instance, is marriage, and what is its purpose? McCarthy answers these questions by quoting Andrew K. M. Adam, who wrote that "the central theological importance of marriage—as the church's institution for the blessing and support of human intimacy—lies in *constancy*."[40] George, to the contrary, hewing closely to recent official teaching, defines marriage as "a one-flesh communion of persons . . . the union of two sexually complementary spouses."[41] It is obvious that those holding George's view will find themselves unwilling to admit same-sex couples to the sacrament of marriage. Authors who, with recent official teaching, further hold that the private, nonprocreative sexual acts of unmarried persons cannot contribute to the public good, likewise deny that same-sex couples have a right to marry civilly.[42] At the other end of the spectrum, those who support the possibility of civil and/or sacramental marriage between persons of the same legal sex have relied on positive theological arguments such as Salzman's and Lawler's notion of "sexual orientation complementarity," critiques of the institutional church's arguments against same-sex marriage, the testimony of same-sex couples about their life-giving relationships, and the negative consequences (identified by one writer as "either promiscuity or emotional isolation") that have historically followed from society's and many churches' refusal to allow same-sex couples to avail themselves of the institution of marriage.[43]

Priesthood and ministry. The Roman Catholic Church's global public advocacy for what church leaders have described as the preservation of the institution of marriage—advocacy that has included promulgating documents such as those we have surveyed above, financially and morally supporting campaigns designed to enact or restore prohibitions on same-sex marriage, and engaging in lobbying activities at the United Nations aimed at blocking statements that enshrine "sexual orientation" and "gender identity" as categories in international law—represents perhaps its most prominent set of public interventions with regard to issues of sexual diversity.[44]

Yet within the church, questions about ministry by and ministry to LGBTQ persons remain at least equally controversial.[45] In this vein, our contributor Mark Jordan has provocatively observed that "you will not understand modern homosexuality unless you understand Catholic homosexuality, and you cannot understand Catholic homosexuality unless you begin with the clergy."[46]

In 2005, the announcement by a Vatican dicastery that homosexual men—or, precisely, men "who practice homosexuality, present deep-seated homosexual tendencies or support the so-called 'gay culture' "—should not be admitted to Catholic seminaries or be ordained in the Catholic Church marked a striking new development in at least a decade of intraecclesial conversations about the ordination of gay men.[47] These conversations are not, of course, unique to Catholicism: one of the catalysts for recent controversies in the Anglican Communion was the installation in 2003 of an openly gay man in a noncelibate relationship, V. Gene Robinson, as Episcopal bishop of New Hampshire, and the Evangelical Lutheran Church of America has also recently found itself divided with regard to the ordination of gay and lesbian ministers. Catholic discussions, however, reflect the influence of at least two factors not shared with other Christian denominations. First, unlike Protestant clergy, Catholic priests are required to take vows of celibacy. And second, recent revelations concerning the sexual abuse of minors by Catholic priests in a sordid record stretching over more than half a century have led some commentators to connect clergy sexual abuse in Catholicism with the presence of significant numbers of homosexual men in the priesthood.[48] Others, while acknowledging that many priests currently in ministry are gay, have strenuously resisted such connections, charging instead that these men have been made into scapegoats for a crisis not of their making.[49] Jeannine Gramick's and Gerard Jacobitz's essays in this volume are two of the most recent contributions to an ongoing conversation about gay Catholic priests and religious.

Some bishops and theologians, and even the former Vatican spokesperson Joaquin Navarro-Valls, have argued that for gay men, taking a vow of celibacy is not the same act of sacrifice that an identical vow would represent for a heterosexual man.[50] Andrew Baker, a priest who in 2002 served on the staff of the Vatican Congregation for Bishops, offered other reasons why those with what he called the "serious *disorder*" of "same-sex attraction" should not be ordained: that same-sex attraction often co-occurs with "other serious problems such as substance abuse, sexual addiction and depression"; that homosexual candidates for the priesthood might not be willing to disseminate or adhere strictly to church teaching about sexuality; that a priest with same-sex attraction would be more likely to approach other men "as a possible sexual 'partner'"; and that same-sex-attracted seminarians might form cliques in which "effeminate affective manners and a certain 'acceptability' of the disorder are often promoted."[51] For Baker, then, there are anthropological underpinnings to the prohibition of gay men in Catholic seminaries and religious life that became official church teaching in 2005: if homosexuality is an intrinsic disorder, then those who struggle with that disorder are all but certain to manifest disordered conduct and relationships.

Those who have vehemently disagreed with Baker have also built their arguments on anthropological foundations. Thomas Gumbleton, the retired auxiliary bishop of Detroit who has contributed to our companion volume, *Voices of Our Times*, wrote in the same publication as Baker that "I insist that we must reject any suggestion that a gay priest or bishop cannot make the same celibate commitment a heterosexual man would make. It is a very inadequate understanding of celibacy to say that . . . [only] a heterosexual priest is 'giving up a good thing, the desire to have a family.'" Gumbleton proceeded to articulate a series of reasons why "we must reject attacks on homosexual priests and value their ministry in the church." He argued that gay men often bring to their ministry experiences of marginalization and suffering that most of their heterosexual counterparts cannot; that gay priests often possess "an exceptional ability and courage to proclaim the truth," just as they have done by coming out. He concluded, "What a loss if we drive these 'gifted' people from our midst!"[52]

Jordan's observation that, in Catholicism, homosexuality and the clergy are inextricably bound up with the other has been borne out in a variety of other, often highly personal testimonies. In his 2004 study of autobiographical writings by Catholic gay men, Dugan McGinley reported that "if I had to pick one phrase or sentence which popped up more frequently than any other in the course of reading these . . . autobiographies, it would have to be, 'I wanted to be a priest.'"[53] A former seminarian, Jeffrey J. Kripal, articulated a somewhat different perspective: describing his departure from the seminary, he wrote that "it was not that I found the homoerotic culture of the seminary or even the church morally objectionable. . . . What hurt, and what still hurts, was the awareness, dimly felt in my thoughts but clearly seen in my dreams, that the church's homoerotic structure excluded my very being from its most intimate forms of community. I could not possibly fit. I was a religious exile by virtue of my heterosexuality."[54] Mary Hunt, responding to Jordan's work, has built upon his contention that homosexuality and the Catholic priesthood cannot be studied apart from the other, adding that her own experiences as a feminist theologian and an alumna of a Catholic theological school reveal that with regard to the church, "deeper even than its homosexual nature is Catholicism's structured duplicity." The duplicity encouraged by the church, Hunt argued, makes itself known as an economic as well as a theological issue: lay people cannot offer input as to how their contributions to the church are utilized, and Hunt observed that "millions" are spent to fulfill what she takes to be the aesthetic preferences of closeted, or not-so-closeted, gay clergy. She concluded, most provocatively: "Perhaps the single most obvious conclusion I draw from Mark Jordan's analysis is that Catholic priesthood and its theological arm is really a large system of gay male prostitution, perhaps more economic even than sexual. Catholic seminaries and religious orders are tax-exempt institutions that discriminate legally against women and non-homo-conforming men."[55]

Each of the discourses we have been tracing here—moral and ethical theological perspectives on LGBTQ persons and same-sex sexual activity, debates over civil and sacramental marriage for same-sex couples, and controversies involving gay Catholic clergy—is far more extensive and complex than these few pages have permitted us to describe. Yet we hope that even our brief forays into these conversations help drive home the validity of two observations. First, that while many church officials have recently pronounced on a variety of matters related to sexual diversity, there is no single position with regard to same-sex sexual activity, same-sex marriage, or gay clergy that every Catholic, whether a scholar or a person in the pews, shares. In that sense, there is already more than a monologue. Second, however, because contemporary Catholic thinkers and leaders employ often distinctive or competing sets of terms, concepts, and theological and anthropological assumptions when they talk about sexual diversity, attempts at conversation frequently remain more like competing monologues or, to revert to our earlier metaphor, like monological ships passing in the night. In the next section, we aim to demonstrate that these competing narratives about sexual diversity also exist in the public opinion of lay Catholics.

Catholic Opinions on LGBTQ Issues

According to the doctrine of reception, which "asserts that for a law or rule to be an effective guide for the believing community it must be accepted by that community," lay Catholic opinion about a set of church teachings is one way of gauging the reception of those teachings by the People of God.[56] Although it is an ancient doctrine in the church, the "role of the whole church in 'receiving' new formulations of doctrine and discipline" was "rediscovered" in the years after Vatican II.[57] Jean-Marie Tillard referred to the recovery of this principle as "one of the most important theological rediscoveries" of the twentieth century.[58] Indeed, the Council Fathers provided foundational support for this doctrine in describing the *sensus fidei* (or "understanding of the faith") given to the entire laity by Christ in order that the power of the Gospel "might shine forth in their daily social and family life."[59] Tillard's notion of reception articulated a communal, reciprocal relationship between the faithful and their bishops: "The ministers of *episkope* [oversight] receive from the *sensus fidelium* the Church's awareness that something is needed for the well-being and the mission of the community, or the conviction that what has been declared still needs to be refined."[60]

Abundant qualitative expressions of this awareness that something more and different is needed can be found in the range of narratives from Catholics and post-Catholics on LGBTQ identity/concerns and the church. These can be discovered, among many other places, in our companion volume and in McGinley's collection of gay Catholic autobiographies.[61] It is also possible to ascertain a quantitative description of contemporary Catholic reception of teaching on these matters. The snapshots of Catholic opinion that follow offer some glimpse of this important *sensus fidelium* on LGBTQ issues.

First, Catholics are on the whole more accepting of homosexuality than the members of every other Christian tradition in the United States. A Pew Forum study reported in 2008 that by a margin of more than two to one, Catholics believe that homosexuality should be accepted by society

(58%, compared to 30% who believe homosexuality should be discouraged by society). This compares to 50% for the general population, 56% for mainline Protestants, and less for other Christian denominations.[62] When the same question was posed in 2012, 63% of all Catholics said homosexuality should be accepted by society, and 23% said it should be discouraged by society, compared to 56% (accepted) and 32% (discouraged) in the general public.[63] A 2011 study by the Public Religion Research Institute found that 74% of all Catholics agreed that gay and lesbian relationships should be accepted by society (compared to 25% who disagreed, a 3:1 margin).[64] In a 2010 Gallup study, 62% of Catholics regarded gay and lesbian relations as "morally acceptable," representing a sixteen-point jump from the same question in 2006 and nearly three times the increase seen during that period among Protestant respondents.[65]

Over the period from 1996 to 2007, American Catholics were consistently less opposed than the general population to allowing legal same-sex marriage.[66] In 2008, 60% of Catholics supported civil unions that grant many of the same rights as marriage, a substantial increase from the 46% of Catholics who expressed that view in 2003 and a significantly higher figure than the 51% support that civil unions garnered among the general population in 2008.[67] An ABC News/*Washington Post* poll in 2011 found that 60% of Catholics of all races supported same-sex marriage, with 38% opposed.[68] Among white Catholics, support for same-sex marriage grew from 40% to 63% between 2006 and 2011.[69] In another research study in 2012, 59% of all Catholics favored allowing gay and lesbian couples to marry legally, with 36% opposed, while 52% of the American population favored legal same-sex marriage.[70] A different poll in 2012 found 53% of all Catholics favoring same-sex marriage with 37% opposed, compared to 48% favoring and 44% opposed in the general public.[71] In March 2013, a *Washington Post*/ABC News poll showed a rise among the general public favoring legalized same-sex marriage, with 58% in favor and 36% in opposition. In that same poll, Catholic opinion remained stable with 59% in favor and 35% opposed.[72] When the issue of civil unions is added to the mix (resulting in three possible responses: favoring marriage, civil union, or neither), studies indicate that nearly three-quarters of American Catholics favor some form of legal recognition for same-sex couples: 43% say gay couples should be allowed to marry, and an additional 31% say gay couples should be allowed to form civil unions but not marry.[73] More than two-thirds (69%) of Catholics agree that same-sex couples in "long-term committed relationships should have the same rights as married couples in the areas of hospital visitation, health insurance and pension coverage."[74]

When asked in 2006 whether "gay and lesbian people who meet all other qualifications should legally be able to adopt children," 57% of all Catholics agreed, with 38% disagreeing.[75] In 2011, 60% of Catholics favored "allowing gay and lesbian couples to adopt children," with 32% opposed. This compares to the 36% of white evangelicals and 44% of black Protestants who favored such rights.[76]

In 2007, 58% of Catholics supported the Employment Non-Discrimination Act, which would prohibit workplace discrimination based on sexual orientation or gender identity.[77] In 2011, 73% of Catholics favored laws that would "protect gay and lesbian people against job discrimination."[78] A Pew poll in 2010 demonstrated a 68% approval of allowing gays and lesbians to serve openly in the military, compared to 23% who opposed such practice—a 3:1 margin. In 1994, the approval figure for Catholics was 58%.[79] A 2011 survey on this question demonstrated that 63% of Catholics favored open service by gays and lesbians, with 21% opposed.[80]

The majority of Catholics believe that gays and lesbians are facing "a lot of discrimination" in society.[81] When Catholics are asked about their church's "handling of the issue of homosexuality," they rate their own church lower than other Christian groups rate theirs. Only 39% of Catholics give their own church a grade of either "A" or "B" on this subject, with 32% giving either a "D" or "F" to the church.[82]

It is clear from this review of opinion data that Catholics have for nearly two decades been measurably more supportive of a range of LGBTQ issues than the general population and than their counterparts in other Christian denominations. These issues include social acceptance, marriage equality, and a variety of rights with regard to relationships, adoption, employment, and military service. More than a simple majority of lay Catholics clearly holds views of support for their LGBTQ neighbors on a variety of issues, although these data also demonstrate a diversity of opinions among Catholics. Many of the supportive views are directly contrary to the views expressed by the episcopacy as Catholic teachings. Given the increasing trend of such support, the prognosis for the reception of those teachings seems apparent. The implications of these dimensions of the *sensus fidei* for the development of the institutional church have not yet been fully realized.

Essays in Ministry, Law, Ethics, and Theology

The Catholic Church asserts that it ought to be "enriched by the development of human social life" so that it may understand its constitution in Christ "more penetratingly, express it better, and adjust it more successfully to our times . . . for whoever promotes the human community at the family level, culturally, in its economic, social and political dimensions, both nationally and internationally, such a one, according to God's design, is contributing greatly to the Church."[83] Academic and pastoral work must also contribute to the development of the church in its consideration of this range of issues related to LGBTQ persons. The authors whose work is assembled in this volume are engaged in that very promotion of the human community in its various dimensions, and we are pleased to present their contributions to this evolving conversation. In this section we introduce the work of a distinguished group of scholars in theology, ethics, law, and ministry.

We begin with a series of essays on ministry and ministers that explore from various perspectives the silencing of voices within the church. Kelby Harrison focuses on the themes of language and queer voices as she wrestles with the subject of what it is possible to say about sexual diversity in the context of the dominant forces of church, institutions, and society in postmodern times. She posits that LGBTQ Catholics and post-Catholics live amidst the tension between minority sexual identities/discourse and the silencing authority of the Roman Catholic Church. She explicates the paradox that both sides in this battle are foundationally oriented toward the good yet remain at odds. She does so through careful analysis of the generation and control of discourse by regimes of power, the implications of understanding queer orientation as a spatial reference of embodiment, and narrative theory in which all persons orient their life stories toward the moral good. Harrison calls first for the recognition—by government and religious organizations—of sexual identities subject to social contempt. Then she asserts the need for the church to provide language for

LGBTQ identity that aligns with the good, as a way of nourishing its people and helping them find their voice.

Mark Jordan starts with a thought experiment in which he contemplates the range of doctrines that would need to be altered if the Vatican decided to change its teaching on homosexuality. But such contemplation, he concludes, is not likely to bear fruit in the end because of the futility of continuing to advance pastoral, historical, philosophical, or theological arguments with the powers that suppress speech about homosexuality within the church. Jordan compares the historical trajectories of the Anglican and Roman Catholic churches in their considerations of homosexuality as part of his analysis of the underlying conditions and mechanisms of the silencing of speech. His essay reflects upon the need for transformation of the structures of power in a gendered organization in which such power is the object of strong desire. Rather than continuing to engage in the tired debates of past decades, he invites and encourages us to develop new language about Catholic homosexuality as the way to move forward.

Elizabeth Dreyer, in response to Jordan, connects his discussion to the silencing of women. She promotes an appreciation of Christian community as being always on its journey to fuller truths and thus needing to be open to new understanding and new language. She lifts up the faithful witness of LGBT Catholics to the Gospel and offers a program of universal faithfulness for all people of the church, drawing this program from a reflection on Acts 10, in which Peter is awakened to God's message of acceptance and inclusion.

Jeannine Gramick broaches the subject of extensive public silence about the lives of lesbian religious women. She describes decades of ministry and dialogue that have nonetheless taken place within New Ways Ministry and other groups. Gramick explores three main themes that have been part of this development in the lives of lesbian nuns since the 1970s: sexual identity, coming out, and celibacy. Within these developments, she explores the hidden treasures of intimate friendship as symbol for the love of God; of countercultural witness, service, and education aligned with the marginalized and rejected; and of mentorship and role modeling for those coping with rejection and pain.

In her response to Gramick, Jamie Manson notes that lesbian nuns, like all women, have also been excluded from significant voice or function within the Roman Catholic Church by virtue of their biology as women. She emphasizes vectors of ministry that reach out to the margins and to the voiceless, territory with which pioneering religious women and queer ministers have long been familiar. Manson laments the fact that much of this important ministry is carried out invisibly, but she also lauds lesbian nuns as possible role models for young adult lesbians. She describes the recent decision of the U.S.-based Leadership Conference of Women Religious to engage in dialogue with the Congregation for the Doctrine of the Faith as yet another example of the courageous, pioneering efforts of religious women from which the church and all people have profited.

Gerard Jacobitz describes a range of problems that conflicting church teachings create for seminarians and their vocation directors, for practicing priests, and for the Vatican. He argues that the church extols the foundational principles of the essential dignity of the person and the reliability of human reason informed by practical experience but that these together militate against the arguments the church advances in its teachings about homosexuality. Jacobitz analyzes theological anthropology, the fruits of human sciences, and the human experience of sexual orientation as dilemmas for the church in attempting to retain its notion of homosexuality as intrinsically disordered. He argues that the rigid exclusion of gay men from seminaries presents a similar dilemma, especially in the light of the human experience of lay Catholics who demonstrate increasing support for LGBT issues. Finally, Jacobitz discusses the implications for considering the charism of celibacy apart from the call to priesthood.

In the essays occupying the middle portion of this volume, the subject of same-sex marriage, or marriage equality, is considered from the perspectives of law and ethics/theology. Michael John Perry addresses the legal dimensions of same-sex marriage from the vantage of the legal categories of religious and moral freedom as well as of widely accepted international doctrine on human rights. In a penetrating analysis, he turns on their head the assertions frequently advanced by the church hierarchy in the political actions it has undertaken to combat—on moral grounds—the legalization of same-sex marriage. As Perry argues, the religious or moral claims of one sectarian group may not be legitimately used by governments to displace the moral freedom of other groups or persons, especially in societies in which various religious groups may differ on the question at hand. There is, indeed, a religious freedom argument to be made about same-sex marriage, but it is not the one championed by the Catholic bishops.

Patricia Beattie Jung explores the theological and ethical landscape of arguments about same-sex marriage. She examines in turn each of the arguments proposed by the Vatican and the U.S. bishops in their opposition to marriage equality and finds them insufficient to justify the church's endorsement of civil discrimination against gay and lesbian couples. Jung advances multiple lines of argument to demonstrate that homosexual couples can be open to the gift of life, that homosexual activity can be genuinely complementary, and that homosexual acts can be natural in the normative sense. She presents descriptions of multiple Catholic perspectives on marriage equality and arguments for why it will not harm marriage, the dignity of persons, or children. Jung provides a number of rationales for promoting marriage equality, including its advantages to couples, families, and society in general—the same advantages that accrue when heterosexual marriage is promoted.

Joan M. Martin provides a response to Jung from her perspective as an African American Protestant minister and ethicist, noting a growing ecumenical consensus on matters of marriage, procreation, and homosexuality. Martin interrogates theologically the assumption underlying the Roman Catholic Church's proscriptions and pronouncements about marriage: that only certain of God's children are "open to life." She explores the confluence of love and life held within the belief that humans are created in the image of a God of "unfathomable" love. She contrasts dominant interpretive discourse with feminist, womanist, and LGBTQ justice liberationist perspectives on sexuality and marriage, comparing these latter experiences with African American experiences. All of these marginal experiences are part of a dynamic meaning of "human beingness" that encompasses difference and particularity in understanding the universal. Martin also reminds us that there are many more complex questions to be faced about human sexuality—whether we feel ready or able to do so or not—when we consider bisexual, transgendered, and transsexual persons as well as those with other forms of sexualities that do not fit within traditional dualistic constructions.

Lisa Sowle Cahill reminds us that Catholicism is not embodied primarily in its formal institutions, offices, or teachings—reaffirming that dialogue among the laity and between the laity and ecclesial hierarchy is a critical element of the Catholic Church envisioned by Vatican II. As she writes, "All of the faithful are both teachers and learners." From that understanding proceeds the theological significance of increasing support among U.S. Catholics for same-sex unions and marriage and an acknowledgment of the chasm between Catholics and their bishops on these topics. Sowle Cahill also surveys the diverse theological terrain of current discussions, including the development of the concept of natural law as a product of practical reason rather than rigid and static legalisms. She describes three examples of inadequate hierarchical responses to contemporary theologians and the laity. She also traces the modern evolution of official Catholic teaching on marriage and its purposes, with its recent shift to proclaiming the importance of love—thus creating a plausible Catholic argument for same-sex marriage. Inductive reasoning and pastoral concern both speak to the procreative and intergenerational family-building value of marital relationships, forms of value that promote the public good and are justifiably applicable to same-sex marriages and families.

In the final set of essays in this volume, we turn to broad issues of ethics and theology in consideration of LGBTQ individuals and their treatment by and within the Roman Catholic Church. These essays explore themes of language and voice in a variety of analyses about the place of homosexuality in church history, thought, and authority. These authors examine critically the ambivalences of the institutional church's posture toward LGBTQ individuals.

In his essay, Michael Sepidoza Campos adopts a strategy of avoiding the language of official teaching in order to permit greater theological imagination to inform his discussion. This is the very strategy recommended in this volume by Mark Jordan as the way forward in Catholic discussions of homosexuality (see Chapter 2). Sepidoza Campos uses the symbol of the stranger to investigate the relationships of LGBTQ Catholics with the church. His intention is to broaden ecclesial discourse not only to examine those standing at the margins but to develop a relational theory that involves all persons in a process of opening themselves to the mystery of otherness. As he puts it, "Touching God's transcendence, one is rent open to the mystery of others and of one's world." Sepidoza Campos details the ambivalent welcome of the church to the stranger and describes how encounters between stranger and host reveal a network of relationships, which add layers of richness and complexity to existing theological monologue, upholding both familiarity and mystery. As Sepi-doza Campos concludes, the welcome of the stranger is inherent to the identity of the Catholic community; the welcome of the hosts by the stranger is the paradox that reminds the community of its own profound mysteries.

Patrick S. Cheng draws parallels between the classroom bullying of LGBTQ youths (with its resultant harms) and the "theological bullying" by the Roman Catholic hierarchy of those who dissent from the church's teachings on homosexuality (with its resultant harms). By its ongoing and deliberate actions, Cheng argues, the hierarchy intends to silence dissent-ing voices through the use of terror (spiritual, economic, and political) and unbridled authority. Cheng notes the need to stop this repetitive cycle of bullying and the importance of witnesses who speak out and demand that all people be treated with dignity and respect as beings created in the image of God. He finds hope in the development of queer theologies, especially by theologians of color; the courage of queer theologians who have stayed within the Roman Catholic Church; the appearance of the many new voices of nonacademic Catholic theologians; and the emergence of new genres of affirming queer Catholic writings.

Frederick S. Roden provides an expansive accounting of the implica-tions for the church and its faithful members of the divine commandment to love, particularly in the context of Catholic ministry to LGBTQ youth. Like Harrison in her indictment of the oft-used slogan "love the sinner, hate the sin," Roden confronts the deceptiveness of a church that pro-claims both the evil of homosexual activity and the evil of hate crimes directed at homosexuals. He traces the hierarchical silencing of dissident Catholic voices on sexual morality resulting in the inhibition of develop-ment of new moral theologies since the early twentieth century. The de-velopment of Catholic theologies of homosexuality was then, as now, left to the laity. Meanwhile, as Roden argues, the souls of LGBTQ youth cry out in suffering for the mercy of God and are left without the comfort of a receptive Catholic moral theology that might be found in Christ's loving identification with the suffering and marginalized.

Finally, in the Afterword, Paul Lakeland takes further forward the theme of finding voice in a discussion of theological development from the margins rather than from Rome. He examines the essays in this volume and the conferences from which they were born from the perspective of ecclesiology. Lakeland concludes that this work bears significant meaning for the Catholic Church, insofar as it presents new places for theological reflection and widening understandings of who constitutes the church. Looking beyond the confines of the contributions of scholars in this volume, Lakeland argues for the theological possibilities of sacramental same-sex marriage within the church, based in Catholic notions of divine love and theological anthropology. What makes human sexual relations holy is their reflection of the love of God—a love open to all human beings. Lakeland points out that sacramental marriage, by design, points a couple outward, toward the good of the community and the world, a good that the church should desire for and from all its faithful.

In the end, we share with Paul Lakeland the desire that the More than a Monologue conferences and the volumes that have resulted from it will foster continued, open, and honest conversation about sexual diversity within the Catholic Church and other communities of faith. We place our trust in the work of the Spirit to enliven and sanctify all such efforts, and we hope that you, the reader, will appreciate what these essays have to contribute to that vision.

1 Learning to Speak

KELBY HARRISON

Union Theological Seminary

The Catholic Church is a part of my sexual subjectivity[1]—in fruitful and insidious ways, some of which reach my conscious awareness and some of which do not. I am an openly queer woman, a scholar concerned with the history of sexual identity discourses, concerned with the various discourses of ethics, and predominantly concerned with thinking through constructive ethics for LGBT/Q[2] people. The Catholic Church, perhaps to its chagrin, is a part of all of that. It has required a long process of deconstruction and reconstruction to find the strength and useful intellectual pathways to undertake this scholarly work. The influences of my Catholic upbringing and education linger.

The Catholic Church remains most legible in the patterns of my thinking and in my unexpected mimicry of its values. But what strikes me as interesting—in this briefest of self-narratives—is that despite the idiosyncrasies of my life, there is nothing unique in my narrative of learning how to articulate a new conception of sexual self in a culture deeply rooted and influenced by religious ideology. All queer people—Catholic, post-Catholic, and many religious others—learn to articulate new sexual identities. This is peculiar because the institutions and religious discourses that have most strongly shaped our subjectivities have offered next to nothing in terms of language to shape the articulation of sexual subjectivity.

To begin, yes, the church must learn to listen. But how and where do we—as lesbian, gay, bisexual, transgender, and queer people—learn to *speak*? The sexual ideologies of religion and the Catholic Church that have shaped us are ideologies that often render us invisible and/or "intrinsically disordered."[3] Where in this space do we find narratives to articulate ourselves as created in the image of God, beloved and good, and at the same time to embrace and celebrate our embodied eros?

As I was thinking through and struggling with what I wanted to say in my opening remarks for the Fordham University conference on sexual diversity and the Catholic Church on the theme of "Learning to Listen," I realized my concerns were much more about what is possible to say. I mean this in a theoretical way. How is it possible for a group of the faithful (or previously faithful, or even religiously influenced though secular) to speak up and back to a dominant and primary source of their own subject formation? This is an especially vexing question when we consider that our new discourse[4] of sexual subjectivity must also be capable of critiquing the very premises of that subject formation. This is more than just speaking truth to power; it first requires an ability to figure out how to speak at all.

In a sense, this speaking is miraculous—a kind of speaking in tongues. Yet clearly LGBT/Q people speak—and in abundance—about their senses of identity, their sexual insights, and their sense of self. The task cannot be as simple as appropriating the new discourses of sexual subjectivity that make space for minority perspectives, although that is, of course, a part of the task. What I want to try to do in this essay is to look at the theoretical space of sexual subjectivity that must first open up before narratives of LGBT/Q sexual identity can take root. In order to do this, I will employ continental philosophy to begin to describe the contours of this space. Because lesbian, gay, bisexual, transgender, and queer identities are contemporary identity versions of very old human sexual behaviors and gender nonconformities, it is important to frame how we theorize identity in our most modern of times—a time academics in the humanities refer to as postmodernism.

Postmodernity includes the appraisal that we—as subjects—are a product of discourses. Discourses are modes of organizing knowledge, ideas, and experience that are rooted in language and its concrete contexts of history and institutions. Discourses infuse our bodies in various ways; we become aware of some and remain unaware of others. We are constructed, socially, by the historical forces and disciplinary conversations of fields such as medicine, religion, philosophy, sociology, and culture that precede our existence yet define the parameters of both our experience of ourselves and our possibilities of identity. This history is an amalgamation, a continual building upon previous understandings and insights. Contemporary notions of identity may be quite recent, but the historical depth of their development is often richer than can be seen at a first, or even a considered, glance.

The Catholic Church can rightly claim deep history. It can claim a history that is much longer than the history of contemporary sexual identity. The Catholic Church is older than the "heterosexual,"[5] it is older than the "homosexual,"[6] and it is certainly older than the ambiguously ostensive "queer."[7] The contemporary church works hard to define the parameters of new questions in human sexuality,[8] even when the results seem antiquated and ill-fitted to contemporary concerns. It is a historical and contemporary influence on the discursive modes of the social construction of human identity.

Contemporary LGBT/Q Catholics and post-Catholics[9] live at the intersection of two discourses at war with each other: the liberative political discourses of minority sexual identities and the moral authority of the Catholic Church that seeks to limit embodied expressions of those identities. Oftentimes it is a silent war, where one side assumes it has won and the other side avoids the conflict because it knows it has not. The gentle negotiations that already wounded souls attempt to make with the hierarchy often do not produce change—sometimes they simply create safer spaces on the periphery of the church, engaging the ritual and the meaning without engaging the social hostility. But this cannot be enough for the future trajectory of social justice for LGBT/Q people. It will not be enough.

In what follows, I will articulate what I see as a foundational paradox in LGBT/Q (post-)Catholic subjectivity. This paradox is created by directly conflicting notions of morality in each of the two identities entwined to make a single subjectivity. On the one side there is the discourse and moral influence of the church—driven by the Vatican—that seeks nearly complete silence about nonheterosexual sexuality in tension with a counternarrative of LGBT/Q identities that are mostly secular and focused on identity pride and political and social recognition. Both of these identities—Catholic and politically LGBT/Q—are identities underpinned by an orientation toward the good. Both of these identities see the other as a hindrance to the achievement of that good. To create a deeper articulation of this paradox, I will engage Foucault and theories of subjectivity formation under discursive regimes, Sara Ahmed on ideas of queer orientation, and Charles Taylor on narrative theory and articulation of self as the good. I will conclude with some thoughts on why the church needs to learn to help LGBT/Q people speak, not just to listen to what we have to say.[10]

Foucault on Discourse, Subject Formation, and the Christian Pastorate

Michel Foucault, a French philosopher of the mid-to-late twentieth century, argues that our very conditions of possibility as sexual subjects arise within and under the scope of discourses and regimes of power. These discourses of sexual normalcy, salvation, moral rectitude, faith, and human value/dignity/worth crafted by institutions like the Catholic Church create sexual subjects who think of themselves as morally correct, valuable, and created in the intended image of God or as morally inferior, unworthy, and not in alignment with natural law. To understand how institutions create and control subjects, I will examine four aspects of Foucault's theories of power: sexual repression as discourse proliferation, the construction of truth, the Christian pastorate, and docile bodies. All of these aspects of his understanding of power will help illuminate the Catholic influence—intended or otherwise—on sexual subjectivity.

Sexual Repression as Discourse Proliferation

One of the primary arguments of *The History of Sexuality* (volume 1) is that the Victorian era of repression did not in fact silence sexuality. Instead, Foucault argues, there was an incitement to discourse via the attempt to repress the discussion of sex; there was a "veritable discursive explosion."[11] Foucault writes:

> sex was driven out of hiding and constrained to lead a discursive existence. From the singular imperialism that compels everyone to transform his sexuality into a perpetual discourse, to the manifold mechanisms which, in the areas of economy, pedagogy, medicine, and justice, incite, extract, distribute, and institutionalize the sexual discourse, an immense verbosity is what our civilization has required and organized.[12]

Thus in the Victorian era we begin to see the conversation around sexuality develop in professionalized secular spaces, among experts who create secular institutions for the medicalization of sexual behavior. Sexuality ceases to be a moral issue but begins to become a psychological issue, an identity issue, a medical issue, and a social problem.

Also around this time, the Catholic Church began to lose its secure and tight hold over sexual discourse. Foucault writes, "the secure bond that held together the moral theology of concupiscence and the obligation of confession (equivalent to the theoretical discourse on sex and its first-person formulation) was, if not broken, at least loosened and diversified."[13] Now, individuals weighed down by guilt or concern over their sexual behavior did not solely have to go to priests to confess; they could go instead to doctors or psychiatrists. The first-person narrative of sexual desire was now under the purview of discourses outside of and away from the world of theology and ecclesial control.

The discourse of sexual identity began to take root in the science of sexology. The narratives available (first for the "invert," then the "homosexual," eventually the "lesbian" and "gay man," and finally the "queer person") were becoming purely secular. Perhaps the contemporary disease between the Catholic Church and the LGBT/Q community is left over from exactly this separation. Perhaps the current silencing of LGBT/Q people by the Catholic hierarchy is a resentment created by and retained from the loss of control over the discourse of sexual deviancy that began in the 1800s.

At that time a split developed in how and by whom truth was established in the area of sexual morality. The discourses of sexology, psychology, and contemporary culture have defined the parameters of subaltern sexual identities, providing narratives of sexuality identity and certain kinds of frameworks for making sense of sexual experience— for example, "coming out of the closet." These discourses are all contemporary constructions. The Catholic Church, however, is still employing moral theologies that have not realigned with these contemporary cultural discourses. Both sets of discourses cling to claims of truth that are backed by their distinct claims of power or expertise. In many ways, LGBT/Q Catholics and post-Catholics are still living at the intersection of this split. These observations ought to lead to an immediate set of questions about how power employs itself over bodies via claims of truth.

The Construction of Truth

Foucault argues that we need to see truth as a function of the politics of this world. We have been sold a myth of truth as a retrieval of fact created via study and increasing human insight. This myth misdirects how we ought to see the development of truth through its mechanisms of production and its impact. Foucault writes:

> Truth isn't outside power, or lacking in power: contrary to a myth whose history and functions repay further study, truth isn't the reward of free spirits, the child of protracted solitude, nor the privilege of those who have succeeded in liberating themselves. Truth is a thing of this world: it is produced only by virtue of multiple forms of constraint. And it induces regular effects of power. Each society has its regime of truth, its "general politics" of truth: that is, the types of discourse which it accepts and makes function as true; the mechanisms and instances which enable one to distinguish true and false statements, the means by which each is sanctioned; the techniques and procedures accorded value in the acquisition of truth; the status of those who are charged with saying what counts as true.[14]

This focus on the techniques and procedures of truth allows Foucault to isolate what he sees as five important traits of truth in the "political economy" of our contemporary society. Truth is (1) "centered on the form of scientific discourse and the institutions that produce it," (2) "subject to constant economic and political incitement," (3) an object of "immense diffusion and consumptions" through education and information technologies, (4) produced and "transmitted under the control . . . of a few great political and economic apparatuses (university, army, writing, media)," and (5) constitutive of "'ideological' struggles."[15]

I draw attention to these five mechanisms of truth production because they describe the growing bodies of literature and discourse on LGBT/Q identities and experience. Truth about sexual identity in the secular world is governed by these kinds of techniques of knowledge as power. I wish to emphasize the point that power—as Foucault sees it—is not a matter of repression. Power is not the process of saying no and policing prohibitions. Power "traverses and produces things, it induces pleasure, forms knowledge, produces discourse." This productive aspect of power cannot be overlooked. The power of the Catholic Church produces Catholic people. The power of social and medical discourse produces LGBT/Q people. Each of these regimes of power can be seen as a "productive network which runs through the whole social body."[16] The points of social location one occupies will determine which productive strains of those interwoven networks one experiences.

The Christian Pastorate

Foucault also describes the techniques of the power of the Christian pastorate, which deviates from these productive norms. Through multiple means—each different from the others—the Christian pastorate infuses power into the docile bodies it influences (more on the latter below). Foucault specifies four characteristics of Christian pastoral power:

It is not territorial.
It is concerned with nurturing its own rather than vanquishing others.
It entails responsibility to the point of self-sacrifice.
It is exercised over individuals, one by one.[17]

In Foucault's model, we can recognize any major church institution, such as the Catholic Church, as well as its relationship to adherents across geographical and political borders by its investment in certain bodies over others, because of identity ties, the depth of responsibility of its leaders (including celibacy, poverty, and willingness to travel), and the individual nature of its influence.

Compare this to the power of knowledge production in which discourse is produced via institutions, subject to economic and political control, diffused and consumed, limited in its production, and foundational to ideological struggles. The Catholic Church produces truth in these ways and then disperses it through global infusion of nonterritorial influence over those it has baptized and confirmed with individual attention. Knowledge production is nonindividualistic, but the Christian pastorate directs itself at the shaping of particular bodies. Both sets of discourses influence and produce bodies. This individualized care and influence makes the relationship between the Catholic Church and LGBT/Q people globally particularly important. Political recognition can aid in the

advancement of self-care to LGBT/Q communities within particular regions, but the ability of the Catholic Church to transgress those borders
and reach within and have influence over unique persons means that a
pro-LGBT/Q Catholic Church would have the power to strengthen individual people despite political persecution. In its current anti-LGBT/Q
theological mindset it also has the ability to reach inside political borders
and weaken individual people despite advancements in equality.

Docile Bodies

"A body is docile that may be subjected, used, transformed and improved."[18]
Human bodies are docile under discourses and regimes of power. Under
forms of knowledge, Foucault explains, bodies are "offered up," "manipulated by authority."[19] Bodies become useful insofar as they receive training.
This "docility-utility" is what he calls a discipline.[20] Disciplined bodies are
diminished in terms of their political viability; obedience decreases the
forces of the body. But at the same time, the docility of these bodies creates
economic returns as utilized bodies oriented toward the discourse of power.[21]
Docile bodies work for the regime of power, yet docile bodies cannot defend rights that those with power deem disoriented from that regime.

Interestingly, disciplinary power works "through its invisibility; at the
same time it imposes on those whom it [creates as] subjects a principle of
compulsory visibility."[22] The forced visibility of the subjects means that
the disciplinary regime can be assured of its ability to hold power over the
individual subjects. Here we can begin to see the historical and juridical
importance of the visibility of LGBT/Q identities within the Catholic
Church, for the church, as well as the inherent risks of that visibility for
LGBT/Q people, if the parameters of Catholic moral theology of sexuality
do not shift. The current invisibility of LGBT/Q people within the church
means that the disciplinary power over these bodies does not effectively
render them docile. The disciplinary power of the church cannot properly
infuse itself into LGBT/Q bodies, because the church does not render them
first as fully formulated subjects—created fully in the image of God, fully
participatory in the body of Christ and the life of the church while simultaneously honoring the full subject formation of LGBT/Q bodies created by
the medical, psychological, and social discourses that have shaped and
literally created them with a particular set of cultural and spiritual needs.

What the church does provide is a limited set of teachings on same-sex sexuality that pushes against the literally orienting (narrative providing, political location establishing, cultural resource making) discourses of contemporary sexuality. The teachings of the church establish same-sex attractions as intrinsically disordered. This claim of "disordered" serves literally to disorient LGBT/Q people; it severs them from knowledge of self, produces or mandates complex self-deception, hinders access to life-giving sexual relationship and partnership.

These metaphors of orientation and disorientation suggest possibilities for movement on a map. If the cartography of sexuality is carefully plot-ted, with both the Catholic placement of its sexual ethics grid and the secular overlay of the grid of social justice, one sees a complex matrix through which an LGBT/Q person may or may not be able to find a path toward what is good.

Orientation

The notion of orientation conjoined with sexuality is meant to specify the direction of desire. As the term functions in contemporary society, it im-plicates both the sex of the persons toward whom attraction is directed as well as the sex of the individual with the attractions. The trajectory of this attraction as a connecting line has certain identifiable qualities—represented in the colloquial ways we discuss desire—and is also sugges-tive of theoretical and theological implications. For example, a straight orientation suggests a direct pathway between two persons, where a queer orientation implies an indirect movement, a deviation. This sym-bolic idea of the movement of desire is readily embraced and displaced unconsciously.[23] In the following sections I want to expose some of the implications of this talk of movement and its impact on one's sense of a spiritual or moral path.

Catholic Disorientation

Oftentimes the Catholic teaching that same-sex sexuality is intrinsically disordered is reduced to "love the sinner, hate the sin" in popular discourse and culture. The actual teachings by the church on "homosexuality" are of course more complexly worded. Here are two representative teachings that frame both sides of this trenchant theological statement. The first statement was written by the Vatican's Congregation for the Doctrine of the Faith in 1986. It clearly condemns LGBT/Q bullying and implicitly advocates for pastoral intervention: "We recognize that these persons [homosexuals] have been, and often continue to be objects of scorn, hatred, and even violence in some sectors of our society. Sometimes this hatred is manifested clearly; other times, it is masked and gives rise to more disguised forms of hatred. . . . Such treatment deserves condemnation from the Church's pastors wherever it occurs."[24] The recognition of and advocacy against social mistreatment of LGBT/Q persons is one active way in which the church can "love the sinner." While I commend the church's condemnation of social mistreatment, it is unclear how the church can say "I love you" and "you are a sinner" at the same time—knowing that the latter assertion, in this instance, is an intrinsic assessment of character and identity solely in the case of LGBT/Q persons. The church maintains that all human beings are sinners; however, the attribute of "sinner" is here attached to a state of character and identity in a way not paralleled with heterosexual sinners who are sinners based on behaviors rather than an intrinsically disordered state. In this statement of love, the immediate rejoinder mitigates and minimizes the affective assertion. Love ought to entail at minimum an affirmation of goodness, especially an affirmation of the ways in which we find and create love.

Here is the other side of the equation, from a document entitled "Ministry to Persons with a Homosexual Inclination: Guidelines for Pastoral Care": "The homosexual inclination is objectively disordered, i.e., it is an inclination that predisposes one toward what is truly not good for the human person."[25] This is often simplified into "hate the sin," but here we actually see the more insidious side of the "love the sinner" framing. A homosexual inclination is considered a disordering, a deviation from the good. It richly implies that the homosexual orientation orients the homosexual off the spiritual path that leads to the good or a place of moral wholeness. The statement of "love the sinner, hate the sin" has a fundamental slippage in its conception of moral orientation. Instead the phrase could read "love the inert homosexual orientation; hate the reactive homosexual orientation." The first half implies a condition warranting moral pity; the second half implies the inability to act morally. This frame almost explicitly claims that the "orientation" in sexual orientation is what establishes the proper direction of one's moral compass toward the good; it certainly implies as much. I want to explore this dis-orientation that the church promotes to see if we can discover a possible theoretical space for reorientation. In so doing, I will also explore what it means to articulate oneself as directed toward the good.

LGBT/Q Orientation

Orientation implies space. Sara Ahmed argues that "bodies are sexualized through how they inhabit space."[26] As a way of explaining how discourses of power become embodied, like the writing of a text, we see that our sexuality is writ as gestures, formulated as embodied style, seen through physical movement, and mapped through movement in space. Queer sexuality is framed as counterembodiment within compulsory heterosexuality. Ahmed writes: "Compulsory heterosexuality shapes what bodies can do. Bodies take the shape of norms that are repeated over time and with force. Through repeating some gestures and not others, or through being orientated in some directions and not others, bodies become contorted: they get twisted into shapes that enable some action *only insofar as they restrict the capacity for other kinds of action*."[27] To become queer under this kind of normative force is to reorient oneself, utilizing significant energy. As embodied work, the "work of reorientation needs to be made visible as a form of work."[28] To appropriate new discursive regimes of identity under systems where those scripts are dominantly unavailable or must be sought and uncovered and to rework already wrought bodies is to undertake a reconstructive task of significant proportion. And given the limited availability of prewritten scripts of realignment from "moral" authorities, this task can produce unpredictable effects.

The contemporary popularity of the term "queer" may be an attempt to capture something about this dis-alignment and limited availability of morally aligned scripts. Ahmed writes, "the etymology of the word 'queer' . . . comes from the Indo-European word 'twist.' Queer is, after all, a spatial term, which then gets translated into a sexual term, a term for a twisted sexuality that does not follow a 'straight line,' a sexuality that is bent and crooked."[29] The bending or twisting of the work of reorienting oneself toward objects of same-sex desire does not remain as legible in the more traditional terms of "lesbian," "gay," or "bisexual" as it does in the term "queer." "Queer" retains a history, a trace of the work first undertaken to disorient, before reorienting.

Queer is not the only spatial term suggesting deviation. According to Ahmed, "perversion is also a spatial term": it often describes the "willful determination to counter or go against orthodoxy" and also to turn away from "what is right, good, and proper."[30] The Catholic claim of "intrinsically *disordered*" from the good becomes a polite way of establishing homosexuality as perversion. Human beings want to think of themselves as seeking out the good and as finding orientation—or as being ordered—toward those things that will help them achieve a state of flourishing. To be excluded from those narratives is to be excluded from something that is deeply humanizing, as we will see in the next section.

Reorienting to the Good

In *Sources of the Self*, Charles Taylor identifies two key components of personal identity that situate and direct the energies of an individual: an orientation to the good and a life narrative that articulates that orientation. One's sense of self is dependent upon one's conception of the good. Taylor argues, "To know who you are is to be oriented in moral space, a space in which questions arise about what is good or bad, what is worth doing and what not, what has meaning and importance for you and what is trivial and secondary."[31] Some sort of operative or tacit definition of the moral is the psychological touchstone for organizing life activities and decisions. It is interesting that Taylor describes this in spatial terms. In this space, questions "arise" that provide orientation for movement toward a particular goal. The use of the word "space" may be a simple rhetorical shorthand referring to a kind of focused mental space. But it is also worth noting that this moral space provides physical and metaphorical movement through the landscape of one's life.

Taylor connects this orientation to the good to the concept of a narrative. He writes:

> in order to make minimal sense of our lives, in order to have an identity, we need an orientation to the good, which means some sense of qualitative discrimination, of the incomparably higher. Now we see

that this sense of the good has to be woven into my understanding of my life as an unfolding story. But this is to state another basic condition of making sense of ourselves, that we grasp our lives in *narrative*.[32]

I agree with Taylor that in the story of our lives, the role of "the good"[33] must be a storyboard or framework within which the self operates. Perhaps it would make more sense to view the good as that which provides the contours and style of our individual narrative. However we are to conceive of it, the good is something that provides the basic recognizable character of a life, although not necessarily the basic recognizable attributes of an individual. It is that which provides the story line, the plot, the arc of the trajectory/ies of the individual's directive aim. This transitional and interdependent relationship between personal identity, the good, and narrative is foundational—for Taylor—to any analysis of the self.

If Taylor is correct, if "the good" can be found within the style of any life narrative, then a few things result. First, we have a ubiquitous structure in which the good must operate for all individuals. Second, it must always produce some basic structural life components. Third, it allows for an individualized contingency, so that the good can manifest in unique and individualized ways without needing to be radically individualized.

This also means that LGBT/Q persons will struggle with and against their articulations of self in order to produce a narrative of the "good" that captures the broadest stretch of their life experience. In this all-too-human endeavor, Catholic identity literally impedes the flourishing of the self because it defines the "homosexual inclination" as "intrinsically disordered . . . toward what is truly not good." This authorial definition of the self as disordered both inhibits articulation of sexual identity and continues to keep LGBT/Q identities from the communion table of full human recognition.

Politics of Recognition, Orderly Catholic LGBT/Q Subjectivities

Identity demands recognition from the population at large and from institutions in particular. This recognition is of value, Kwame Appiah asserts, because "it will be uncontroversial among those who have normal human relations that the responses of other people play a crucial role in shaping one's sense of who one is."[34] The idea is that our intimate relationships help us in developing an inward sense of identity by enabling us better to recognize who we are. Appiah and Taylor, among others such as Habermas,[35] think that it is the government's job to recognize identities that are otherwise subject to social contempt. This sustaining of recognition through the state helps reduce the risk of possible self-contempt on the part of individuals who are shunned by those they love. This, in short, is the idea behind a "politics of recognition." In addition to the value of the government providing recognition of identities, it ought to also be clear that institutions that provide education or claim access to the sacred ought also to engage in this politics of recognition. This entails a moral obligation for the Catholic Church.

Recognition is the first step. Recognition ought to be a central sacred function within the church. The experiences, political tribulations, theology, and social plight of LGBT/Q persons must be recognized and supported by the church. The second step is the provision of scripts of LGBT/Q sexual identity in alignment with the good, ordered toward this good. This ought not to be seen as expanding the productive sense of power over additional docile bodies but instead as a pastoral concern of "nurturing its own" rather than vanquishing them. The Catholic Church—every church—needs to help its faithful learn how to articulate their own sexual subjectivities in authentic ways. This is broader than a claim for passive inclusion; this is about creating active, productive inclusion of LGBT/Q people of faith.

Closing Words

To discern the contours of my sexual subjectivity I have had to look elsewhere than the church. This search is ongoing. During my years of Catholic education, some of the most important years in my individuation and subject formation, there was a dearth of resources provided to me to find my own voice. This would still have been significantly true if I had been a heterosexual woman. To take up the Catholic symbolic, I cannot speak as an imitation male or an imitation heterosexual. To be "listened to," I cannot be heard as an imitation male or an imitation heterosexual. So, in learning to speak, there are systems of ideological privilege, dominance, and theological repression that I had to unlearn first.

Everything I learned about being a queer woman I learned in gay bars or in graduate school, when after many hours of studying regular white male heterosexual philosophy I would consume the writings of feminists and queer thinkers. In part, I spent many years in school trying to accumulate resources and skills to articulate my subjectivity, a subjectivity that is shared and diversified by the LGBT/Q communities of which I have been a part. We should not be alone in these explorations or have to rely solely on secular sources. An institution of pastoral concern should be involved.

As Foucault asserts, our sexual subjectivities are some of our deepest and most controlled subjectivities. Desire is central to subjectivity and a regime that denies/forbids articulations of desire denies the very subjects themselves. Until all the pastors of the Catholic Church understand our queer desires, they will not understand our subjectivity. Until they understand us, they cannot help us on our path to find God or in our narratives of self framed by the good.

2 Talking About Homosexuality by the (Church) Rules

MARK D. JORDAN

Danforth Center, Washington University in St. Louis

Imagine this. Overnight, God changes the hearts of a majority of officials in the Vatican. They awake in the morning convinced that the Roman Catholic church's condemnations of "homosexual acts" are both untrue and unjust. They resolve to revoke them. What would they have to revise in church doctrine or practice in order to correct the teaching about gays and lesbians?

. . . Let us suppose that God has worked a change in the pope himself. . . . [At last the pope] has decided to right a wrong done to homosexuals over centuries. His advisers have persuaded him at least to go slowly—to "study" the problem before acting on it. Rumor rushes down the clerical layers: The moral teaching about homosexuality is to be corrected by papal command. . . . The Holy Father asks, "What is required for the thorough correction of the teaching?"[1]

Those are pieces from the opening of a book I wrote a few years ago. The introduction struck some people as irreverent. Perhaps they were right—though there are much more irreverent pages later on in the book. What they could not know is that the opening was the remnant of another book I started to write and then threw away.

In that discarded text, I had asked myself just the question I imagined for the Vatican: What else would have to change in Roman Catholic teaching if the pope did awake one morning, resolved to reverse the condemnation of homosexuality? Some connected changes are obvious. The prohibition of artificial means of contraception would fall away, for example, because you would lose the linchpin argument that restricts genital activity to physical procreation. You would also have to rethink prohibitions of masturbation and a range of other sexual acts. Either the restriction of sex to marriage would have to be modified, or else you would have to include same-sex couples within marriage—thus changing received accounts of the sacrament's ends or purposes. Still other changes, less obviously related, seemed to be entailed. For example, once it becomes possible to talk about same-sex love as a created good, much of the gendered language about love in moral or mystical or Trinitarian theology might require revision—or at least a second hearing. So too would contrasts between love and communal charity or love and friendship.

After spending some months tracing obvious and not so obvious changes, I stopped writing.

I stopped first because I realized that changing magisterial teaching did not depend on producing better arguments. There were good arguments already on the table when I was writing in the late 1990s: pastoral arguments from John McNeill, historical arguments from John Boswell, and philosophical or theological arguments from Richard Woods, Mary Hunt, Elizabeth Stuart, and James Alison, to mention only a few.[2] But those good arguments had not changed official teaching—except perhaps to make it worse. The last forty years have seen both the flowering of LGBT-affirming Catholic theologies and the intensification of official repression. Magisterial teaching against homosexuality is now more fully articulated than before, and disciplinary controls over LGBT life in churches, seminaries, and religious communities are tighter now than they were around 1970 when McNeill's courageous articles began to appear in the *Homiletic and Pastoral Review*.[3] So covering the same ground with more arguments was not the way forward. This was my first realization—it stopped me in mid-manuscript.

I also stopped for a second reason. I realized that the issue of homosexuality was not just one example of the exercise of churchly power. It is a privileged example—an example directly implicated in current forms of that power. Changing church teaching on homosexuality requires not the revision of doctrines but the transformation of structures of power, since doctrinal or regulatory homophobia is, among other things, the mask of a homoerotic power that animates those structures. So I left off tracing doctrinal revisions in order to compose a meditation on how official Catholicism silences homosexuality so that it can continue functioning in its present institutional form.

The book I actually wrote then is neither clear nor coherent. Yet I stand by the double insight that led to it. Arguments alone will not produce change in Catholic teaching on homosexuality because a distorted form of male-male desire is essential to the present operation of church power. So, here, I will try to describe some connections of prohibited desire and church power more clearly and more coherently than I did. I hope to trace some of the processes that undo serious Catholic speech about homosexuality. These processes do their work by preventing speech, if possible; by discrediting it when prevention fails; but above all by hardening the shells around words before emptying them of meaning.

A note to polemicists: Any regular participant in church "debates" about homosexuality not only learns the opposing speeches but begins to internalize them as a cautionary voice. While writing the book I did publish, I worried about how it might be misused to stigmatize gay priests or to fuel some versions of anti-Catholicism. In fact, it was misused in both ways. I did not anticipate so clearly the attacks on my honesty, my intelligence, my morals, or my faith. The book's reception by "conservative" Catholics has given my naïveté a rough education.[4]

I begin this essay by talking about myself to acknowledge that the most obvious rebuttals of it will take the form of ad hominem *attacks. It is not hard for a busy polemicist to assemble such an attack from pieces already posted on the web—some of the most elaborate disguised as reviews or responses to that earlier book. I do not mention them to bewail my singular fate. I mean instead to underscore how familiar such attacks now are—how trite libel has become in church exchanges over homosexuality.*

Some libels are predictable when attacking anyone who questions or criticizes church teachings on sexuality. Such a person must be consumed by disgusting passions, must have committed unspeakable crimes, must be an abomination in the sight of God. These charges recycle medieval characterizations of the sodomite. Following medieval precedent, a polemicist can also know in advance that any dissenter from church teaching on sexuality is not a true Catholic—is already a heretic who is doubtless guilty of one or more unforgivable sins against the graces of the Holy Spirit bestowed in baptism.

I want to concede at least a part of the last charge. Since publishing the book on Catholic homosexuality, I have in fact left the communion of the Roman Catholic Church. I now worship as an Episcopalian—though friends frequently remind me that I am indelibly Roman Catholic in my theology and my ecclesial reflexes. (You will see that I have just provided fresh material for an ad hominem *dismissal of this essay—though this is hardly the first time I have talked about being an Episcopalian.) Does this change in my community of worship mean that I can no longer write about Catholicism—even though I have spent decades as a Roman Catholic, teaching in Catholic schools on Catholic topics, and even though I continue to teach and write as an academic specialist on Catholicism?*

I can see that my present position imposes special considerations of charity. But I do not see any rules that prohibit my speech—or, rather, the rules I can see seem to me unjustified. I especially resist the rule that the only persons who can credibly speak about church power are those currently licensed by that very power. Something like that rule is implied every time an "orthodox" Catholic blog claims that "dissenters" have no right to speak about a church they have already departed through their very infidelity. A rule that preemptively disenfranchises anyone who would disagree is not a rule of speech but of silence. It is not a rule of charity but a sure index of tyranny.

Unfortunately any speech about Catholicism, sexuality, and clerical power is so vexed—so scandalous—that I cannot proceed without underlining three cautions against misunderstanding.

First, I propose to describe an ecclesiastical system of power over sexuality, not the individual lives under it. Of course people can lead a Christian life of unstinting love, of vivid witness, of embodied grace under the present system of Roman power. I am hardly trying to set absolute limits to all lives within the system or, indeed, to calculate a limit on any of those lives in their pursuit of holiness. I describe a configuration of clerical power because I think that it sets impossible conditions for serious public speech about Catholicism and homosexuality—or about Catholicism and gender more generally.

Second caution: I want to talk about this clerical power as homoerotic. I do not mean to imply anything about the sexual acts or fantasies of individuals who participate in this power. I apply the term to the charge or energy circulating through a system—what helps constitute it as a system. Some writers use the word "homosocial" rather than "homoerotic" when referring to social relations rather than to genital acts—to make clear, say, that they are talking about male bonding rather than male-male copulation. I stick with the word "homoerotic" because this form of clerical power is the object and the instrument of sharp longing, of desire.

Third and final caution: I speak of the configuration of homoerotic power in the Roman Catholic clergy at particular times and places. The "church" does not possess the immutability or eternity that classical theology attributes to God (even if some who exalt the church wish that it did). Across church history, there are interesting analogies or repetitions, and there are striking structural similarities among church cultures in a given time. (There are also important dissimilarities, and the Roman Catholic Church at any single moment—in this moment—is a much more complicated cluster of institutions than any description can capture.) But power has to be described in the particular—both because of the limits of our imagination and its language and because power has a history. It mutates as it extends itself, as it enters different bodies, as it encounters other forms of power. Moreover—to quote that ancient Catholic, Michel Foucault, whom I have just been paraphrasing—"power is tolerable only on condition that it mask a substantial part of itself."[5] Power makes new masks—or redecorates old ones. They have to be deciphered one by one.

A further note to polemicists: The mention of Foucault opens another line of attack against this essay—that I am evidently relying on relativistic, nihilistic, and atheistic ideologies that blind me to truths both of nature and of revelation.

This rhetorical strategy is another sort of argument ad hominem, this one against my sources rather than against me. Interestingly, this strategy too will resort to biographical caricatures in order to avoid engagement. (So, for example, a polemicist may proceed to point out that Foucault was, of course, a well-known homosexual who [stage whisper] engaged in sadomasochistic practices.) The strategy wants to save itself the trouble of having to read—of having to consider, for example, the extraordinary intelligence that Foucault devotes to analyzing the transit from confession or spiritual direction to psychiatry, from the older Catholicism of the flesh to the contemporary Catholicism of idolized procreation.

The polemical effort to dismiss powerful thinkers as fundamentally corrupt always looks to me like a reflex of fear. Certainly it is the opposite of the courage in truth that has animated the strongest periods of Catholic intellectual life—in the twentieth century or the thirteenth.

I want to characterize the system of Catholic power that prevents speech about homosexuality by an admittedly hasty comparison of the course of recent debate in the Anglican and Roman Catholic churches. I present the two trajectories in order to raise the question: *Why has the debate gone so differently?* I then want to pursue only one of the many answers to that question—the one that has to do with the relation of same-sex desire to modern structures of Roman clerical power.

In the early 1950s, Derrick Sherwin Bailey was employed by the Church of England's main social agency, the Moral Welfare Council, to be a traveling lecturer on sex and marriage for theological colleges and other church schools.[6] When news stories about sensational homosexual scandals began to attract public attention, he realized that rising controversy over sodomy laws would require fuller answers from the Anglican Church. He undertook to find them. In April 1952, Bailey proposed to the Moral Welfare Council a study group on homosexuality—what would later be described as "a small group of Anglican clergy and doctors, with legal advice," who were "alone . . . responsible for the views . . . [they] expressed."[7] An officially unofficial group, able to speak candidly.

Bailey was only one of several authors for the study group's interim report, published in 1954, but many passages in it echo or agree with his views, especially about the inadequacies of sexual terminology. For Bailey and for the report, a person who suffers the condition of homosexuality is an invert. *He* (the pronoun is appropriate) is to be distinguished from the bisexual and the pervert, that is, "a heterosexual who engages in homosexual practices."[8] The condition of inversion cannot generally be altered, either because there is no therapy for it or because therapy is resisted. Note the basic distinction here, between curable and incurable same-sex desire, with the incurable kind called "inversion."

The pamphlet puts men and women together when it is time for moral judgment: adolescent fixation "will exempt an invert from responsibility for his homosexual condition *but cannot absolve him from responsibility for immoral homosexual practices.*"[9] This generalization of condemnation to cover both men and women—when the analysis had been preoccupied with men—is both typical and interesting. It is typical as an application of one misogynistic prejudice: women have no real sexuality, so they can always be added to sexual morality as an afterthought, especially when it comes time to judge. (For another version of Christian misogyny, by contrast, women are designated the polluting bearers of sexuality.) The shift to general condemnation is interesting as a way to detach the imagination from male-male desire at the moment of pronouncing judgment. Indeed, one function of abstract categories like "invert" or "homosexual" is to prevent any overly vivid imagination of particular forms of male-male love—especially in a male-dominated institution.

If the Anglican report is remembered at all, it is usually for distinguishing this moral conclusion from the punishments of criminal law. The report is clearly arranged to favor decriminalizing consensual homosexual acts between adults—and Bailey himself had already written of a "Christian duty to press for the removal of this anomalous and shameful [legal] injustice, which has done untold harm and has achieved no good whatever."[10] I think this is a remarkable claim—even if it raises many questions (say, about the relation of sexual law to moral judgment). Still I want to stress the other side of the story: the report qualifies this policy recommendation by reiterating its moral judgment—this time on theological grounds. "Homosexual acts are sins against God, whether or not they are also crimes against the State." Homosexual acts deflect "the activity of the sexual organ from its proper end."[11] They cannot be excused on a plea of love any more than sexual acts between other unmarried lovers. The only space for erotic life among Christians is in marriage. Since inverts should not marry partners of the other sex, and since approving same-sex marriage would undermine society, those who suffer the condition should follow the example of (heterosexual) women who cannot find a husband: they should "*accept their condition, and by seeking to sublimate their sexual lives in various socially useful ways achieve personal fulfillment.*"[12] They should avoid homosexual bars, form chaste friendships, and rely on the sacraments. Meanwhile, society will try to correct the causes that produced them.

Roman Catholic readers who have never heard of the Moral Welfare Council or its interim report may find this language oddly familiar. It is in fact much like language used two decades later by the Vatican.

In 1975, the Congregation for the Doctrine of the Faith (CDF) issued a declaration on human sexuality that contained what many regarded—what some still regard—as a significant paragraph on homosexuality. The declaration is not primarily concerned with homosexuality. Its purpose is more encompassing. It wants to reassert "natural law" arguments against a variety of sexual sins, including extramarital sex, homosexuality, and masturbation. (Why homosexuality should now receive so much more church attention than masturbation or extramarital sex is part of my interest here.) As regards "the sexual inclination of man and the human reproductive power," "natural law" precepts teach that genital acts "do not have their true significance or moral force outside of legitimate marriage."[13] Any other genital activity, including any activity involving "artificial means" of contraception, is an abuse of human sex. It is not hard to predict how this teaching will apply to "homosexual relations." Both the "perpetual teaching" of the church's officials and "the moral sense of the Christian people" refuse to excuse "the homosexual relations of some persons."[14] Note the claim for the timelessness of doctrine and the implied exclusion from "the Christian people" of those whose "moral sense" does not refuse to excuse homosexual relations. These might, in all charity, be called wishes rather than truths.

There is one other piece in the paragraph—the most important for some readers. The declaration allows indirectly that there may be grounds for distinguishing between curable and incurable homosexuals, between those who have a homosexual "proclivity born from bad education or damaged sexual maturity or habit or bad example"—all of whom are counted curable—and those who are homosexuals "in perpetuity" because of "some kind of almost innate impulse" or "a vitiated constitution."[15] The document admits this distinction in the most roundabout way: while paraphrasing a position it will oppose, in an aside, it notes that a distinction between curable and incurable homosexual desire "seems to be made not without reason."[16] This is an astonishing circumlocution. Is it meant to concede a point without conceding it—or to test reactions to a possible concession—or to register a disagreement among the paragraph's authors?

The declaration then directs that such perpetual homosexuals are to be treated gently in pastoral care. Their moral culpability should be judged prudently. Of course, neither the distinction between kinds of homosexual desire nor the ensuing pastoral directive gives permission for homosexual acts. "According to the moral order of objective things homosexual couplings are acts that are deprived of their necessary and essential ordering." Again, "acts of homosexuality are disordered by their very nature, nor can they be approved in any way whatever."[17]

This paragraph was hailed as a breakthrough. You can take that as a sign of the beleaguered conditions of queer Catholic life, but you can also imagine that some activist Catholics might have heard echoes of the older Anglican report, which had been widely publicized throughout the late 1950s and 1960s in American groups working on homosexuality and religion. Although both documents conclude that it is never morally permissible to enact homosexual desires, an optimistic reader might want to construe Rome's recognition of an incurable condition as a first step along a road that had, even by 1975, brought queer Episcopalians to happy results. Within the Episcopal Church, plans were by then already afoot for its 1976 General Convention to declare "that homosexual persons are children of God and have a full and equal claim with all other persons upon the love, acceptance, and pastoral concern and care of the Church."[18] If it would take another three decades of disagreement for the Episcopal Church to sort through the consequences of affirming "homosexual persons," that church has indeed welcomed them into sacramental participation—not yet fully, and not, of course, without causing various splits in the United States and abroad.

The story of Roman Catholic debate since 1975 goes rather differently. In 1986, the CDF issued a letter that corrected overly optimistic readings of the 1975 declaration and expelled groups like Dignity from church property, while alluding to AIDS as a consequence of homosexuality and describing violence as an understandable reaction against queer political activism.[19] In 1992, the CDF urged Catholic bishops to argue that sexual orientation should not be protected from discrimination on analogy to race or other categories because homosexuality is an objective disorder.[20] In 1998, the CDF forced the American bishops to revise and reissue "Always Our Children," their "pastoral message" to the parents of homosexuals.[21] In 1999, the CDF issued a notification against Jeannine Gramick and Robert Nugent for refusing to sign a profession of faith that included, among other things, discredited readings of the biblical passages supposedly about homosexuality.[22] Beginning at least in the spring of 2002, members of the hierarchy publicly blamed clerical sexual abuse on the presence of homosexuals in the priesthood.[23] And in 2005, the Vatican's Congregation for Catholic Education issued an instruction denying ordination and even seminary admission to "those who practice homosexuality, present deep-seated homosexual tendencies or support the so-called 'gay culture.'"[24]

If the words looked the same in Anglican and Roman documents at certain moments, the ensuing histories diverged sharply. Why this different history? Why the unflagging and intransigent reaction of the Vatican dicasteries and other official voices?

There are many answers to such questions, but I want to continue with just one, the relation of debates about sexuality to Roman structures of clerical power.

Another note to polemicists: My highly abbreviated comparison is open to various rejoinders. An obvious one would contrast the disunity visible in the Episcopal Church or the worldwide Anglican community with the serene unity of Roman Catholicism. Episcopalian disunity is real and painful. So too is the present disarray of the Anglican communion. But it may be that evident disunity is at least one degree better than fictional unity. Too much of the unity of Roman Catholicism is an illusion created by processes for silencing and excluding. It is the "unity" of enforced monologue.

Another rejoinder to my comparison would see in it proof that the only antidote to a "liberal" slide into heresy or apostasy is the robust assertion of traditional values by an authoritarian hierarchy. Here, of course, we move beyond debates over sexuality into larger questions of faith—though perhaps not the questions that an "orthodox" polemicist might imagine. (One question, for example, is whether a God who took flesh as a renegade rabbi, who left behind memories of scandalous sayings and the command to recall him by hosting an indecently open table, really intended to teach the kind of truth captured in a universal catechism and a code of canon law.) But by now it should go without saying that our debates "about sexuality" are mostly not about sexuality.

Looking back to the Anglican and Roman documents in view of their divergent effects, we might now notice certain other features in their treatment of sex and gender. For example, while the CDF's 1975 declaration ties homosexuality to artificial contraception, the Anglican Church had already begun in the late 1920s to modify its teaching on the regulation of birth in marriage. We could notice that as the Anglican committee was working on issues of homosexuality, other Anglican groups were already pursuing the ordination of women. We should notice, most of all, that the early leader of Anglican efforts to rethink homosexuality, D. S. Bailey, was a married man with children.

Roman Catholic debates about homosexuality cannot be understood except in relation to a priesthood that is all male and, in the Roman Rite, normatively celibate. The importance of this relation is confirmed even within the Anglican example, since Bailey's work was hardly greeted with enthusiasm on all sides. There were evangelical Anglicans who opposed him because of their reading of the Scriptures. But much opposition came from Anglo-Catholic quarters, that is, from groups that advocated priestly celibacy and opposed women's ordination. These were also the groups notorious for attracting large numbers of closeted or not-so-closeted homosexual men. Public homophobia often goes along with private homosexuality. Or public homophobia is, for some men, the only secure container for their disconcerting desires.

This duality of public stigma and private passion is hardly confined to churches. We see it in other all-male institutions, such as the military. Indeed, there is a long literature on military schools that resonates uncannily with tales from seminaries and religious houses at precisely this point. But in "high" Christian churches the duality of homophobia/homoeroticism takes intense forms, because it is mixed with ideals of liturgical purity and embodied submission to divine authority. In "high" churches, the duality of this version of masculinity is intensified because the most admirable woman is a perpetual virgin and because God's male body can be produced and handled only by male hands. I mention a few elements in a complex system of symbols, and I rush to assure you that I am not contesting basic doctrines so much as pointing to their familiar gendering—so familiar that most adherents hardly remark it. They fail to notice how quickly this theological gendering is fused into the rhetoric of power—say, in the phrase, "Holy Father." In Roman Catholicism, in Anglo-Catholicism, the fusion of gendered doctrine and church hierarchy is so seamless, so fluent, that it becomes invisible—which is not to say that it ceases to operate.

How can we understand the forms of desire that flow through this religious system of gendered power? One way would be to narrate the psychological mechanisms that bring individuals into the system or allow them to succeed within it. There are plausible stories to be told about how easily a young man suffering from homosexual desires is attracted to an institution that certifies his sexual purity—and, in a curious way, his official heterosexuality—while exempting him from heterosexual activity.

I have learned from these stories. I have told some of them about myself. Still, psychological explanations seem to me to focus too exclusively on individuals and, indeed, to put blame on individuals. More importantly, they shift attention to genital acts, as if the pursuit of particular sexual encounters were the cause rather than the result of the system of power. But the homoeroticism of modern clerical power is only secondarily about the kind of desire we call sexual. It is primarily about the gender of desire for incontestable authority—the gender of desire for this very form of power. I am not asserting a form of "gender essentialism," according to which there are immutable characteristics of male and female in all times and places. I am suggesting instead that the required maleness of the priesthood and the further distancing of women by mandatory celibacy puts some cultural stereotypes of masculinity into strict connection with Catholic priestly power. When a church system requires that its priests be men, it is important to ask immediately: Which constructions of masculinity are thus imported into church life? The answers vary, of course, by time and place. The masculinity of the village priest I knew as a boy in Mexico is not the same as the masculinity of a celibate colleague in the American academy. No composite picture of the required masculinity of the Catholic priest can be painted for a single time and place, much less for all times and places. But it is possible to notice something of the range, as it is possible to watch the changes across historical spans. So I do want to say, for example, that contemporary articulations of Catholic clerical power have been shaped by late modern notions of totalitarian control—and that these notions have brought with them certain declamations of masculinity.

Current Roman Catholic teaching on the priesthood is many things, some of them quite beautiful. Whatever else it is, it is also a teaching about gender—about the necessary correlation of culturally available ideals of masculinity with a particular form of priestly power. To allow priests in the Roman Rite to marry would change this power and this masculinity. So too, more decisively, would the ordination of women. The peculiar geometry of this form of male-on-male power—its demands for absolute certainty, its attraction to regimented purity, its tastes in humiliating surveillance—depends on the exclusion of women.

The geometry is entirely ideal. It consists of fantastic demands or attractions or taboos, not lived realities. Still, the fantasies matter, because they solicit and shape certain forms of desire—especially desire for unqualified obedience as the entryway to power. Unqualified clerical obedience operates *within* the clergy before it can be demanded outside of it. It is based on the promise of an eternal reward—but more immediately on the promise of a share in power. "Submit to this power in order to gain this power." For clerical power to continue from generation to generation, it must persuade some men that their own desires are found within it.

There are many costs to perpetuating such a system of masculine desire, but one of the most interesting is the silencing of male-male love. That love must be suppressed because it lies too close to the fantasy circulating in the system of power—because it risks exposing the fantasy as fantasy. The fantasy of obedience-authority dissipates before the lived reality of embodied desire, of the democracy of shared vulnerability, of the equality of our need for care and our call to take care. Precisely because Christian tradition overwhelmingly associates same-sex lust with men, and because a fantasy of male-male power motivates certain forms of clerical power, there can be no permission for speech about same-sex love.

To speak positively in a Catholic setting about homosexuality is more than an offense against official teachings on morals or an act of doctrinal dissent (since modern notions of *magisterium* have effectively abolished the epistemic distinction between morals and dogma). To speak about homosexuality as a created good or a divine calling risks exposing a deep fantasy about church power. It risks violating the most important rules for Catholic speech.

Again, to the polemicists: A clever polemicist might respond to my analysis by shrugging his shoulders and smiling with a puzzled shake of the head. Do I really think that the Catholic priesthood or the church itself is nothing but a system of suppressed homosexual desire? What a sadly cynical view of a grand institution!

Perhaps the clever polemicist senses my own discomfort. Whenever I write about the homoerotic character of certain systems of clerical power—or the special significance of public speech about homosexuality within them—I become uncomfortable. I remember the many Roman priests who were models for me of generous intellect and unstinting service. I think of my friends now who are remarkable priests and who are comfortably gay. I pull back from my own generalizations—as a writer of history, as a writer simply. I wish that I did not have to write so bluntly, so clumsily about these questions.

At the same time, I see that these sentiments, while genuine, serve under the present rules only to perpetuate silence around the gender of church power. It is embarrassing to speak about power so crudely, but both the crudeness and the embarrassment are themselves so many effects of power. We stumble when we try to talk about the power around us, not least because it ridicules and hardens—it empties—any languages we might use to name it. If all speech about clerical homoeroticism ends by being crude and loud, that itself is the best evidence for how fully the clerical system has corrupted certain speech. The scandalous excesses of this essay are, after all, only echoes of the old violence of churchly rhetoric about sexual sinners. More: they are the ongoing effect on language of the prevailing clerical systems.

The reason that there is so little progress in official Catholic debates about homosexuality is that a fantasy of male-male desire is a motive force in prevailing systems of clerical power. The fantasy sees its fulfillment not in sexual relations but in the rewarding of absolute (male) obedience with uncontested (male) authority. The fantasy must be masked, so (male-male) homosexuality cannot be discussed publicly—except in forms of speech that serve silence.

In one of the series of lectures he delivered at the Collège de France in the spring of 1975, Foucault made a first effort to describe early modern changes in Catholic pastoral practice and then the transfer of those techniques—of that power—to the new sciences of psychiatry. The effort is a rough draft of what becomes, in the last decade of his writing, an increasingly nuanced meditation on the origins, progress, and afterlife of the Christian pastorate. Still, the rough draft contains some memorable formulations. The desiring body—the concupiscent body, to use the technical term—is coded or charted as a flesh that can be endlessly monitored and copiously described.[25] Indeed, the flesh, like sexuality, is defined by its relation to speech: "The flesh is what one names, the flesh is that of which one speaks, the flesh is what one says. Sexuality is essentially . . . not what one does, but what one confesses."[26]

This is a deliberate provocation—an inversion of the contemporary "secular" conviction that sexuality is the most real thing of all, the innermost truth, the self-certifying experience. The provocation is quite deliberate: Foucault repeats it. He has already told his lecture audience, for example, "In a general way, I would say this: sexuality, in the West, is not what one keeps silent, it is not what one is obliged to keep silent, but what one is obliged to confess."[27] I do not want at present to explicate the various meanings of these dicta, much less to defend either their truth or their pedagogical prudence. I want only to add the notion that sexuality arises in or around speech to my analysis of the conditions for Catholic speech about homosexuality.

Mandatory celibacy is mostly a rule not about bodies but about speech. When a priest speaks a vow of celibacy, he is supposed to be vowing not to do certain things, but he is certainly promising not to *say* certain things.

The prohibited speech acts include avowals of his sexual desires or acts—but also the proud naming of his lovers. Mandatory celibacy further imposes a practice of silence on the pious faithful, who are not supposed to speculate about priestly sex, to name anything they might see as priestly sex, or to denounce the sexual abuse of themselves or their children.

I keep speaking of silence, but of course I mean public silence. The other side of this system is a set of intricate compulsions to speak one's sexuality privately—to cultivate disciplines of self-description and self-accusation, to learn a list of approved terms or their euphemisms, to memorize an interior map on which every desire is supposed to have a place and eventually to take its place. The public silencing of speech about sexuality is supposed to be complemented by the endless murmuring of the confessional. I say "supposed to be," because American confessional discipline has largely broken down in recent decades, especially when it comes to sex. The church's teaching on sex has become so unconvincing—so widely and regularly disregarded—that even "good Catholics" boast of keeping silent about it in the confessional.

There are doubtless connections between the emptying confessionals and the bombast of magisterial condemnations of homosexuality. But it is more important to ask about the Catholic Church's reaction to other public discourses about homosexuality. No church can now control all the publicly available speeches about homosexuality. There are too many of them, and they arrive through too many channels. Favorable speeches come in news and entertainment, of course, but also in school curricula, clinical settings, political debates, or gossip. They are heard most forcefully over the Thanksgiving table. Faced with this swell of speech, the Catholic Church, along with many others, has adopted tactics of silencing and exclusion—or silencing until exclusion. What it cannot control, it excludes and then covers over with an endless flow of insult. The faithful are not supposed to debate homosexuality; those who debate homosexuality are no longer part of the faithful, and so they can be treated to various forms of condemnation and ridicule.

I have sketched these processes very schematically, but even a simplified sketch may suggest how they produce a double emptying of speech. Inside the church, silence about priestly homosexuality means in practice a constant misnaming or misnarration. Since officially priests may not be homosexual (especially with each other), any signs of homosexual activity must be kept silent—frequently by shouting denials or denunciations. Meanwhile, positive speeches about homosexuality outside the church are dismissed as both false and anti-Catholic.

These rules or processes operate within a much larger history of prescribed Christian speech about sexuality. Many of the prescriptions are actually ways of producing silence, not least by denaturing language. That is a basic lesson from Foucault: endless talk about sexuality can be a means of muzzling pleasures—of denying them access to speech by gibbering ventriloquism. We have centuries of Christian speech about sexuality, and we have so few Christian truths about our sexed bodies.

A final note to polemicists: The most clever polemicist would object just here that the very same line of reasoning could be used to argue against holding Catholic conferences about homosexuality or publishing books on the topic. To declare oneself a homosexual, to advocate acceptance of homosexuality on progressive grounds, is only to participate in the modern system of compulsory speech about sexuality. That system, according to Foucault himself, is an inheritance of early modern forms of pastoral practice in the confessional and spiritual direction. So, the polemicist would conclude, proclaiming oneself a Catholic homosexual and arguing for sexual liberation within the church is, in the end, only indenturing oneself to a debased form of pastoral practice. Resistance should in fact keep silence.

I would concede much of what this Foucault-reading polemicist says, but I would deny the conclusion—not least, by appeal to Foucault's example as a writer. Serious conversation about homosexuality in Catholicism does not consist only of coming-out stories or endorsements of liberationist platforms— though personal testimony and caucus platforms have their good effects. Catholic conversation about homosexuality must show enough of the churchly operation of gendered power to guide the making of fuller speech.

If certain key forms of clerical power are at stake underneath church debates over homosexuality, what is the best way forward?

It is not the mounting of more arguments. Making and remaking arguments within a field of speech in which the language has been emptied of content is a game that cannot be won.

There is a better form of linguistic resistance. It is resistance felt first not as endless counterargument but as interruptions by bodies that cannot bend anymore. It is the abrupt refusal of bodies to speak the lines or to keep the silences that the fantastic rules of power assign.

The sequel to this interrupting resistance is language making. Fuller language for speaking what we now label "Catholic homosexuality" does not yet exist—though there have been remarkable anticipations of it. But it is still too soon for Catholic homosexuals to say who they are to be—or even what names they are to be called. There has not been enough time for freedom, for stammering.

If this essay should somehow elude the polemical responses prepared for it and other speech like it, its best effect would be to save the time and energy of those who feel themselves called to say something on behalf of LGBT people in the Catholic Church. Heed the call, but avoid the debates! Give your time and such graces as come your way to the artistic work of making other languages, so that they can draw forms of life after them.

This is my better answer to my long-ago question for the Vatican—and for myself. To change the teaching on homosexuality, you have to resist the gendered structures of clerical power that demand silence, that empty speech. To change the teaching, find other language.

Response to Mark D. Jordan

ELIZABETH A. DREYER

Fairfield University

I am grateful for the opportunity to consider further some of the issues raised by Mark Jordan in his essay on the teachings about homosexuality in the Catholic Church. Participating in the More than a Monologue conference at Fairfield University, as well as writing this paper, have involved me in reading, reflection, and conversation with many persons—an enriching experience that has evoked memories of my ministry with and to members of Dignity, an organization of lesbian, gay, bisexual, and transgender Catholics, in Toronto in the 1980s, and has also projected me forward into new and provocative intellectual territory.

I want to thank Professor Jordan for having the courage to address these issues in a public conversation. It is dehumanizing to refuse to discuss crucially important issues because we do not want to upset people, because we fear rejection or reprisal, because we want to control others, or because our speech is not yet perfect. It is no secret that silence can be violent and sinful, contributing to our diminishment as a community—a way to quench the Spirit (1 Thes 5.19).

In response to Professor Jordan, I offer five brief points of reaction and extension and then conclude with three questions.

First, I would like to underline Professor Jordan's comments that link the oppression of homosexuals with the marginalization and silencing of women. In this vein, I call attention to an October 2011 column in the *National Catholic Reporter* by Joan Chittister, entitled "Lack of Women Will Irreversibly Harm the Church."[1] Chittister cautions about the cost to a church that prohibits conversation about women's ordination, cuts feminine language from its public prayers, prohibits young women from being altar servers, and removes women from church boards. Michelle Dillon, a Catholic sociologist at the University of New Hampshire, has documented the exodus of adult women from the church in the last twenty-five years, a pattern repeated among gay and lesbian Catholics.[2] It is imperative to seek solutions to stem the tide of these departures. Homophobia and misogyny are co-conspirators against life in the body of Christ. Jordan holds these concepts together, and so should we.

Second, doctrinal positions, including those on homosexuality, depend in part on the interpretation of scripture. I have always liked Gregory of Nazianzen's fourth-century argument for the divinity of the Holy Spirit, in which he notes how God reveals Godself progressively, in time— perfection is reached by additions, he argues. The Hebrew scriptures revealed the first person; the New Testament revealed the second; in God's own time, the Spirit "supplies us with a clearer demonstration of Himself" by dwelling among us. As the season becomes ripe for human readiness, God confers fuller news about God and creation. "You see light breaking upon us, gradually."[3] The message of this fourth-century insight is that the Christian community is *always on the way* to a fuller truth about God, humanity, love, life, and sin. The More than a Monologue conferences took place because the time has come to receive and name a broader truth about the life and faith of gay, lesbian, bisexual, and transgendered persons.

Third, metaphor offers another way to expand the truth of reality. Twenty years ago, Xavier Seubert, an American Franciscan theologian and priest, wrote an article, "The Sacramentality of Metaphors: Reflections on Homosexuality," in which he invites believers to identify a wide range of meaningful metaphors used for heterosexual love and then apply them, *mutatis mutandis*, to homosexual love, as a way to broaden the scope of how we might think and speak about homosexual love.[4] In addition to this use of metaphor to expand our horizons about the meaning of love, the community also needs to listen to the love language of those with differing sexual orientations. What imagery, metaphors, art, and music are used to express the experience of homosexual love? How do gay and lesbian people describe their experience of God, grace, and the goodness of their existence? This larger space, this stretching of language, then needs to be heard and received respectfully by the rest of the church. Through such a mutual process, heterosexual and homosexual experiences of God, love, life, sin, and goodness can be expanded and deepened.

The German theologian Jürgen Moltmann reminds us that the Holy Spirit is present always as the Spirit of particularity—in this or that concrete life.[5] The limiting, ecclesial language of "condition" and "inclination" blocks our ability to see the flow of life that is the Holy Spirit being poured forth into every Christian heart (Rom 5.5). I suggest a parallel situation between heterosexual experience within marriage and that outside of it. When the latter is silenced by the narrow yet universalizing descriptor "promiscuity," we learn nothing about this particular expression of love. Nor can we enter into an open process of discernment about what is life giving and what is death dealing in this love. These are questions we must ask about all kinds of love. A universalizing descriptor shuts down even our ability to know the contours and experiences of these expressions of love, which have been created by a good God.

My fourth point relates to the question Jordan asks at the end of his essay, about how to advance the cause of gay and lesbian Catholics. He rejects reasoned argument in favor of artistic work, as well as resistance and refusal to acquiesce to what the fantasies of power demand. I support his methodological suggestions, but I want to hang on to reasoned argument as well; the fact that some people refuse reasonable dialogue should not prevent the rest of us from continuing to engage in it. Perhaps the most powerful strategy is faithful witness to the Gospel. I am not alone in being edified by the loving, intelligent, and generous lives of so many gay, lesbian, bisexual, and transgendered Catholics. Stopping short of canonizing this community, I suspect that their witness will indeed be effective in advancing the journey toward truth.

Finally, I wish to reflect on the tenth chapter of Acts, which proposes a model for the first-century church. In this story, a devout, Jewish centurion named Cornelius has a vision in which God tells him to invite Simon Peter to his house. Meanwhile, Peter is having his own vision, in which a sheet filled with all kinds of animals, reptiles, and birds is let down by its four corners. He hears a command to "kill and eat" (v. 13).[6] Right in character, he says: "No, Lord, I have never eaten anything that is common or unclean" (v. 14). No doubt a vexed God says: "What God has cleansed, you must not call common" (v. 15). Just in case Peter did not catch on, this happens three times—a familiar pattern in Peter's life. A perplexed Peter then hears Cornelius's servants at the gate. The Spirit tells him to go with them *without hesitation* because they were sent by the Lord. When Peter arrives, Cornelius falls down at his feet, but Peter says: "Stand up; I too am a man. . . . You yourselves know how unlawful it is for a Jew to associate with or to visit any one of another nation; but God has shown me that I should not call any man common or unclean" (vv. 26, 28). Then to all present in the sight of God, Peter says, "Truly I perceive that God shows no partiality, but in every nation anyone who fears him and does what is right is acceptable to him" (vv. 34–35). Peter then recounts the story of how Jesus commanded his disciples to preach and testify *that he is the one ordained by God* to judge the living and the dead and that everyone who believes in him receives forgiveness through his name. "While Peter was still saying this, the Holy Spirit fell on all who heard the word. And the believers from among the uncircumcised who came with Peter were amazed because the gift of the Holy Spirit had been poured out even on the Gentiles. For they heard them speaking in tongues and extolling God" (vv. 44–46). The story ends with Peter saying: "'Can anyone forbid water for baptizing these people who have received the Holy Spirit just as we have?' And he commanded them to be baptized in the name of Jesus Christ. And they invited him to remain for some days" (v. 48).

With this text as a foundation, I offer a nine-step program for all people of the church today:

1. Aim to live in an upright fashion.
2. Listen *humbly* to the Spirit.
3. Invite each other over—particularly those who are different from us.
4. Remember that we are all mortal.
5. Trust God's word that nothing is unclean.
6. Imitate a God who shows no partiality.
7. Do not quench the Spirit.
8. Be ready to notice and be amazed at the Spirit's work in *all of* us.
9. Work to create a new community in the Spirit, a new, inclusive body of Christ.

In conclusion, I would like to raise three questions. The first has to do with power. Jordan protests manipulating, silencing power and ends his essay with a reflection on sacramental power. I wonder if further exploration of types of power would be fruitful for this conversation. In particular, I am thinking of the New Testament's language of "power," which points to the dynamism and energy of the Spirit that enlivened the first Christian communities—words such as *energeia, dynamis, exousia*.[7] The Spirit's power was real and tangible, banishing fear and infusing the community with new life. Other resources include Bernard Loomer's scholarship on power. He distinguishes between relational and unilateral power. The first type points to the respectful power of the Spirit; the second to abusive "power over" others.[8] By attending to these various types of power, we can bring clarity to the discussion, enhancing our ability to promote and practice collaborative power while exposing power that silences.

Second, Jordan proposes a hermeneutic of homoerotic power as a way to understand the hierarchical power of the Roman Church. While the dynamic of silencing makes it difficult to gather data, we need to ask about additional grounding forces of the Roman Catholic hierarchy. Examples might include forces such as economics, ambition, celebrity, and control. Extending the parameters of the present conversation will give us a fuller, more adequate picture of this organization and its use/abuse of power.

Third, this conversation about the relationship between totalizing power and the homoerotic structure of the Roman Catholic hierarchy leads me to raise questions about this dynamic beyond Catholicism. For example, is power exercised in comparable ways in other branches of Christianity and in Judaism and Islam (taking into consideration the significant differences on topics such as natural law and celibacy)? By expanding the discussion beyond the Roman Catholic Church, we may find more effective ways to address problems and work for change.

In my final thoughts, I return to my time in Toronto, when I was working in a ministry with and for members of Dignity and helping plan a Dignity retreat. During the liturgy, at the prayers of the faithful, my only petition was to ask this prayerful, loving, gay community of Catholics to forgive us, the straight community, for our blindness, our hardness of heart, and our arrogance. So few in the church look to this talented, nurturing, generous group of people as models of holiness—individuals who can help straight believers become ever more fully the body of Christ. My prayer has not changed.

3 Lesbian Nuns: A Gift to the Church

JEANNINE GRAMICK

New Ways Ministry

Homosexual issues have gained increasing prominence on the Catholic Church's agenda in the last several decades, but when the topic of homosexuality and church ministers is raised, inevitably the conversation focuses on gay priests and male religious. This may be so for a variety of reasons. Gay priests and male religious are certainly much more visible or "out" than lesbian religious sisters. It may be that there are greater numbers of gay priests and brothers than lesbian nuns,[1] but the attention paid to gay priests and brothers may also reflect a sexist culture that is more interested in males than females.

Because so little public attention has been given to the subject of lesbian nuns, I believe they are the most invisible and silent subgroup in the community of lesbian and gay Catholics. This article will summarize the topic as it has surfaced in the public arena and in more closed circles in the United States since the latter part of the twentieth century and then will analyze what significance these events might have for the wider church.

Three books allegedly or peripherally dealing with lesbian nuns appeared in the 1980s. Judith Brown's scholarly book, *Immodest Acts*,[2] tells the story of Sister Benedetta Carlini, a nun in Prescia, northern Italy, in the seventeenth century, who was elected abbess of the Mother of God Convent largely because she claimed to have visions or apparitions from an angel and from Christ. A church investigation brought to light not only her faked stigmata and bogus religious claims but also her erotic behavior, which she forced on another nun in her convent. The book's subtitle, *The Life of a Lesbian Nun in Renaissance Italy*, given by the publisher presumably to increase sales, is misleading. The subtitle, as well as the book's content, unfortunately reinforces the false notion that what defines a nun, or any woman, as "lesbian" is sexual activity with another woman. Furthermore, the book's descriptions of erotic behavior confuse the category "lesbian" with "rapist" or "sexual predator."

The *New York Times Book Review* thought the book presented "a vivid picture of convent life and the Roman Catholic Church during the upheavals of the Counter-Reformation."[3] While the picture may have been vivid, I like to think it was not typical because it paints a bizarre picture of seventeenth-century convent life. The descriptions certainly do not fit contemporary convent life or present-day lesbian nuns.

Another book, *Lesbian Nuns: Breaking Silence*,[4] was published in 1985. Through a successful appearance on the Phil Donahue show and a subsequent national media tour, the book's editors, Rosemary Curb and Nancy Manahan, propelled the book to national attention. Interest in and sale of the book increased when the Catholic hierarchy in Boston influenced the NBC affiliate there to cancel the editors' appearance on a television show. In one interview, the publisher stated that after only three months, the initial run of thirty thousand books had been increased to 150,000. After four printings of the book, the small, lesbian-owned publisher sold the distribution and printing rights, and the book subsequently appeared in Australia, Brazil, England, France, Germany, Holland, Ireland, Italy, and Spain.

Lesbian Nuns: Breaking Silence consists of brief stories by fifty contributors. The title is somewhat misleading because all but nine of the fifty narratives were contributed by former nuns. Moreover, many of the women did not realize they were lesbian until after they had left convent life. Readers desiring salacious stories of lurid cloistered love affairs were disappointed with the book because relatively few of the articles contain references to physical contact or occasional kissing. Most of the stories describe platonic friendships, many from a feminist point of view.

The work received only two reviews from the Catholic press: from the *National Catholic Reporter* and *Sisters Today*.[5] Both reviews were less than enthusiastic and essentially claimed the pieces in the book were superficial. Given the brevity of each testimony, such a critique was probably inevitable. The real value of the book lay in drawing public attention to the neglected subject of lesbianism, using "nuns" as the hook. Lesbian leaders acknowledged that many lesbians were inspired to come out as a result of reading the book. Furthermore, it was the first time that lesbianism was discussed openly in the mainstream media of television, radio, and newspapers in the United States and abroad.

A third book, entitled *Homosexuality in the Priesthood and Religious Life*,[6] presented historical, theological, pastoral, and ministerial dimensions of homosexuality in the clerical and religious life. Within this analysis, and at the heart of it, were seven lesbian sisters who told their stories of the dawning awareness and affirmation of their sexual identity. More substantial in length than the accounts in *Lesbian Nuns: Breaking Silence*, the chapters were authored by sisters who were still members of religious congregations. In most of these pieces, the authors used pseudonyms because they feared negative reactions from church authorities to their self-disclosure. The sisters tell of the integration of sexuality, celibacy, and spirituality in their lives. Some speak of the feelings of isolation they experienced in their journeys to self-acceptance. One sister said very simply, "I maintain that love is the greatest offering we lesbian religious have to bring to the Church."[7] In one review, a lesbian sister commented that the essays by the lesbian nuns "mirrored for me examples of faithfulness, authenticity, integrity, and my own goodness and gifts."[8]

As these books were appearing in the public forum, two organizations were serving the needs of lesbian sisters. Both groups, Communication Ministry, Inc. (CMI); and New Ways Ministry, began in 1977. While the mission of CMI was to minister with both male and female religious or clergy, less than 5 percent of the six hundred members it had at its peak were female. Because of the heightened publicity of the clerical sexual abuse crisis in 2002, the Vatican's 2005 instruction from the Congregation for Catholic Education that basically said gay men should not be ordained to the priesthood and the subsequent fear among gay priests and religious, the membership of CMI dramatically declined in the 2000s. In 2009, the group dissolved and invited New Ways Ministry to continue its mission, an invitation that New Ways Ministry accepted.

As part of New Ways Ministry's mission of working for justice and reconciliation of lesbian and gay Catholics with the wider church, it fostered dialogue about lesbian nuns among Catholic institutions. The ministry's staff conducted workshops about lesbian religious for such groups as the Religious Formation Conference and contributed articles to the publications of the National Assembly of Women Religious,[9] the National Sisters Vocation Conference,[10] and the National Religious Vocation Conference.[11]

In 1979, New Ways Ministry held its first retreat for lesbian nuns. This was followed by a series of regional workshops for lesbian women religious in 1984–1985 and three conferences for the leadership of women's congregations the following year. Every five years, New Ways Ministry sponsors a weekend symposium, usually drawing about five hundred church leaders, at which there is always a session about lesbian nuns.

Toward the end of the 1980s, small support groups for lesbian nuns appeared in a number of large cities. To foster these groups and to assist isolated sisters, New Ways Ministry published the first edition of a newsletter called *Womanjourney Weavings* in 1990. Over the years, the circulation of the newsletter has remained at about four hundred, with the mailings going to some heterosexual congregational leaders, formation directors, and vocation ministers, as well as to lesbian sisters. One of the most important features of this newsletter, which gives increased visibility to lesbian nuns, is a list of contact sisters in various geographic regions. This enables sisters who feel isolated to meet and have conversations with other lesbian sisters in their geographic area.

In 1997, Sister Fran Fasolka IHM formed an online discussion group with approximately seventy-five lesbian sisters subscribing.[12] Before her death in 2009, Sister Tobias Hagan CSJ conducted annual retreats for lesbian sisters for about twenty years. Between 2005 and 2011, New Ways Ministry sponsored annual conferences for lesbian sisters, their congregational leaders, and vocation and formation ministers to support lesbian sisters and to provide education within the Catholic community about the gifts that these women offer the church.

What is the significance of all this private and public discourse about lesbian nuns in the landscape of recent church history? What did these events mean for the Catholic community in general, and how did they affect lesbian nuns in particular? As I reflected on the historical overview I have just been tracing in the context of these questions and on my own involvement in this ministry for the past forty years, three issues emerged. The overriding question that surfaced for women religious during the first twenty years, that is, during the 1970s and 1980s, was sexual identity. During the next twenty years, "coming out" dominated the agenda, both in society and in the church. The topic of celibacy remained prominent in both periods. These three issues become a lens through which we can appreciate the gifts that lesbian sisters offer the church.

Celibacy

Sister Benedetta Carlini, the Italian Renaissance abbess in Judith Brown's work, is called a lesbian nun because of her erotic activity with another nun. In the 1970s and 1980s, many people believed, and some still believe today, that sexual activity defines a lesbian woman. At the time of the first retreat for lesbian nuns in 1979, it was evident that Vatican officials believed this idea. In a communication to the leadership of my religious community, the Congregation for Religious claimed that the published description of the retreat used the word "celibate" as a "slogan." To be lesbian, the congregation's communiqué implied, meant that a woman was sexually active. It is possible that many nuns would not name themselves lesbian because they too hold this idea and do not engage in sexual behavior. With such an activity-based definition, all celibates, whether lesbian or heterosexual, would lack a sexual identity. Both the scientific community and sisters themselves testify that this is obviously not true. Still, there is a lingering but misguided suspicion that lesbian sisters cannot or do not live celibately.

A similar misgiving or hesitation comes from some heterosexual religious community leaders who ask, "Does a lesbian identity affect one's ability to be celibate?" or "Isn't it more difficult for a lesbian sister than a heterosexual sister to live in a community of women?" In my discussions with religious community leaders over the years, questions like these have surfaced. The assumption beneath these questions is the false notion that lesbian women are attracted to all other women. Such universal attraction is no more accurate for lesbian sisters in relation to women than it is for heterosexual women in relation to men. The important or relevant question is: "How do both lesbian and heterosexual sisters live out their celibacy in healthy ways?"

In preparation for writing this essay, I asked a small group of lesbian sisters this question, and all the responses were similar.[13] Most felt that living a healthy *celibate* life meant living a healthy *balanced* life. They nurtured themselves with good books and films, sufficient exercise and leisure, rest, play, garden work, and enjoying nature. One artist said she used painting and creative expression to channel her sexual feelings. They believed that a principal aid for a healthy celibate lifestyle was fidelity to a life of prayer. Many spoke about a rich contemplative life, personal solitude, being centered in God, or having an understanding spiritual director.

The obvious charism of a life of celibacy is that it enables a person to dedicate herself to the service of humanity. Without the obligations of spouse and family, she has more time to devote to others. But celibacy offers the community other gifts that may not be as apparent. All the lesbian sisters I know say that a key component of their celibate life is the ability to form close and warm friendships. Most have been blessed with intimate and trusted friends with whom they could share their journeys and natural frustrations, as well as the ups and downs of life along the way. Lesbian sisters can teach us the value of friendship.

In our society, so much emphasis is placed on the physical and sexual aspects of relationships. Television, films, novels, and other mass media are saturated with sex and imply that there can be no intimacy without sex. Physical closeness is often confused with and substituted for the intimacy of spiritual or psychological closeness.

This relationship of intimate friendship is, I believe, the preeminent symbol for the God-human relationship. Unlike the spousal relationship, which has historically been used as the principal icon for the God-human relationship, friendships can flourish without genital involvement; however, no deep spousal relationship can survive without genuine friendship. Friendship is the bedrock. Human companionship or friendship is the true meaning of the creation story. In Genesis 2:18, God says, "It is not good for the human to be alone." Persons need companionship and intimate friendships to quench the thirst of the human spirit. People can live without genital satisfaction, but it is difficult to imagine a psychologically healthy person who can live a fulfilled life without at least one good friend.

In addition to witnessing to the gift of intimate friendship, the celibacy of lesbian nuns reminds us of the personal boundaries that we must establish for ourselves and others. Those in recovery from addiction soon learn that boundaries are important and that setting them is a first step in loving oneself. Finding appropriate boundaries may be difficult because of deep inner wounds from childhood. The child within is terrified of fixing boundaries for fear the other will leave. At the other extreme, the inner child can set up huge boundaries to keep the other from getting too close or too intimate because of fear of being hurt again.

Over the course of life, we learn to put up walls and take them down. If we never become skilled at establishing proper boundaries, we will never define who we really are. Hopefully, if we learn how to manage our boundaries, we can feel self-worth, attain greater self-awareness, and form healthy relationships. The celibacy of well-balanced lesbian sisters is a sign of that need for appropriate personal boundaries.

Their celibacy is also a countercultural witness. In a society where sex is glorified, a celibate lifestyle is considered deviant. Lesbian sisters understand what it means to be considered abnormal or on the edge. They are in good company because Jesus also stood on the edge. Like Jesus, they empathize and connect with those outside the mainstream or dominant culture. Their unusual sexual status enables them to identify with the less-valued members of society.

For example, lesbian sisters have felt the hurt of exclusion or invisibility when heterosexual women comment on the charisma or sex appeal of male movie stars, and they feel unable to voice their comparable feelings toward female celebrities. They have compared such experiences to incidents Hispanic persons have when they are in an environment with predominantly white people and white privilege is unconsciously accessed. Both lesbian sisters and Hispanic people simply feel that they are invisible and their worth is unacknowledged. The outsider sexual status of lesbian sisters thus enables them to relate to and be in solidarity with minority racial groups, the economically poor, religious minorities, and others outside the powerful or dominant group.

Sexual Identity

Conversations about sexual feelings were not even entertained among women religious before the 1970s; however, the sexual revolution, the feminist movement, and the gay rights movement of the 1960s and early 1970s eventually affected women's congregations and the wider church. For the most part, women who entered religious life before the 1960s (who constitute the bulk of women in religious life today) presumed they were heterosexual because that was the assumption of society. Today, of course, there is greater awareness of sexual orientation, but this was not the case before the sexual revolution in the United States.

How sisters came to discover their sexual identity is part of the charism of lesbian religious. They teach us the meaning of sexual identity and how to understand it. Sisters who had buried their sexual feelings and desires with their secular clothes when they donned a traditional habit began to question their sexual identity as they traded their long robes for modern dress. Because they generally lived, worked, and found emotional satisfaction in an all-female environment, some began to wonder if they were lesbian. Others asked, "If I am celibate, how do I know if I am lesbian or heterosexual? If I have had sexual relations with other women, am I lesbian? Are *all* nuns lesbian because they live with other women? If my emotional and social needs are met primarily by women, am I lesbian?" In short, who *is* a lesbian nun?

In the 1980s, I spent a great deal of time counseling individual sisters and conducting workshops to clear up the confusion surrounding sexual identity. Data at that time indicated that about one-third of lesbian women had been married, and more than half of these were biological mothers. So engaging in sex with men did not mean that these women were heterosexual. Today, far fewer lesbian women marry heterosexually because of less rigid social expectations, but the point is clear: sexual behavior is neither an essential indicator nor a determiner of sexual identity.

Sisters teach us that living or working in a homosocial environment does not necessarily mean that a person is lesbian or gay. Social relationships are not necessarily sexual. Having one's affective needs for touching, hugging, and dispassionate kissing met by another woman is not necessarily an indicator of lesbianism, because all human beings need to express affection. One of the hazards of a celibate lifestyle is the risk of losing natural warmth through fear of expressing affection through touch.

The crucial difference between a relationship of friendship and a lesbian relationship is eroticism. Psychological studies tell us that eroticism is not the most important part of a relationship for most women, whether they are heterosexual or lesbian. Women want to feel understood, to share stories and confidences, to enjoy common values, to feel close to another person. This valuing of the emotional over the erotic can lead a sister to conclude falsely that she is lesbian. The emotional component is the stuff of friendship. The erotic component is the necessary factor of a lesbian identity.

Psychology says that sexual identity is characterized by the gender direction and strength of romantic feelings, erotic desires, and sexual fantasies, but this definition sounds very clinical. Lesbian sisters give us an easier and more human way of understanding sexual identity. They encourage us to ask the question, "With whom have I fallen in love?" What defines a nun or any woman as lesbian is some internal sexual longing and desire, and "falling in love" is a good description of this hunger. Lesbian sisters have helped us sort out the pieces of what sexual identity really means.

In addition to educating the wider church about sexual identity, lesbian sisters have mentored others who are learning to embrace their sexuality and trying to accept it as the spiritual and religious gift that it is. This mentoring or spiritual companioning often includes sharing one's own story of discovering sexual identity. One such story, which I summarize here, illustrates these pieces of understanding sexual identity.[14]

Sister Mary described her growing awareness of her sexual identity as progressing through three stages. The first period she imaged as a foggy night in which she felt enshrouded in the clouds of the repression of her affective life. She experienced deep personal inadequacy and a continual state of depression. Her fear of relationships and sporadic attractions to other sisters, coupled with loneliness and a conviction that she was not loveable, were all interpreted as indicators of sinfulness, illness, or inadequacy. She was not aware of her sexuality, only of something alarming that she could not fully articulate but that needed to be controlled. She sought counseling and prayed frequently to a God who seemed distant from such a desolate and shameful person.

Gradually, a kind of dawn arose. In this second period, healing began to occur, which she attributed to God's grace, a certain readiness in her, and a fortuitous blend of people and situations. This was a time when the old structures of religious life came tumbling down, which meant that she could no longer keep life at bay. The departure of some very close friends from religious life brought grief and heartache but also unearthed long-hidden feelings of affection, tenderness, and care. The dawn broke upon her as she became aware that she could love and was indeed lovable. The depression passed, and she began to participate earnestly in life, to assume risks, to care about other people, and to allow them to care about her. She felt well and happy. She now sees this period of her life as God's amazing providence at work, a period when people and events prepared her to accept herself and her sexual identity.

During the turbulent years of this second stage, Mary had three powerful relationships of loving and falling in love that prompted her to think seriously about her sexual identity. Although these experiences were not genital and did not involve lesbian women, she discovered priceless truths about herself. She learned that intimacy meant sharing oneself with another and exposing one's weakness and vulnerability to another. She felt the warmth of holding another person and learned the value of human touch, an embrace, and physical closeness. All this showed her that she was not a disembodied robot and that to be fully human she needed to experience the bodily, as well as the spiritual, part of her nature. Both then and now she has viewed these relationships as treasured gifts and a wellspring of blessings.

The second relationship caused her to wonder more deeply about her sexual identity. With the third relationship she recognized that she was falling in love and named her feelings as erotic, but this was frightening. She described it to the other sister this way: "I know I do love and care about other people in my life, but the way I feel about you seems to have something distinctly different about it, something that has to do with the constancy of your presence to me and the intensity of my feeling for you."[15] In her journal she wrote, "The conversation made me wonder again about the possibility that my own tendencies are more homosexual than heterosexual. I suppose I always wonder how people would react if I said this. Maybe the deeper wonder is in me though—what does or what might the fact mean in terms of my life? What if it is true and I admit and accept it? What are the implications of that for my life here and now?"[16] She began therapy, and after about a year concluded that her sexual identity was lesbian.

During the third period of her religious life, when Mary was in her forties, the fog totally lifted, and the dawn gave way to a bright day. She was elected to the leadership team of her congregation. She felt she had integrated the intense relationships into her life in a healthy way and felt no need to think or talk more about it.

Then one day a sister in her community came to the Leadership Council to say that she wanted the council to know that she was attending a retreat for lesbian and gay Catholics. This information jolted Mary into realizing that she needed to take steps to deal with her sexual identity with more than intellectual acceptance. She had commented on her feelings in her journal and had acknowledged her sexual identity to herself as a result of therapy, but she had never mentioned it to another person. Now she was confronted with a sister who was attending a retreat with other lesbian and gay Catholics!

Mary reread her journals and letters, studied all kinds of materials about homosexuality, and began therapy again. She said, "It was as if the floodgates were finally opened and all the thoughts, fantasies, and feelings I had never admitted or been able to articulate tumbled out. . . . I began to consider the implications of anything more than a detached intellectual understanding of being lesbian."[17]

The therapist helped Mary trust and validate her own experience. Her Leadership Council gave her personal affirmation and enabled her to become more involved with lesbian and gay groups and events.

She felt like the woman in the Gospel who had found her lost coin (Luke 15:8–9). Like the woman who called her neighbors to rejoice with her, Mary needed to tell her friends and some co-workers about her sexual identity. About six months later she attended a retreat for Catholic gay and lesbian religious sponsored by CMI and soon began to attend weekly liturgies with a chapter of Dignity, an organization for lesbian and gay Catholics. Little by little, she told more members of her community that she was lesbian.

For more than a few decades now, Mary has been providing Catholic resources, educating her own community, and talking with others about the goodness of lesbian and gay people and the gifts of a lesbian identity.

Coming Out

In 1999, a staff member of New Ways Ministry conducted an informal survey of ninety-four lesbian sisters from the United States and five other countries about the reality of being a lesbian in religious life.[18] Fewer than 15 percent of the respondents said that they were generally known as an "out" lesbian. As 14 percent of the respondents had completed initial formation in the preceding decade, being fully out as a lesbian sister may depend on the time period of entering religious life. Unfortunately, there was no data analysis of correlation between the time of entrance to religious life and being out. Whether or not it is the newer members of religious life who tend to be generally out, indications are that more and more sisters, including those who have been in religious life for many decades, are coming out.

This increase in coming out was evident in the annual conferences for lesbian sisters and congregational leaders that New Ways Ministry held between 2005 and 2011. Each program included a sharing of coming-out stories by two lesbian sisters: one who came to realize her lesbianism while in community and another who was aware of her lesbianism before she entered the convent. At one event, a congregational leader was astonished and touched when a tiny, quiet, gray-haired woman in her seventies stood up and told the group that they were the first to know that she had just discovered she was lesbian. The participants felt that her coming out was a gift to them.

One sister described coming out of silence and into speech as a sacrament—an outward sign and a source of grace.[19] She said that "*Out of Silence*," a phrase that became the title of a book she later wrote, describes what is happening among lesbian sisters more and more often in the twenty-first century. Some lesbian sisters are even providing sample coming-out rituals for others as one way of modeling the sacrament of coming out.[20]

Lesbian sisters can be role models for those who meet rejection when they come out to family members. These sisters, who consider themselves within the religious family of the institutional church, find it extremely difficult to deal with a church hierarchy that calls them intrinsically dis-ordered. Feeling depressed, resentful, or angry over these labels, some have written respectful letters to bishops or other church officials about the hierarchy's stance. One sister told me she learned to "just consider the source" of hateful speech. She felt that there is a great deal of shame to be borne by the organizational church but that it is Jesus Christ and Gospel values that anchor her to her religious family, which she said is the entire People of God. For the most part, lesbian sisters resist the hierarchy's labels by ignoring them and working in supportive and nourishing church environments, such as their religious communities. Many say that the sacraments, the social teachings of the church, and a worldview of openness and the honest search for truth promoted by Vatican II give them hope and reason to stay in their Catholic family.

Except for some lesbian women who entered religious life in the last couple of decades, most lesbian sisters experienced a time when their orientation was hidden from the people with whom they lived and worked. They learned how to keep a deep and personal part of their humanity secret. While priests were taught that the "seal of the confessional" applied to sins confessed during the Sacrament of Reconciliation, it seems that many lesbian sisters applied this kind of seal to their sexual identity.

A priest friend of mine once told me that an eighty-year-old nun came to him for the Sacrament of Reconciliation because he was a visiting priest unknown to her or her community. She confessed the sexual desires she had felt toward women, which she had carried in her heart for her entire adult life, distressed by the fact that she thought these were "sinful" feelings. Not coming out to another person until age eighty can be considered a tragedy, just as all suffering is tragic. No human being can escape suffering or pain, whether emotional, physical, mental, or psychological. This is the suffering that Christ showed us how to endure. "Father, if it be possible, let this chalice pass from me. But not my will, but thine be done" (Matt 26:39). The long coming-out process of lesbian sisters, even at age eighty, teaches us to be strong, courageous, and faithful in the face of seemingly unbearable suffering. In hiding from the temple authorities who were pursuing him, Jesus knew the fear of exposure, just as he now understands the worry and apprehension experienced in hiding one's sexuality.

Coming out has been a recurring theme in the *Womanjourney* newsletters for lesbian sisters. In one essay, a sister describes how she navigated the bumpy waters of coming out in a quiet way and came through the process with a renewed enthusiasm about life. Her story is quoted extensively below because it poignantly illustrates how the witness of others can ultimately overcome the fear of coming out.[21]

> I was sitting in my room one day, watching the sunshine pouring through the windows and feeling rather gloomy. I was thinking how I had lived in the closet as a lesbian for almost fifty years and how afraid I was of being out. I felt discouraged because I like being a sister and I like being a lesbian and I could not see how I could openly be both. It was not because I wanted to have a partner. It was because, somehow, it didn't seem as if a person is supposed to be a sister and a lesbian at the same time. I was afraid that being out as a lesbian would lead to my being out of the community, and I felt much pain over that possibility.

When I was younger, knowing I was lesbian had been a secret about the size of a penny inside my pocket. I would take the penny out and think about it once in a while, but mostly I was just as happy to leave it hidden in my pocket. . . . I was afraid of people's reactions. Only after I met lesbian women who were happy and excited about being lesbian did my feelings begin to change. Gradually, my penny became as large as a Susan B. Anthony dollar and, in time, filled every nook and cranny of my thoughts and feelings. There weren't pockets enough to hold it! At this time in my life, I came to a turning point.

As I sat in my room, I thought about going into my bedroom closet and praying. Why not pray in that small closet with two louvered French doors since that was where I was living? Wondering how it would feel to go inside, I squeezed myself into the closet and closed the doors. . . .

I began to notice little cracks of light showing through the louvers of the door. As I looked through the louvers into my room, I could see light flooding my room. I thought, "Why am I here in the dark when I could be out enjoying the sunshine?" I imagined one of the sisters in the house saying through the louvers, "Linda, what are you doing in there? Come on out!"

. . . I felt a profound sadness. My efforts to avoid everything that could identify me as lesbian had led me to be only half known by all but a few people in my life. I thought about the gay and lesbian people I knew who were out and who were risking everything to be themselves. I wanted with all my heart to be like them. I thought, "I don't want to die in the closet."

Praying in the closet that day was the beginning of a steady resolve to take steps to live out and to find ways to integrate being lesbian with being in a religious community.

Linda began to conquer her terror and take some risks. She participated in social, spiritual, and political activities with other lesbian and gay people, introduced herself by name, and shared that she was a sister. Linda gained strength to come out because of her association with and admiration for other lesbian women.

Linda's story confirms some of the findings of a research study of the lives of fifty-seven lesbian sisters.[22] The analysis in the study showed that the model for coming out is relational; moreover, progress in sexual development is made through key relationships. Just as Linda gained strength from key relationships with lesbian and gay people who were out, her coming out as a lesbian sister now gives courage and strength to others to come out.

Linda is fully out. She no longer fears being out. She knows she can be a lesbian and a religious sister at the same time. Like other lesbian sisters, Linda is currently experiencing a contentment and enthusiasm about life that she had not known before.

What Lies Ahead?

If lesbian sisters experience such a sense of freedom and grace in coming out, why do more lesbian nuns not come out? There are certainly many reasons, all centering around the perceived risks involved. Sister Linda said she was afraid that she would be dismissed from her religious community. Sister Mary wondered how people would react. Other lesbian sisters fear losing the ministries they care deeply about. Some are worried they might taint the reputation of their communities because some in society may assume they are sexually active. If more lesbian sisters came out more publicly, there would be opportunities for religious congregations to educate society about lesbianism and celibate commitment. If being lesbian is as good as being heterosexual, why would the community's reputation be harmed? This is the question that the leaders of women's congregations are asking the church to consider.

The Vatican has not commented on the merit of admitting lesbian women to religious life. Not surprisingly, because it is more concerned about males than females, the Vatican has taken a position on admitting gay men to priesthood or religious life; essentially, men who have "deeply rooted" homosexual tendencies should not be accepted into seminaries, but those who have overcome "transitory" homosexual tendencies can.[23] Such a policy treats homosexual identity as shameful and gay persons as reprehensible. Faced with the extension of such a possibility to their communities, the leaders of women's congregations would most likely attempt to engage in dialogue with the Vatican about the intrinsic dignity and worth of a lesbian or gay orientation.

Lesbian women who are already open about their identity have been accepted into many women's congregations for the last several decades. Leaders in these communities have come to understand that a homosexual identity is natural and normal for some people, just as a heterosexual identity is normal and natural for others. They reject the outsider status to which the male hierarchy has relegated lesbian and gay people.

The advocacy position of these leaders was one factor that induced the Vatican's Congregation for the Doctrine of the Faith (CDF) to initiate a doctrinal assessment of the Leadership Conference of Women Religious (LCWR) in 2008.[24] LCWR has approximately 1,500 members, who are elected leaders of their religious orders, representing approximately 80 percent of the 57,000 Catholic sisters in the United States. This group has been at the vanguard of social justice and Catholic Church renewal since it began in 1956.

The CDF was concerned about certain areas of dissent, it said, that had been expressed at various LCWR assemblies. For example, Sister Mary Ann Zollmann BVM, in her presidential address at the 2003 LCWR assembly, told the story of conversations she had with some bishops about an alternative ethic to the traditional church position on homosexuality. In her remarks, she said:

> As some of the participants made their appeal to ethical directives based in natural law and the intrinsically disordered nature of homo-sexuality, I found myself tapping into a place of grief and alienation. In my heart's eye, I saw faces of men and women I know whose sexual orientation is gay or lesbian and who live compassionately, justly yearn-ing for a return of compassion and justice on the part of a church they love. I thought of men and women whose passion for wholeness in re-lationship is lived in deep commitment to life-long same-sex partners. I heard deep in my own being, their struggle to find a home in our church.[25]

Another mark against the sisters of LCWR was their support of New Ways Ministry. The CDF was displeased that the LCWR officers, in addition to the leadership teams of various sisters' congregations, had written letters supporting New Ways Ministry and its programs. The letters, the CDF said, suggested that the sisters do not agree with the church's traditional teaching on human sexuality.

In making its displeasure public in April 2012, the CDF, in one sense, did an enormous favor for lesbian sisters and the entire church, because the news that the leaders of U.S. nuns are advocates for lesbian and gay people soon spread across the globe. This public support will, I believe, give further courage to lesbian sisters to come out in greater numbers in the future.

When a lesbian sister overcomes the fear of coming out, she gives the church a myriad of gifts. As described more fully above, she becomes a mentor for others who struggle to acknowledge their sexual identity. She gives the gifts of service to humanity and identification with the marginalized. She is an educator in the truest sense, as she is teaching us the meaning of sexual identity and the value of intimacy, friendship, and personal boundaries. She becomes a role model for dealing with rejection and pain and for finding an enormous passion for life. She is an example that the sense of freedom, peace, and joy she experiences in coming out far outweighs the pain or anguish she felt in the days of being hidden.

While there are other examples of healthy and integrated sexuality, lesbian nuns model this sexual integration in a way not found elsewhere in the church. The gifts that lesbian sisters offer the church are authentic, desirable, and valuable. One sister told me simply and humbly, "I have something of great price to offer." In many ways, lesbian nuns are the church's pearls of great price. They are treasures that have been hidden in our convent fields for centuries but that are now being unearthed. I believe that increased public discussion about lesbian sisters, which seems inevitable, will bring these gifts and many more to further attention and much deserved recognition.

The Prophetic Life of Lesbian Nuns:
A Response to Jeannine Gramick

JAMIE L. MANSON

National Catholic Reporter

It is rare to hear a discussion of lesbian Catholics, let alone lesbian nuns. We talk often of LGBT Catholics, but often these discussions lump gay and lesbian experience together. I believe it is important to note that the experience of lesbians and the experience of gay men in the church can and do have some marked differences. I make these distinctions not to create a suffering contest between gays and lesbians, with the prize going to the group that is most oppressed. We all share in a deep oppression.

For lesbians, the experience of being Catholic affects more than their sexual orientation. It relates to the anatomy itself. Women, by the very fact of their bodily reality, are excluded from the most significant forms of religious authority and spiritual leadership. Lesbians, therefore, face exclusion not simply because of their sexual orientation but also because of their sex.

By banning women from serving as priests, the hierarchy says essentially that, when it comes to performing the sacraments, God cannot work through the body of a woman. One can never stress enough how corrosive it is to a woman's spirit not to have ever seen her own bodily form wear a stole, stand behind an altar and raise the bread and wine, place her hands in the waters of a baptismal font, or step through the center door of the confessional in a Roman Catholic church. For many lesbians and straight women, this leads to feelings of isolation and disempowerment.

On the other hand, there are some priests who are out to their congregations and communities. These situations are rare, of course, and there are far more priests functioning from within the closet. Nevertheless, there exists the possibility that gay men will have the opportunity to watch another gay man celebrate the sacraments. They are able to see a reflection of their bodies and their sexual orientation function sacramentally and with spiritual authority. Given the number of gay men who have served as priests throughout the centuries, there is little doubt that gay clergymen, both progressive and conservative, have had some role in shaping church doctrine.

So, when one of the sisters whom Gramick quotes says of the Vatican's harsh speech about gays and lesbians, "consider the source," she is acknowledging this reality. The question for Catholic lesbians is not so much *what* the teaching is but *who* created the teaching.

Women, and lesbians in particular, have never had and still do not have any voice in creating any of the teachings of the Roman Catholic Church. They have never been given a place at the table. There has never been an opportunity for their thoughts or experiences to be considered.

If one is a lesbian, one is in double jeopardy with the church. Lesbians are alienated because of their bodies and also because of the way their bodies respond to desire and love in erotic relationships. Genitals themselves, not just genital activity, stand between a lesbian and full acceptance into the Roman Catholic Church.

But there can be grace in being marginalized. As Gramick observes, lesbian nuns understand what it means to be on the edge of society. And that understanding helps them reach out to those who struggle, particularly who struggle with accepting their sexuality. Furthermore, it should never surprise any of us that there are gays and lesbians in ministry, that they gravitate toward ministry and, in many cases, excel at it. Gay, lesbian, bisexual, and transgendered people have a history with ministry that goes back to ancient times.

As Christian de la Huerta pointed out years ago, there is a long tradition, particularly in tribal religions, of LGBT people serving the tribe or village as the

> shamans, the healers, the visionaries, the mediators, the peace keepers, the "people who talk between the worlds," the keepers of beauty. The two-spirited people of native American tribes such as the Lakota, Navaho, Omaha, and Zuni. The Zulu and Dagora in Africa, the Hijira in India. People whom we would today label LGBT were honored, respected, and even revered for the spiritual roles they fulfilled.[1]

I do not think this reality is as distant from our contemporary experience as we might think. Spending eight years at Yale Divinity School taught me time and again that ministry, if anything, is a queer enterprise.

If we understand the word *queer* the way in which queer theorists and queer theologians use it, ministry seems really to fit that description. Patrick Cheng, whose essay on theological bullying and Catholicism appears later in this volume, defines queer as an undertaking that is a "self conscious embrace of all of that is transgressive of societal norms. It is subversive, seeing things in a different light, and reclaiming voices and sources that previously had been ignored, silenced or discarded."[2]

Ministry by its very nature, therefore, is a queer endeavor. So many seminarians, ministers, priests, and nuns that I have met over the years—whether gay or straight—have always been sensitive, countercultural. They are idealists and visionaries; they are committed to reaching out to the margins and giving voice to the voiceless.

What I also find striking is how many gay and lesbian people who are not in formal ministry are also doing the traditional work of the church. Many of them do not affiliate with a church. If anything, they identify as spiritual but not religious. Yet LGBT people and nuns seem to gravitate toward the healing professions. They are theologians, ethicists, scientists, and artists, spiritual directors and hospital chaplains, healthcare professionals and leaders of nonprofit organizations, advocates for immigrants, and outreach workers to the homeless and imprisoned.

These commitments to healing and social service seem to be a place of deep connection between women religious and LGBT persons. Yet, particularly in the case of young adult lesbians, a chasm often exists between them. This is particularly sad because nuns possess certain treasures that I think young adult lesbians, in particular, long for: community and spiritual life. What I think leads lesbians, especially young adult lesbians, to distance themselves from nuns is, first, celibacy, and, second, their ties to the Roman Catholic institution.

Gramick rightly points out that the bulk of sisters ministering today in the United States entered their communities prior to the 1960s. At that time, our culture was still based on the traditional communal structure. People still lived in communities, in a village. Many Catholics identified their parish as their neighborhood. People lived close to family, if not in the same home as extended family. Their communities, their religious traditions, gave them their identities; they told them what their values were and what to believe. It was a social climate that did not openly discuss sexuality and a church that demanded that they bury their sexual feelings. Thankfully, most women religious in the past few decades have moved beyond these repressed beginnings.

Today's young adult women came of age in a culture that speaks much more freely about sexuality and in a society where gender roles have loosened significantly. The notion that being in a loving, committed relationship might somehow compromise a person's capacity to serve God fully is foreign to most of them.

More importantly, they were raised in a postcommunal, individualistic culture in which the needs and demands of the individual are superior to the needs and demands of the community. Most did not grow up surrounded by extended family or in a traditional parish or neighborhood. Their community did not necessarily tell them what to believe or give them their identities. Most were raised to believe that individuals have the right to decide what they believe in, what their values are, and how they are going to live their lives. Therefore, for this new generation, a partner or a spouse—not community—provides a crucial part of their identity and their support network. It is possible that the need for a partner may be stronger and more crucial to their emotional stability and spiritual health than it was for previous generations.[3]

But even if the celibacy mandate were lifted, the ties that Catholic religious communities still have to the institutional church will continue to be problematic for many lesbian women, regardless of how called they feel to live a life of ministering on the margins. It is on this particular point that I have a contention with Gramick's essay. Many lesbian nuns, she writes, survive by learning to ignore the teachings of the hierarchy. Yet, at the same time, some of them are afraid to come out, for fear that they might lose their ministries or taint their communities. Even though, I am sure, many sisters are out to their communities, they still cannot come out publicly. I know many women religious, and they all have made me feel accepted as a lesbian. Yet I am not aware of any one of them being openly lesbian herself. Has the hierarchy truly been ignored if some sisters still fear that they will taint their communities by coming out?

There is a part of me that understands why lesbian sisters ignore the hierarchy's teaching: the hierarchy ignores the voices of all women, lesbians in particular. But if you attempt to ignore the hierarchy and hesitate to come out publicly, then very often you have little option other than doing ministry "under the radar."

Too much good and just work in the church seems to have to happen under the radar. The problem is, if it is under the radar, many of the people who need to know about it never get to hear about it. Under the radar means that the hierarchy, apparently, does not hear about it. But too often it is not *just* the hierarchy that does not hear about it. Many of the LGBT people who are most hungry for a loving, nurturing experience of church do not hear about it either and, as a result, remain spiritually deprived. I know so many gays and lesbians, young and old, who still believe that if they were to even walk into a church, either they or the church would burst into flames, apparently because the guilt of their sinful life is so great.

The truth is, the hierarchy is getting harder and harder to ignore. They are channeling millions of dollars through the Knights of Columbus to prosecute their agenda against same-sex marriage.[4] Some continue to deny communion to those who come to the table wearing a pride flag.[5] Bishops are forcing Catholic Charities to abandon foster children rather than face the possibility of allowing loving, stable, same-sex couples to adopt them.[6]

Interestingly, the hierarchy's battle against same-sex marriage has even affected sisters themselves. The Congregation for the Doctrine of the Faith's April 2012 "Doctrinal Assessment" of the Leadership Conference of Women Religious specifically names the sisters' "failure" to oppose same-sex marriage publicly as one of the aspects of LCWR in need of reform. Not surprising, the CDF also criticizes "certain radical feminist themes" among women religious, though the hierarchy neither defines what those themes are or what they mean by radical feminism.[7]

Four months after the doctrinal assessment was handed down, members of the LCWR decided to use the opportunity presented by their General Assembly to be a prophetic witness to the bishops on behalf of those marginalized by the institutional church. Then-LCWR President Sister Pat Farrell told the media in a press statement that the "expectation is that open and honest dialogue may lead not only to increasing understanding between church leadership and women religious, but also to creating more possibilities for the laity and, particularly for women, to a have a voice in the church."[8]

Women religious have always been trailblazers. In the eighteenth century, they crossed the Atlantic in small ships, fending off pirates along the way, to get to this country. Once they were here, they ministered to the wounded on the battlefields of the Civil War and provided aid to victims of the great San Francisco earthquake and the influenza epidemic. From humble beginnings, they managed to establish the largest private school system in the country, 110 colleges and universities, and over six hundred hospitals in the United States.

The battle against gays and lesbians that the church hierarchy is waging may be the twenty-first-century frontier where our sisters are most desperately needed. More than ever, we need their prophetic voice to help open up a true and just church.

Religious life is "a prophetic life form," as Sandra Schneiders said in 2010.[9] Women religious consecrate their lives not only to living out the teachings of the gospels but also to following Jesus' command to "read the signs of the times." The work that women religious do is decades, if not centuries, ahead of that of the male hierarchy. They have created among themselves the church that so many restless Catholics long for: small, supportive, nonhierarchical, intimate communities grounded in sacramental life and outreach to the poor and marginalized. In many ways, the sisters have built the church of our dreams.

Given what I have read in Gramick's essay, I am convinced that heterosexual sisters must continue to build that supportive environment for lesbian sisters so that lesbian sisters can feel safe coming out not only to their communities but also to the many LGBT people who have been broken by the institutional church. Lesbians, suffering both as women and as same-sex-attracted persons, are particularly hungry for communal life and a meaningful experience of spirituality. Having "out" sisters would also have a significant impact on the straight community, who would be able to appreciate the meaningful contributions that lesbians make to the life of the church.

If coming out is a sacramental experience, as one sister to whom Gramick referred suggested, that sacrament needs to find a deeper, fuller life among these wounded Catholics who are leaving the church in droves—many of them over women's and LGBT issues. Gramick mentions that lesbian sisters find life in the supportive and nourishing church environments that communities of sisters create and sustain for themselves through their work. Perhaps lesbian sisters in particular are called to bring forth that life-giving model of church to the ever-widening margins of wounded Catholics that the hierarchy is creating. They can continue in greater and more public ways to embody what a true and just church looks like. In doing so, lesbian nuns will provide yet another great gift to the church.

4   Seminary, Priesthood, and the Vatican's Homosexual Dilemma

GERARD JACOBITZ

St. Joseph's University

The ongoing clergy sexual abuse crisis in the Catholic Church has focused attention on the disproportionately high percentage of homosexual priests and seminarians compared to the general population.[1] Estimates as to the precise number of gay seminarians and priests are as controversial as they are varied.[2] And perhaps the Vatican's 2005 ban on any future gay seminarians was introduced in part to put an end to the speculation. But current official Catholic teaching on homosexuality, which I will argue in this paper to be inherently unstable, coupled with the continued requirement of celibacy for priests of the Roman Rite, has resulted in an ironic situation in which gay men are welcomed into the clerical ranks so long as they remain closeted. The true nature of homosexual orientation as a deep and abiding dimension of human personality is either ignored or completely denied, while evangelical celibacy, one of the Catholic Church's unique gifts to Western spirituality, which in its monastic origins had no connection with the clerical state or church hierarchy, is in danger of extinction because of its near total identification with priesthood and repressed sexuality. There are, no doubt, many factors contributing to the steady and precipitous decline of the Catholic priesthood, but certainly the Vatican's insistence on enforced celibacy along with its current teaching on homosexuality are among the most prominent. I will first consider the instability of current teaching on homosexuality and then show how this teaching has led to a situation that is both unhealthy and unsustainable in the current life of the church.

Instability of Catholic Doctrine on Homosexuality Since 1975

One of the many unexpected gifts of the Second Vatican Council was the affirmation of a principle implicit in Catholic tradition but not often enough articulated: that there is a hierarchy of doctrines. This is the doctrine that says not all doctrines are created equal. The clearest expression of the principle appears in the Council's Decree on Ecumenism, *Unitatis Redintegratio*, where it is proposed as a means for reconciling Christians who have not yet found a way to agree on everything:

> In ecumenical dialogue, Catholic theologians, standing fast by the teaching of the church yet searching together with separated brothers and sisters into the divine mysteries, should do so with love for the truth, with charity, and with humility. When comparing doctrines with one another, they should remember that in Catholic doctrine there exists an order or "hierarchy" of truths, since they vary in their relation to the foundation of the Christian faith. Thus the way will be opened whereby this kind of friendly rivalry will incite all to a deeper realization and a clearer expression of the unfathomable riches of Christ.[3]

The placement of the principle in the Decree on Ecumenism should not give the impression that it is of peripheral significance. The hierarchy of doctrine was, after all, the only hierarchy the council fathers endorsed without qualification, and they did so as a means of promoting reconciliation and unity among Christians. The pronouncement should thus be understood in line with the council's radical departure from the language of condemnation, which had been characteristic of the previous twenty ecumenical councils starting with Nicaea, in favor of an inclusive and exhortatory style, which John W. O'Malley, in his recent study of the council, has identified with the elusive "spirit of Vatican II." O'Malley shows how the council's promotion of the radical solidarity of all peoples, the essence of the Christian gospel, is to be found primarily in the remarkably consistent *form* of the council's documents rather than their varied *content*. This solidarity, therefore, should be understood as a pervasive and central theme of the council.[4] In this respect, the hierarchy of doctrines, with its goal of solidarity, should be counted among the council's most important teachings. It is founded on a theology of the human person, deeply rooted in scripture and tradition, which affirms that human beings are endowed with an unearned and unsurpassable dignity by virtue of their being created in the image and likeness of God.

For the better part of forty years, the Catholic Church has attempted to develop its official doctrine on homosexuality. The Congregation for the Doctrine of the Faith (CDF) broke new ground in 1975 with its "Declaration on Certain Questions Concerning Sexual Ethics," which distinguished "between homosexuals whose tendency comes from a false education, from a lack of normal sexual development, from habit, from bad example, or from other similar causes, and is transitory or at least not incurable; and homosexuals who are definitively such because of some kind of innate instinct or a pathological constitution judged to be incurable." Only homosexual acts, which the declaration refers to as "intrinsically disordered," are subject to moral evaluation, and a stipulation is added for these "incurable" homosexuals: "their culpability [for these acts] will be judged with prudence."[5] This new teaching was promulgated during Cardinal Franjo Seper's prefecture of the CDF late in the papacy of Paul VI, and it is perhaps no surprise that within ten years, under a new pope, John Paul II, and a new prefect, Cardinal Joseph Ratzinger, subtle qualifications were considered necessary. According to the CDF's 1986 "Letter on the Pastoral Care of Homosexual Persons," the "homosexual condition," however blameless it is per se, is nevertheless to be understood as an "objective disorder" because it is a more or less deeply rooted tendency to engage in acts that themselves can only be understood as intrinsically evil.[6] Since the promulgation of the 1986 "Letter," the very concept of sexual orientation—as it is has emerged in the secular context, informed not only by the behavioral and social sciences but also by the experience, over time, of a great number of men and women of good will, both homosexual and heterosexual—has been downplayed by the Vatican in favor of an approach that treats homosexuality simply as a tendency or inclination immediately ordered to a set of specific genital acts.

Already in the 1986 "Letter" there appear the statements that "the human person, made in the image and likeness of God, can hardly be adequately described by a reductionist reference to his or her sexual orientation" and that "today, the Church provides a badly needed context for the care of the human person when she refuses to consider the person as a 'heterosexual' or a 'homosexual' and insists that every person has a fundamental identity: the creature of God, and by grace, his child and heir to eternal life."[7] By 1992, the CDF had placed the term "sexual orientation" in scare quotes, with the caveat that "homosexual persons who assert their homosexuality tend to be precisely those who judge homosexual behavior or lifestyle to be 'either completely harmless, if not an entirely good thing.'"[8]

THE VATICAN'S HOMOSEXUAL DILEMMA 89

Finally, in what seems to be the latest moment in a trajectory, the 2005 instruction of the Congregation for Catholic Education (CCE) on the admission of homosexual candidates to seminary and Holy Orders never once mentions the words "orientation" or "condition," and the phrase "homosexual person(s)," which had occurred some twenty-nine times in the CDF's 1986 statement, is altogether absent from the instruction.[9] Thus, sexual orientation, introduced into Catholic teaching about the same time it became current in the social sciences, has been all but abandoned by the church while it has gained wide acceptance in contemporary secular culture.

I would like to propose that what has consciously or unconsciously motivated the Vatican's idiosyncratic approach to the concept of sexual orientation is ultimately traceable to the hierarchy of doctrines affirmed at Vatican II. In this case, faithfulness to the church's teaching on the intrinsic goodness and dignity of the human person, which includes a thorough confidence in the compatibility of faith and reason, necessarily trumps anything that the church has to teach about the moral status of particular sexual acts. It is precisely these two aspects of the church's teachings on the human person—first, the intrinsic and unconditional dignity of the person, and second, the essential reliability of human reason informed by practical experience—that come into conflict in the Vatican's teaching on homosexuality since 1975. These two features of Catholic theological anthropology are so deeply ingrained in Catholic sensibility that they function almost as grammatical rules for doctrinal statements—consciously or unconsciously—such that lesser doctrines cannot depart from them without becoming incoherent. But this is exactly what has happened since the CDF decided in 1975 to take some initial steps in acknowledging the existence of sexual orientation.

Theological Anthropology Catholic and Protestant

The radical humanism of Catholic theological anthropology came into clearest relief when it was juxtaposed with the quite opposite theology of the human person proposed by the Protestant reformers. Michael and Kenneth Himes present a nice comparison of Roman Catholic and Protestant theological anthropologies in their study *Fullness of Faith: The Public Significance of Theology*:

However much the reformers differed among themselves on issues such as Eucharistic theology and ecclesial polity, they agreed on the utter corruption of the human person as a result of the sin of Adam. Luther's description of the human being as "turned in on himself" expressed the conviction that the fall had destroyed the capacity for genuine other-directedness. The Formula of Concord (1576) held original sin to be "so profound a corruption of human nature as to leave nothing sound, nothing uncorrupt in the body or soul of man, or in his mental or bodily powers." In 1619 the Synod of Dort, which set the main lines of Calvinist orthodoxy, taught that after the fall the human being was left in "blindness of mind, horrible darkness, vanity, and perverseness of judgment; became wicked, rebellious, and obdurate in heart and will, and impure in all his affections." Although some glimmers of natural light remain by which humanity has some knowledge of God, natural things and morality, human beings pollute this light and are incapable of using it correctly "even in things natural and civil." This is echoed in the Westminster Confession's declaration that fallen human beings are "dead in sin and wholly defiled in all the faculties and parts of soul and body," and have become "utterly indisposed, disabled, and made opposite to all good, and wholly inclined to all evil." The individual, radically turned in on himself or herself and closed to any possibility of agapic community, is locked into selfishness.[10]

Even the Anglican *Thirty-Nine Articles* of 1563, which to this day are published on the website of the Anglican Communion, reflect a theological anthropology firmly situated within this extremely negative Protestant approach:

Original sin standeth not in the following of Adam (as the Pelagians do vainly talk), but it is the fault and corruption of the nature of every man that naturally is engendered of the offspring of Adam, whereby man is very far gone from original righteousness, and is of his own nature inclined to evil, so that the flesh lusteth always contrary to the Spirit; and therefore in every person born into this world, it deserveth God's wrath and damnation. And this infection of nature doth remain, yea, in them that are regenerated, whereby the lust of the flesh, called in Greek *phronema sarkos* (which some do expound the wisdom, some sensuality, some the affection, some the desire, of the flesh), is not subject to the Law of God. And although there is no condemnation for them that believe and are baptized, yet the Apostle doth confess, that concupiscence and lust hath of itself the nature of sin.[11]

These theological anthropologies from the period of the Reformation are fully consonant with the nominalist emphasis on the utter transcendence of God and with the independence of the natural order so central to the Enlightenment philosophy and political theory that laid the groundwork for the secular age. Perhaps if it had not been for Luther, Catholicism too would have followed this trajectory. But in response to the Reformation, the Roman Church held fast to its roots in the divine immanence and in the teleology of eminently discoverable natural essences.

The Council of Trent acknowledged that the first man, Adam, "lost the holiness and justice in which he had been constituted" and as a result of original sin "was changed in body and soul for the worse."[12] Yet despite original sin, the essential nature of the human being was left completely and marvelously intact; it was in no way utterly corrupted. "Free will, weakened as it was in its powers, and downward bent, was by no means extinguished in them,"[13] such that even before justification in Christ, not all human actions could be declared without merit.[14] Furthermore, baptism was understood at Trent as removing the entire essence of sin, such that "for those who are born again [at baptism] God hates nothing."[15] Whatever belongs to human nature after justification is completely restored. The baptized are made "innocent, immaculate, pure, guiltless and beloved of God, *heirs indeed of God, joint heirs with Christ*" (Rom 8:17).[16] It is not simply a matter of God refusing to register human evil despite its continued presence. Whatever evil is incurred by original sin is completely eradicated by sanctifying grace, of which baptism is the tangible sign. Concupiscence, or the inclination to sin, remains in the baptized, but it is not to be understood as an evil; "it is left for us to wrestle with" for our greater good, such that "he who shall have *striven lawfully shall be crowned*" (with reference to 2 Tim 2:5).[17]

This perspective was only strengthened, as the Himes brothers note, in the Counter-Reformation theologies that followed the Council of Trent:

Later in the sixteenth century, disputes about the sovereignty of grace and the status of human freedom led to the teaching that the original justice and holiness of Adam were "accidental" [in the Aristotelian

sense], not intrinsic to the human person as human. This original justice and holiness were lost as a result of original sin, but since they
were accidental qualities, human nature remained essentially unim-
paired. As some counter-reformation Catholic theologians phrased the
point, the human person, created in the image and likeness of God,
might lose that likeness, consisting in original justice and holiness, but
retained the image of God.[18]

This latter distinction, so characteristic of the classical church Fathers,
serves as a reminder that Catholic teaching on the intrinsic goodness of
the human person was present in the tradition long before the Reformation. Its roots, for example, were already well established in the theology
of Thomas Aquinas, as the Belgian Dominican, Servais Pinckaers, has
shown by surveying all occurrences of the term *dignitas* in Aquinas's corpus. Aquinas frequently places the term in relation to *persona*, with its
most creative and effective instances pertaining to the *persona humana*.[19]
The "dignity of the human person" as a principle of Catholic doctrine
becomes a staple in the post-Tridentine theology that leads into the
nineteenth-century Thomist revival, canonized by Leo XIII in his 1879
encyclical *Aeterni Patris*. It then becomes a predominant theme in the
abundantly productive tradition of modern papal social teaching, which
the same pope initiated with the encyclical *Rerum Novarum* in 1891. From
there, the French Thomist philosopher Jacques Maritain would make the
dignity of the human person, without explicit mention of its theological
underpinnings, the focus of his crucial input on the drafting committee
of the United Nations' Universal Declaration of Human Rights in 1948.[20]
It plays a central role in John XXIII's encyclical letter *Pacem in Terris*
(1963), a prominence that would only be magnified by its place in the
Second Vatican Council's "Pastoral Constitution on the Church in the
Modern World," *Gaudium et Spes*.[21]

In light of this historical development, the gay Catholic writer Andrew
Sullivan rightly notices something revolutionary in the title of the CDF's
1986 "Letter on the Pastoral Care of Homosexual *Persons*":

> To some, the use of the term "homosexual person" in a Catholic text
> might seem a banality. But the term "person" constitutes for Catholic
> moral teaching a profound statement about the individual's humanity,

dignity, and worth. It invokes a whole range of rights and needs; it reflects the recognition by the Church that a homosexual person deserves exactly the same concern and compassion as a heterosexual person, has as many rights as a human being, and is as valuable in the eyes of God.[22]

But within the course of the same 1986 "Letter," the CDF, in a move that almost seems an attempt to compensate for this positive assessment, invents a new moral category, the "objectively disordered" inclination: "Although the particular inclination of the homosexual person is not a sin, it is a more or less strong tendency ordered toward an intrinsic moral evil; and thus the inclination itself must be seen as an *objective disorder.*"[23] The inclination is judged to be objectively disordered simply because it may lead to an intrinsic moral evil—an evil morally wrong under all circumstances. From a Catholic perspective, however, the simple *desire* to do something wrong can only be identified with the concupiscence, or inclination to sin, that the Council of Trent acknowledged as remaining in the baptized after justification. But, as we have seen, Trent not only refused to call the inclination to sin evil; it also did not consider it objectively disordered. Such a desire may indeed contribute to the growth and greater good of the person. Only acts can be *objectively* disordered in Catholic moral theology; there is no such thing as intrinsically evil or objectively disordered human desire.[24] Even if everything that is meant by "homosexual orientation" were reduced to the desire to engage in specific prohibited genital acts, it would make no sense to call this desire *objectively* disordered unless there were an *essential* connection with the acts, as if there were no free moral agent standing between the inclination and the execution of the acts, which clearly is not the case. Homosexual desire may or may not lead to the acts in question.

Why then did the CDF introduce this new moral category, the objectively disordered inclination? Given the most authoritative Catholic teaching that human desire in and of itself can only be considered good and that original sin did not compromise the image of God at the core of the human person, it seems the CDF wants to distance itself from any understanding of homosexuality that would identify it too closely with the human person (and this despite the use of the term "homosexual person" in the document) because anything that reaches to the core of the human person *has to be good* simply by virtue of that proximity. Such is the logic of Catholic anthropology. To the extent that official Catholic teaching would consider homosexuality an orientation of the person, the morality of homosexual genital acts would have to be reevaluated in terms of whether they might be essential expressions of the orientation. In its attempt to confine "homosexuality" to a tendency immediately ordered to acts that are already presumed to be intrinsically evil, the CDF avoids this reevaluation. The 1986 "Letter" says the introduction of the new moral category is necessary because "[in] the discussion which followed the publication of the [1975] Declaration . . . an overly benign interpretation was given to the homosexual condition itself, some going so far as to call it neutral, or even good."[25] But the real problem arose when the same declaration admitted that, at least for some, homosexuality is "some kind of an innate instinct" or "constitution."[26] Treating homosexuality as an objective disorder is thus consistent with the CDF's subsequent history of downplaying homosexual orientation. But this position causes more problems than it solves when considered in light of a corollary of the same Catholic anthropology, a steadfast confidence in the integrity of human reason.

Homosexual Orientation and the Human Sciences

In August 2009, the American Psychological Association adopted by a 125-to-4 vote a resolution accompanied by a comprehensive report on the effectiveness of "sexual orientation change efforts" (SOCE). The taskforce charged with preparation of the report undertook an exhaustive review of peer-reviewed journal articles, comprising eighty-three separate research studies stretching from 1960 to 2007. The findings of the taskforce were conclusive: "The results of scientifically valid research indicate that it is unlikely that individuals will be able to reduce same-sex attractions or increase other-sex sexual attractions through SOCE."[27] In addition, the taskforce found that "there was some evidence to indicate that individuals experienced harm from SOCE," with negative side effects including "loss of sexual feeling, depression, suicidality, and anxiety."[28] The taskforce published its findings against a backdrop of what it referred to as already established "scientific facts," including the following:

Same-sex sexual attractions, behavior, and orientations per se are normal and positive variants of human sexuality—in other words, they do not indicate either mental or developmental disorders.

Homosexuality and bisexuality are stigmatized, and this stigma can have a variety of negative consequences (for example, minority stress) throughout the lifespan.

Same-sex sexual attractions and behavior occur in the context of a variety of sexual orientations and sexual orientation identities, and for some, sexual orientation identity (that is, individual or group membership and affiliation, self-labeling) is fluid or has an indefinite outcome.

Gay men, lesbians, and bisexual individuals form stable, committed relationships and families that are equivalent to heterosexual relationships and families in essential respects.[29]

The APA resolution is the culmination of a fifty-year history of revisionist thinking on the nature of homosexuality. Already in 1973, under the guidance of such pioneers as Evelyn Hooker, the American Psychiatric Association removed homosexuality from its list of mental disorders and sexual deviations; the American Psychological Association, in turn, declared in 1975 that "homosexuality *per se* implies no impairment in judgment, stability, reliability, or general social and vocational capabilities."[30] In fact, the latest editions of the *Diagnostic and Statistical Manual of Mental Disorders* (DSM) do not even contain the word "homosexual." Dr. Robert L. Spitzer's recent disavowal of so-called reparative therapy for homosexuals, which he had once championed,[31] is just the latest chapter in this remarkable development that has resulted in a clinical view of homosexual orientation that hardly resides on the margins of human personality. Rather, for those who have the orientation, there is every indication that it is as essential a dimension of the personality as sexuality itself. And it should be noted that these findings were established, initially at least, against a strongly negative cultural bias against homosexuality, in a climate where the scientific data had to stand solely on the strength of their objectivity.

That the CDF is aware of this scientific development is evident in its 1986 "Letter," which contains an ambiguous statement on the value of the natural sciences. The claim is made that the Catholic moral perspective "finds support in the more secure findings of the natural sciences, which have their own legitimate and proper methodology and field of inquiry." But a caveat is added:

> However, the Catholic moral viewpoint is founded on human reason illumined by faith and is consciously motivated by the desire to do the will of God our Father. The Church is thus in a position to learn from scientific discovery but also to transcend the horizons of science and to be confident that her more global vision does greater justice to the rich reality of the human person in his spiritual and physical dimensions, created by God and heir, by grace, to eternal life.[32]

Now, it is certainly reasonable to say that faith furnishes a horizon of understanding wider than that of the natural sciences, but in Catholic theology what is understood by faith cannot directly contradict the well-established truths of science. Grace builds on nature. And human reason is competent to discover the truths of the human condition, even competent to discover truths that lie beyond it. The Magisterium cannot, therefore, simply cordon off a field of scientific inquiry and say something to the effect of, "In this area there is nothing further to be learned; we know all there is to know." But this is exactly what has been done in the case of homosexuality. It is akin to the apocryphal story of the pope refusing to look through Galileo's telescope because he "knows" there can be no moons orbiting Jupiter.[33]

Furthermore, in turning away from the natural light of human reason, the CDF turns toward the Bible in a way that is completely strange to the Catholic natural law tradition; that is, it employs an uncritical prooftexting reminiscent of Christian fundamentalism.[34] But any Catholic approach to biblical exegesis proceeds with the recognition that the Bible was written in cultural situations far removed from the modern. Catholics do not pretend that any passage in the Bible can be read without the aid of scientifically informed interpretative techniques. In other words, a fundamentalist-literal reading of Leviticus, as if it referred to modern homosexual relationships, has no more place in Catholic moral theology than a fundamentalist-literal reading of the first three chapters of Genesis has in modern cosmological science.[35]

Human Experience of Sexual Orientation

Perhaps even more important than the scientific discovery of sexual orientation is the remarkable shift in cultural attitudes toward homosexuality that has occurred since the mid-twentieth century, a development that cannot be attributed solely or even largely to advances in the social sciences. Rather it has resulted from the actions of an increasingly vocal homosexual population. In the words of Andrew Sullivan,

> homosexuals themselves challenged the distinction between their private acts and public personae. They argued that homosexuality was an emotional orientation, like heterosexuality; that it presupposed a full and integrated life that could not be easily bifurcated. And the dignity of that full life did not tolerate the notion that it should be shrouded in secrecy, treated with any more discretion than a heterosexual life, or euphemized into invisibility. To tell a homosexual to keep his identity secret in public was equivalent to telling a heterosexual that she should never mention her husband or children in public, or tell of common activities, or relate any stories that might indicate her involvement in a sexual and emotional relationship with someone of the opposite sex. It was equivalent to telling an eighteen-year-old heterosexual male that he could not publicly mention the girlfriend he was dating or his plans for the future or his hopes for marriage. It was, in short, a preposterous burden for any self-respecting human being to bear.[36]

It is understandably difficult at times to fathom the magnitude of this cultural shift. In the CDF's 1992 "Response to Legislative Proposals on the Non-Discrimination of Homosexual Persons," Joseph Ratzinger wrote:

> An individual's sexual orientation is generally not known to others unless he publicly identifies himself as having this orientation or unless some overt behavior manifests it. As a rule, the majority of homosexually oriented persons who seek to lead chaste lives do not publicize their sexual orientation. Hence the problem of discrimination in terms of employment, housing, etc., does not usually arise.[37]

But this argument is clearly invalid in the current cultural milieu because its major premise has been completely undermined. An individual's wish to remain silent about his or her sexual orientation was in fact never simply a matter of personal choice; it always presupposed a society inclined to condone if not enforce that silence. Social complicity in the construction and maintenance of the homosexual closet had already eroded to some degree when Joseph Ratzinger wrote his "Response" in 1992. Today it is almost entirely absent. The days of homosexuality as a social taboo are over. We now live in a society where only the *overtly heterosexual* are automatically assumed to be heterosexual. In fact, the situation today is such that it is no longer viable for gays and lesbians to be closeted in the public forum. For example, the world's largest professional services firm, PricewaterhouseCoopers, encourages, as a matter of company policy, all gay, lesbian, and transgendered employees to be out in the workplace precisely because this transparency improves productivity: people can be better accountants when they are free of the shame and fear that are never absent from a life of covering up.[38] It is perhaps a truism to say that morality is not established by majority vote, but the inductive force of a cultural shift of this magnitude has to be taken seriously by any adherent of the Catholic tradition, which values human experience, especially if sustained over a number of generations, as a reliable measure of truth. The acceptance of gay, lesbian, and transgendered persons is becoming *traditional* in our society, and that certainly has Catholic ramifications.[39]

The Vatican's Homosexual Dilemma

Science, reason, and human experience over the past half-century have confirmed that sexual orientation is a deep and abiding dimension of the personality. But if this is true, then it should be apparent that attempts since 1975 to develop doctrine on the homosexual person have led the official Magisterium of the Catholic Church into a double bind. As we have seen, Catholic teaching makes the human person into something akin to the fabled philosopher's stone: anything it touches turns to gold. If sexual orientation is an essential dimension of the human person, if it is not so much *what* a person is but *who* a person is, then it simply cannot be disordered. But right alongside this is a corollary of the same teaching on the dignity of the human person: the Catholic confidence in the reliability of the natural light of human reason. Catholics are not at liberty to reject the well-established conclusions of scientific methodology nor to discount conclusions from the experience of a truly representative sample of human subjects acting in good will. The larger the sample, the more plausible the possibility that it articulates the *sensus fidelium*, and the size of this sample has been growing exponentially for the past fifty years. The double bind can be succinctly stated: If sexual orientation is understood as an essential dimension of the human person, then, in light of fundamental church teaching, it necessarily shares in the human person's unsurpassable dignity. If, on the other hand, homosexuality is presented merely as a more or less deeply rooted tendency to engage in certain illicit sexual acts, this cannot be squared with the church's equally fundamental teaching that human reason (in this case human reason informed by the science of modern psychology) is competent to discover the truth of the human condition. This is the dilemma. And because of it, recent Roman Catholic teaching on homosexuality should not be considered stable; it is inconsistent with the more fundamental principles of Catholic theological anthropology that affirm both the intrinsic and unconditional dignity of the person and the essential reliability of human reason informed by practical experience. Since in Catholic teaching original sin itself does not compromise these principles, neither could any particular teaching on sexual morality. The anthropological teaching clearly has priority in the hierarchy of doctrine, and when these two higher principles are applied to the lower teaching, they seem to call the latter into question.[40]

The Current Situation in the Catholic Seminary and Priesthood

The effects of the inherent instability of the church's official teaching on homosexuality can most readily be seen among Catholic lay people, who have increasingly chosen to ignore the teaching. A 2011 survey by the Public Religion Research Institute showed support for legal recognition of same-sex relationships to be dramatically higher among Catholics than among members of other American Christian denominations.[41] There is even some evidence from Europe that the laity's acceptance of gay and lesbian relationships is beginning to "trickle up" to the bishops.[42] But it is a different story in the Catholic seminary and priesthood, which, because of the hierarchy's direct control, have been made to bear the brunt of the teaching's problematic nature. Rather than keeping gay men out of the seminary, the CCE's 2005 "ban" seems only to have made life worse for those who continue to be admitted.

In his 2006 book on seminary formation, Gerald Coleman, the vicar for priests of the Archdiocese of San Francisco and a former seminary rector, quotes the key passage from the CCE's instruction:

> The church, while profoundly respecting the persons in question, cannot admit to the seminary or to holy orders those who practice homosexuality, present deep-seated homosexual tendencies or support the so-called "gay culture." Such persons, in fact, find themselves in a situation that gravely hinders them from relating correctly to men and women. One must in no way overlook the negative consequences that can derive from the ordination of persons with deep-seated homosexual tendencies.[43]

But then Coleman provides the following commentary:

> The Congregation discourages discrimination and encourages respect and sensitivity. Ultimately, however, the Congregation warns formation teams to guard against individuals who display deep-seated, disordered tendencies. In other words, like their policy against sexually active heterosexuals, these new norms are meant to protect the Church from homosexuals that are most likely to act out sexually.[44]

Coleman's reading ignores the issue of sexual orientation and assumes that any "disorder" is confined to sexual acts. Implicit in Coleman's approach is the instruction's distinction between types of homosexuals, those who "present deep-seated homosexual tendencies, and those with homosexual tendencies that were only the expression of a transitory problem—for example, that of an adolescence not yet superseded."[45] The instruction says that only those with the deep-seated tendencies are prohibited from entering the seminary; those with the transitory type may be admitted with the provision that "such tendencies must be clearly overcome at least three years before ordination to the diaconate."[46] If what current social science and cultural experience call "sexual orientation" can be reduced to a "tendency" immediately ordered to physical acts, the following reading is possible: There are homosexual acts, and these are intrinsically disordered. There are people who have profoundly deep-seated tendencies to engage in these acts. However, a person simply *does not have* profoundly deep-seated homosexual tendencies when he can demonstrate three years' abstinence from acting on them. Regardless of how Coleman might justify his reading of the CCE, what is clear is that he wants to interpret it in such a way as to allow continued acceptance to the seminary of the "right kind" of homosexual men.

There is anecdotal evidence that such loopholes in the 2005 policy are widely employed by Catholic vocation directors who continue to accept gay candidates. I reported on two such candidates in my response to Donald Cozzens's presentation at Fairfield University's installment of the More than a Monologue conferences.[47] The two were accepted as diocesan candidates for ordination after the CCE's 2005 instruction, despite their admitting to being gay. In both cases they were advised by their spiritual directors to mention nothing of sexual orientation in the initial interviews—not to lie if asked, but not to offer the information. Neither candidate found reason to mention his sexual orientation because neither was asked—until, that is, they were given psychological evaluations. Both then admitted to being gay when asked by their psychologists, who then reported this back to the vocation directors.

One of the psychologists shared a draft of his report with the candidate before turning it in to the diocese. When the candidate saw mention of his sexual orientation in the report, he e-mailed the psychologist saying, "Since the word 'homosexuality' does not appear in the DSM-IV, how is it relevant to a report on my psychological status?" The psychologist wrote back that it was not relevant but that the diocese requires him to ask the question. Both these prospective candidates were accepted into their diocesan programs without further mention of sexuality. The candidates and their vocation directors did not discuss the psychological reports, which, presumably, were kept in the candidates' files.

I also reported at the conference on evidence of a more disturbing trend exemplified by three psychologists who routinely conduct psychological screenings for Catholic seminaries. Again, this evidence is anecdotal because the psychologists do not wish to be identified, but between the three of them, they have evaluated over one hundred candidates for Catholic seminaries over twelve years. What is alarming is that in only one case has a candidate admitted to being gay. Indeed, the psychologists have the impression that some of the candidates are lying, but far more prevalent are candidates who, the psychologists say, exhibit a seriously repressed sexuality, especially in the case of younger men: twenty-year-olds who have not dated, who do not masturbate, who are very pious and seem not to be interested in things sexual. All the psychologists can do in cases like these is report back to the vocation directors how very unusual this lack of sexual affect is in a person. But it does not constitute grounds for disqualification of a candidate in the current ecclesial climate. The candidate's acceptance to seminary is at the discretion of the vocation directors, who themselves may very well be gay.

What happens to these gay seminarians—both the ones who are comfortable with their sexuality and the ones who suffer from a repressed sexuality? The best-case scenario is that at some point they will start talking to one another. But in the case of a clandestine group within a group, every ounce of repression translates into a pound of solidarity. The bonds of union will be stronger among the repressed than elsewhere, which cannot help but be destabilizing and divisive within the larger group, not to mention the wider church. This is what was discovered about the "Don't Ask, Don't Tell" policy in the U.S. military.[48] The worst-case scenario is that sexual repression of this nature would devolve into more destructive behaviors, such as sexual abuse. The most comprehensive study of the treatment of sexuality in American seminaries is that of Paul Stanosz, who reports on nine U.S. diocesan seminaries, one in which he resided for a semester of research, allowing him full access to staff and seminarians. Stanosz found considerable deficiencies in the ability of these formation programs to prepare men for a healthy life of chaste celibacy, and that this was especially true for gay candidates. Drawing on the work of the psychologists Laura Smart and Daniel M. Wegner, who study the effects of stigma, Stanosz found that gay seminarians carried all the marks of a minority with a concealed stigma (a stigma that can be more or less successfully hidden by the victim).[49] When a gay person's sexual orientation is stigmatized, the chief danger is that it will become a preoccupation and source of shame. As shamed individuals, gay seminarians will not seek out support for celibate life in relationships; they will be afraid to make appropriate self-disclosures.[50]

But another aspect of the research on stigma is especially relevant to the current situation of a seminary system and priesthood that condones homosexuality as long as it remains concealed. Smart and Wegner identify three typical strategies for reducing the pain of managing a concealed stigma: first, "automatization of suppression," where a kind of life program is initiated that allows or even encourages suppression techniques to be rehearsed until they become skills; second, "situation management," which entails a careful avoidance of any situation that would require the hiding of the stigma, which, curiously, can be achieved in two opposite ways, either by engaging in only superficial relationships where no real sharing of the self is required or by immersing oneself in a subculture that specifically focuses on the stigma; and third, "redefinition of the stigma," where the hidden stigma is reinterpreted as no longer stigmatizing because it somehow belongs to a "former self" sufficiently distant from the "current self" so as to be irrelevant to any questions that may come up about one's identity (Smart and Wegner use the example of a drug addict who has become a "convert," that is, one who has "come clean").[51] Perhaps it should come as no great surprise that a disproportionate percentage of Catholic seminarians and clerics are gay compared to the general population when it is realized that the clerical culture provides a perfect environment for a person who experiences his homosexuality as a stigma to exercise one or more of these three coping strategies. And given the provisions of the CCE's 2005 instruction, it is no small irony that the church's official teaching on homosexuality, with its "ban" on gay seminarians, has resulted in a clerical culture that not only fails to exclude homosexual candidates but also encourages them to relate superficially to men and women *and* to join gay subcultures. Perhaps it is not going too far to say that the Catholic hierarchy has a vested interest (about which it may or may not be aware) in maintaining a cultural status quo where homosexuality is considered shameful. While the number of priests continues to fall, as long as there are young, devout Catholic men who are ashamed of their homosexuality, there will be a strong motivation for this not insignificant minority to join the priesthood, just so long as priesthood entails celibacy.

Donald Cozzens has presented a formidable argument against mandatory celibacy for priests of the Roman Rite in his book *Freeing Celibacy*.[52] His thesis is that some people are born with a natural disposition for celibacy and that the desire to realize this disposition comes as a charism, a divine gift.[53] For such individuals, celibacy is not a discipline but a path of fulfillment. Since grace builds on nature, if the natural disposition for celibacy is not present in the individual, there will be no place for the gift of celibacy to take root, grow, and flourish. The priesthood, however, is a way of life that is attractive to people who may or may not have this natural disposition for the celibate life. Cozzens thinks that forcing someone without it to live as if he possesses it is to court psychological, emotional, social, and ecclesial disaster. There are *good* reasons for why a person who does not have the charism would still be drawn to priesthood, for example, attraction to a life of service, but there are also *bad* reasons, for example, repressed or stigmatized sexuality. I agree with Cozzens that the church has a responsibility to support those who have been graced with the charism of celibacy and that celibacy will be truly free and freeing only when it is no longer a requirement for priesthood. But I would also argue that celibacy can never be free to function as a true charism until homosexuality is accepted by the entire church (including the hierarchy) as a full and authentic variation of human sexual relating. Without this acceptance, it will be impossible to rule out a person's stigmatized homosexuality as the true motive for his seeking membership in a celibate institution.

Conclusion

Roman Catholic theology is more systematic than that of any other Christian denomination—more, in fact, than that of any other religion. It should come as no surprise that a change in one aspect of Catholic doctrine would result in ramifications rippling through the whole organism. Yet never before in the history of the church has change been a more pressing issue. With its embrace of the historical consciousness that emerged in the nineteenth century, the Second Vatican Council acknowledged that change was not only possible but also sometimes absolutely necessary. The radical change in traditional teaching on the church-state relationship that the council adopted prompted the American Jesuit John Courtney Murray to call the development of doctrine—the possibility of a new teaching going beyond or even contrary to a long-held traditional teaching—"*the* issue under the issues" at Vatican Council II.[54] Echoing Pope John's encyclical *Pacem in Terris*, the Pastoral Constitution on the Church in the Modern World stressed the importance of learning from nature as it presents itself in the "signs of the times."

In every age, the church carries the responsibility of reading the signs of the times and of interpreting them in the light of the Gospel, if it is to carry out its task. In language intelligible to every generation, it should be able to answer the ever recurring questions which people ask about the meaning of this present life and of the life to come, and how one is related to the other. We must be aware of and understand the aspirations, the yearnings, and the often dramatic features of the world in which we live.[55]

Given the very substantial changes that have occurred in the scientific and cultural understanding of sexuality over the past several decades, it would be naïve for a church that expects to learn something from nature to assume that these changes would have no effect whatsoever on church doctrine.[56] The church's teaching on homosexuality will continue to be inherently unstable until it can reconcile this teaching with its more fundamental doctrine on the dignity of the human person. Individual gay and lesbian Catholics suffer because of this instability, but so too does the entire church, whose seminarians and ordained ministers are forced to maintain a conspiracy of shame and silence. It is fair to say that further development of church doctrine will not come overnight, but an acceptance of a sociologically and psychologically sound definition of sexual orientation would be a step in the right direction.

5   Same-Sex Marriage, the Right to Religious and Moral Freedom, and the Catholic Church

MICHAEL JOHN PERRY

Emory University School of Law

In this essay, I explain why what we may call "the exclusion policy"—excluding same-sex couples from civil marriage—violates the internationally recognized right to religious and moral freedom *if the policy is based on the principal rationale that the pope and bishops of the Catholic Church give in support of the policy.*

The Right to Religious and Moral Freedom

The statement of the right to religious and moral freedom that is articulated in the International Covenant on Civil and Political Rights (ICCPR) is canonical in this sense: The great majority of the countries of the world—over 85 percent—are parties to the ICCPR: As of June 2012, 167 of the 195 countries that are members of the United Nations were parties to the ICCPR, including, as of 1992, the United States. Article 18 of the ICCPR declares:

1. Everyone shall have the right to freedom of thought, conscience and religion. This right shall include freedom to have or to adopt a religion or belief of his choice, and freedom, either individually or in community with others and in public or private, to manifest his religion or belief in worship, observance, practice and teaching.
2. No one shall be subject to coercion which would impair his freedom to have or to adopt a religion or belief of his choice.
3. Freedom to manifest one's religion or beliefs may be subject only to such limitations as are prescribed by law and are necessary to protect public safety, order, health, or morals or the fundamental rights and freedoms of others.
4. The States Parties to the present Covenant undertake to have respect for the liberty of parents and, when applicable, legal guardians to en-

sure the religious and moral education of their children in conformity with their own convictions.[1]

The UN Human Rights Committee—the body that monitors compliance with the ICCPR and, under the First Optional Protocol to the ICCPR, adjudicates cases brought by individuals alleging that a state party is in violation of the ICCPR—has stated that "the right to freedom of thought, conscience and religion . . . in article 18.1 is far-reaching and profound."[2] How "far-reaching and profound"? Note the breadth of the right: that according to Article 18 "everyone shall have" the right to freedom not just of "religion" but also of "conscience." The "right shall include freedom to have or adopt a religion *or belief* of his choice, and freedom, either individually or in community with others and in public or private, to manifest his religion *or belief* in worship, observance, practice and teaching." Article 18 explicitly indicates that the right concerns moral as well as religious freedom when it identifies the "belief" that is protected as moral belief: "the State parties to the [ICCPR] undertake to have respect for the liberty of parents and, when applicable, legal guardians to assure the religious *and moral* education of their children in conformity with their own convictions." So, the right we are discussing protects not only freedom to practice one's religion, including, of course, one's religiously based morality; it also protects freedom to practice one's morality—freedom to "to manifest his . . . belief in . . . practice"—even if one's morality is not embedded in a religious tradition, *even if, that is, one's morality is embedded not in a transcendent worldview but in a worldview that is not transcendent.* (By a "transcendent" worldview, I mean a worldview that affirms rather than denies or is agnostic about the existence of a "transcendent" reality, as distinct from the reality that is or could be the object of natural-scientific inquiry.)[3] As the Human Rights Committee has put the point:

> The Committee draws the attention of States parties to the fact that the freedom of thought and the freedom of conscience are protected equally with the freedom of religion and belief. . . . Article 18 protects theistic, non-theistic and atheistic beliefs, as well as the right not to profess any religion or belief. The terms "belief" and "religion" are to be broadly construed. Article 18 is not limited in its application to traditional religions or to religions and beliefs with institutional characteristics or practices analogous to those of traditional religions.[4]

In deriving from Article 18 a right to conscientious objection, the Human Rights Committee explained that "the [legal] obligation to use lethal force may seriously conflict with the freedom of conscience and the right to manifest one's religion or belief" and emphasized that "there shall be no differentiation among conscientious objectors on the basis of the nature of their particular beliefs."[5]

Given the breadth of the right we are discussing—the "far-reaching and profound" right of which the ICCPR's Article 18 is the canonical articulation—we may accurately call it the right to religious *and moral* freedom: the freedom to live one's life in accord with one's religious and/or moral convictions and commitments.

Some ICCPR rights—such as the Article 7 right not to "be subjected to torture or to cruel, inhuman or degrading treatment or punishment"—are unconditional (absolute): they forbid (or require) government to do something, *period*.[6] Some other ICCPR rights, by contrast, are conditional: they forbid (or require) government to do something *unless certain conditions are satisfied*. As Article 18 makes clear, under the right to religious and moral freedom, government may not ban or otherwise impede a practice protected by the right, unless each of three conditions is satisfied:

> *The legitimacy condition*: The ban or other policy must serve a legitimate government objective.[7]
>
> *The least burdensome alternative condition*: The policy must be necessary to serve the legitimate government objective, in the sense that the policy serves the objective significantly better than would any less burdensome (to the protected practice) policy.[8]
>
> *The proportionality condition*: The good the policy achieves must be sufficiently weighty to warrant the burden the policy imposes on those who want to act in a way the policy bans or otherwise impedes.[9]

The relevant condition, for present purposes, is the legitimacy condition.

What government objectives are not legitimate under the right to religious and moral freedom? Article 18 does not call into question the legitimacy of government's acting to protect—to list the most obvious examples—the lives, health, safety, liberty, property, and socioeconomic well-being of the citizenry and other human beings; human rights; the orderly functioning of society, including the orderly functioning of democratic and judicial processes; nonhuman animals; and the environment.

Article 18 explicitly contemplates government's acting to protect even "public morals." However, as the Siracusa Principles on the Limitation and Derogation Provisions in the International Covenant on Civil and Political Rights[10] state:

2. The scope of a limitation referred to in the Covenant shall not be interpreted so as to jeopardize the essence of the right concerned.

3. All limitation clauses shall be interpreted strictly and in favor of the rights at issue.

4. All limitations shall be interpreted in the light and context of the particular right concerned.

So, with respect to "public morals,"[11] the Human Rights Committee has emphasized:

The concept of morals derives from many social, philosophical and religious traditions; consequently, limitations on the freedom to manifest a religion or belief for the purpose of protecting morals must be based on principles not deriving exclusively from a single tradition. . . . If a set of beliefs is treated as official ideology in constitutions, statutes, proclamations of ruling parties, etc., or in actual practice, this shall not result in any impairment of the freedoms under article 18 or any other rights recognized under the Covenant nor in any discrimination against persons who do not accept the official ideology or who oppose it.[12]

As the editors of a casebook on the ICCPR have put the point, in summarizing several statements by the Human Rights Committee concerning protection of "the public morals" under the right to religious and moral freedom: " 'Public morals' measures should reflect a pluralistic view of society, rather than a single religious culture."[13]

It follows, then, that protecting "public morals" is not necessarily an illegitimate government objective under the right to religious and moral freedom. Whether protecting "public morals" in any particular scenario is an illegitimate government objective depends on the following analysis. If the government objective asserted in defense of a ban (or other policy) involves the claim that the conduct at which the ban is aimed is immoral, the government objective is illegitimate, under the right to religious and moral freedom, if the government's pursuit of the objective is based on— "based on" in the sense that government would not be pursuing the objective "but for"—a conspicuously sectarian belief, religious or moral, such as "this conduct is contrary to the will of God." This rule—this understanding of the legitimacy condition—is especially fitting for a democracy that is, as democracies increasingly are, religiously and morally pluralistic. In such democracies, the coercive imposition of sectarian religious and moral beliefs is greatly divisive. That divisiveness might be a price worth paying were there a genuine need for government sometimes to adjudicate sectarian religious and/or moral disagreements. That there is no such need—indeed, that there is a need for government *not* to adjudicate such disagreements—is a premise of the right to religious and moral freedom. The further premise that government's competence to adjudicate such disagreements is at best highly questionable—a premise amply confirmed by historical experience—is additional support for the right.

The Exclusion Policy

A core part of the freedom to live one's life in accord with one's religious and/or moral convictions and commitments—which is the freedom protected by the right to religious and moral freedom—is the freedom to live one's life in a marriage of one's choosing (if one chooses to live one's life in a marriage). So the exclusion policy clearly implicates the right to religious and moral freedom.

Something the philosopher James Griffin wrote in his book *On Human Rights* bears quotation here: It is often unnecessary for government to make it possible for everyone to live precisely the life one "has settled on. Most individual conceptions of a worthwhile life have alternatives, as good or nearly as good, and a person may reasonably be asked to find an alternative, if the form first chosen is costly or reduces options for others."[14] Nonetheless,

> if there are same-sex couples who want to form some sort of union and raise children—who want, that is, to have the rich, stable, recognized, respected relations that are at the heart of most people's conceptions of a worthwhile life—and, because of our ethical traditions, there are no social institutions to allow it, then we should create one or another form of them. This too, I believe, is an issue of liberty. No matter how many options there are already, this one, because of its centrality to

characteristic human conceptions of a worthwhile life, must be added. . . . What is at stake for same-sex couples are several of the most important components of a good life available to human beings. . . . Some persons do not want deep personal relations or to raise children. But the great majority of us do, and the [refusal to extend the benefit of law to same-sex unions denies] same-sex couples some of the greatest, most widely distributed, and most deeply embedded—sometimes even genetically embedded—least easily substituted ends of human life there are.[15]

That the exclusion policy *implicates* the right to religious and moral freedom, however, does not entail that it *violates* the right. The right is not absolute but conditional. The policy violates the right if, and only if, the policy fails to satisfy the legitimacy condition, the least burdensome alternative condition, or the proportionality condition. The exclusion policy, as I am about to explain, fails to satisfy the legitimacy condition—the policy fails to serve a legitimate government objective—and therefore violates the right to religious and moral freedom.

The government objectives that have been asserted in defense of the exclusion policy are of two sorts: *morality-based* objectives, which are objectives whose pursuit by government presupposes that same-sex sexual intimacy is immoral, and *non-morality-based* objectives, which are objectives whose pursuit by government does not presuppose that same-sex sexual intimacy is immoral.

The principal non-morality-based government objectives typically asserted in defense of the exclusion policy are (1) protecting the welfare of children and (2) protecting the health of the institution of traditional (that is, opposite-sex) marriage. Although both are undeniably legitimate (and weighty) government objectives, no credible argument supports the claim that excluding same-sex couples from civil marriage serves either one. Put another way, no credible argument supports the claim that all the countries and states that have thus far admitted same-sex couples to civil marriage have thereby disserved—imperiled—either the welfare of children or the health of the institution of traditional marriage or both.[16] Indeed, excluding same-sex couples from civil marriage disserves—and admitting them to civil marriage serves—the welfare of those many children now being raised by same-sex couples.[17]

The dominant rationale for the exclusion policy—as is well known—involves a morality-based government objective: *Admitting same-sex couples to civil marriage would tend to legitimize—"normalize"—and thereby incentivize same-sex sexual conduct. This we must not do, for same-sex sexual conduct is immoral.*[18] For example, in 2003, the Vatican—specifically, the Congregation for the Doctrine of the Faith, whose prefect at the time was Joseph Cardinal Ratzinger, soon to become Pope Benedict XVI—argued that admitting same-sex couples to civil marriage would signal "the approval of deviant behavior, with the consequences of making it a model in present-day society."[19]

Excluding same-sex couples from civil marriage obviously serves the government objective of not taking a step that would tend to legitimize conduct believed by many to be immoral: same-sex sexual conduct. The serious question is whether that government objective—that *morality-based* government objective—qualifies as a *legitimate* government objective under the right to religious and moral freedom. The answer depends on the reason or reasons lawmakers have for believing that same-sex sexual conduct is immoral. If the only reason they have is a religious reason—for example, and in the words of one evangelical minister, "[same-sex sexual conduct] is in direct opposition to God's truth as He has revealed it in the Scriptures"[20]—then the government objective is not legitimate. As I explained in the preceding section, no government objective is legitimate, under the right to religious and moral freedom, if government's pursuit of the objective is based on—"based on" in the sense that government would not be pursuing the objective "but for"—a sectarian belief, religious or moral, such as "this conduct is contrary to the will of God." However, a religious reason is not the only reason lawmakers have for believing that that same-sex sexual conduct is immoral. Indeed, the path of reasoning runs in the opposite direction for many religious believers, whose position is not that because it is contrary to the will of God, same-sex sexual conduct is immoral, but that because it is immoral, same-sex sexual conduct is contrary to the will of God.[21]

The pope and bishops of the Roman Catholic Church—the "Magisterium" of the Church—are leading opponents of "legislative and judicial attempts, both at state and federal levels, to grant same-sex unions the equivalent status and rights of marriage—by naming them marriage, civil unions or by other means."[22] The Magisterium's reason—its rationale—

for believing that same-sex sexual conduct is immoral is a nonreligious reason: a reason that does not assert, imply, or presuppose any religious premise, even the premise that God exists.

According to the Magisterium, it is immoral not just for same-sex couples but for anyone and everyone—even a man and a woman who are married to each other—to engage in (that is, pursuant to a knowing, uncoerced choice to engage in) any sexual conduct that is "inherently nonprocreative," and same-sex sexual conduct—like contracepted male-female sexual intercourse[23] and every act of masturbation, oral sex, and anal sex—is inherently nonprocreative. Because "what are called 'homosexual unions' . . . are inherently nonprocreative," declared the Administrative Committee of the U.S. Conference of Catholic Bishops, they "cannot be given the status of marriage."[24] As Joseph Cardinal Ratzinger stated in 2003, speaking for the Congregation for the Doctrine of the Faith: Because they "close the sexual act to the gift of life," "homosexual acts go against the natural moral law."[25]

The pope and bishops' position that inherent nonprocreative sexual conduct is, as such—as inherently nonprocreative—immoral is a conspicuously sectarian position. It bears mention, in that regard, that the position is controversial *even among Catholic moral theologians*,[26] not to mention the larger community of religious ethicists.[27] Therefore, whether government's pursuit of the objective of not taking a step that would tend to legitimize immoral conduct is based on a biblical rationale or on the bishops' nonreligious rationale (or on both), the objective is not a legitimate government objective: Again, no government objective is legitimate, under the right to religious and moral freedom, if government's pursuit of the objective is based on a sectarian belief, religious or moral. The evangelical legal scholar Michael McConnell's rhetorical question is relevant here: "Is the Civil Magistrate about whom John Locke wrote more 'competent a judge' of the 'Truth' about, for example, human sexuality than about religion?"[28]

Conclusion

In the mid-1960s, in his "Memo to [Boston's] Cardinal Cushing on Contraception Legislation," the celebrated Jesuit priest John Courtney Murray wrote:

The practice [contraception], undertaken in the interests of "responsible parenthood," has received official sanction by many religious groups within the community. It is difficult to see how the state can forbid, as contrary to public morality, a practice that numerous religious leaders approve as morally right. The stand taken by these religious groups may be lamentable from the Catholic moral point of view. But it is decisive from the point of view of law and jurisprudence.[29]

Father Murray did not explain what he meant by "the point of view of law and jurisprudence." Nonetheless, what Murray said was "decisive from the point of view of law and jurisprudence" *is* decisive from the point of view of *the right to religious and moral freedom*: No government objective that is legitimate under the right to religious and moral freedom warrants a government ban on the use of contraceptives.

Moreover, we may say about the policy of excluding same-sex couples from civil marriage much the same thing Murray said to Cardinal Cushing about Massachusetts's anticontraceptive policy: *Same-sex marriage has received official approval by various religious groups within the community.*[30] *It is difficult to see how the state can refuse to countenance, as contrary to public morality, a relationship that numerous religious leaders and other morally upright people approve as morally good. The stand taken by these religious groups and others may be lamentable from the Catholic moral point of view. But it is decisive from the point of view of the right to religious and moral freedom.*

6   God Sets the Lonely in Families

PATRICIA BEATTIE JUNG

Saint Paul School of Theology

Catholics believe that moral judgments should cohere with sound interpretations of the Bible and the living Tradition, but we also believe that the reasonableness of public policies should be evident to all persons of good will, regardless of their faith or lack thereof.[1] Consequently, Catholic teachings about the common good should be consistent, comprehensive, and cohere with scientifically documented evidence. Since the focus of this essay is on the civil licensing, not the blessing, of same-sex marriages, these shall be the norms for this argument.

The Morality of Homosexual Activity

Today the Roman Catholic Church officially teaches that all homosexual acts are "intrinsically disordered."[2] In 1968 Paul VI argued in *Humanae Vitae (HV)* that the unitive and procreative ends of sexual activity were "inseparably connected."[3] This laid the groundwork for the Vatican to assert that only those sexual activities which simultaneously "express and promote the mutual assistance of the sexes in marriage and are open to the transmission of new life" could be considered moral.[4]

Undoubtedly, over the centuries many Catholics, as well as their confessors and even some bishops, did *not* find this judgment insightful or the reasoning behind it compelling. There may even have been many quiet—*sotto voce*—conversations among the bishops and between theologians and local bishops about this matter. But it was not until the 1970s that such scholarly theological arguments went public.

This monologue was first publicly interrupted in 1970, when John J. McNeill argued that some forms of homosexual activity might well be the "lesser of two evils." Just a year later, Charles E. Curran argued that while same-sex activity fell short of the conjugal heterosexual ideal, some expressions might be genuinely good. In 1976, McNeill argued that homosexuality per se was objectively good, and so, if in other ways it was responsible, homosexual activity could be morally good. Many different versions, especially of these last two arguments, have been articulated in the ensuing decades, with Lisa Sowle Cahill developing a particularly powerful version of Curran's line of reasoning and Margaret A. Farley, Todd A. Salzman, Michael G. Lawler, and others developing more fully McNeill's mature approach.[5]

A 2003 letter from the Vatican, as well as the *Catechism of the Catholic Church* (*CCC*), both give the same three reasons for the proscription of homosexual activity. It is always immoral because (1) it is closed to the gift of life, (2) it does not proceed from genuine affective and sexual complementarity, and (3) it violates natural law.[6] Let us examine the reasonableness of each of these claims.

Homosexual Couples Can Be Open to God's Gift of Life

In *HV* Paul VI taught that "each and every marriage act must remain open to the transmission of life."[7] This meant to him that only coitus is morally permissible. All oral, anal, manual, and intercrural forms of genital activity to the point of orgasm are forbidden to everyone, gay or straight. For the same reason, the church's longstanding proscription of contraception was reaffirmed in *HV* and then reiterated in 2009 in a pastoral letter drafted by the U.S. bishops. Contraception is described as posing a fundamental challenge to the very nature and purpose of marriage.[8] While a natural form of family planning—sexual abstinence during times of fertility—is permitted to heterosexual couples, contraception is not. Only lifelong sexual abstinence is permitted to gay people. At first glance, church officials seem consistent on this point.

But note that the sexual activity of pregnant married women and the marriage of postmenopausal women or of men who are permanently infertile are not condemned, even though all of their sexual activity—whether coital or not—would be biologically closed to procreation. In fact, while the U.S. bishops describe heterosexual marital infertility as a tragedy, they teach that there are many ways infertile heterosexual couples can express their openness to the gift of life. The bishops teach that "when childbearing years pass couples should continue to be life affirming, staying involved in the lives of young people . . . nurturing through the exercise of care for those who are needy, disabled or pushed to the margins of society, and by their support for or participation in works of charity and justice" serve life.[9] Similarly, the CCC recommends that such couples adopt children and organize their life together by serving others.[10]

Why could gay and lesbian couples not do the same? What makes coital infertility natural and noncoital infertility unnatural? James P. Hanigan argues that coital infertility is natural because coitus alone can be iconic of the call to serve life.[11] His argument goes like this: only coitus can be open to the gift of life; only heterosexual couples can engage in coitus; so, only heterosexual couples can symbolically embody this call.

In response to this line of reasoning, others have argued—along the track first laid down by Curran—that even if only heterosexual couples can embody this reproductive ideal, it does not necessarily follow that all of what falls short of this ideal should be judged immoral.[12] Still others follow the track eventually laid down by McNeill. The notion that only heterosexual couples can signify the calling to serve life through loving faithful sexual relationships is mistaken for three reasons.

First, all heterosexual couples do not biologically symbolize openness to the possibility of procreation. All men might at least appear throughout their lifespan to be open to the possibility of reproduction. However, no one links older, postmenopausal women, heterosexual or not, with biological openness to the possibility of procreation. Yet the U.S. bishops recently adopted this line of reasoning and extended it to parenting. They argue that same-sex unions are incapable of physically witnessing not only to the value of openness to the gift of life but also to the unique roles of mothers and fathers in the education of children. Although they are not specific, presumably they mean to say something like no gay man can really "mother" a child and that no lesbian can really "father" one on the (highly contested) premise that these are gender-specific tasks.[13]

Second, openness to the possibility of procreation is not essential to morally good sex. Reproduction is clearly sexual, and reproduction is clearly essential to the flourishing of our species. Still, it does not follow that all sexual acts or all sexual relationships necessarily need be open to reproduction. Church officials now recognize that human sexual activities serve purposes distinct from and beyond reproduction.[14] When we take *all* the natural, biological facts of human embodiment seriously, then it becomes clear that while there is a link between reproduction and sexuality at the level of the species, there is no essential connection at the level of acts or relationships. Several facts cohere with this.

Unlike many other species, humans are—biologically speaking— constantly receptive to and initiating sexual activity. We do not heat up only on an estrus cycle, only or always for reproductive purposes. Some reproductive organs—like the uterus—have no sexual function. Some sexual organs have no reproductive function. While the ejaculation of sperm is usually tied to male orgasm, female sexual pleasure has no connection to ovulation. Though its role in the production of sexual pleasure may indirectly facilitate reproduction, the clitoris is not biologically necessary to it. In fact, it may be positioned in human females precisely so as to facilitate pleasure through both coital and noncoital contact, potentially with either same- or other-sex partners.[15] Homogenital behavior has been documented in over 450 species, including primates.[16] It is commonplace in nature. (Of course, this alone does not mean it is normatively natural.) But by expanding the reach of its bonding function, such diversity in sexual behavior enables species with diverse sexual orientations to use sexual contact to extend kin-like ties and childrearing partnerships to more individuals and to use sexual contact to resolve power conflicts with more individuals, all the while responding with greater flexibility to environmental stresses associated with overpopulation. Evolution favors survival, and survival is facilitated by forms of mating that can both include and exclude breeding, as necessary.

Let me summarize. Good arguments make sense of all the relevant data. If one takes *all* the natural biological facts of human embodiment seriously, then two conclusions can be established as reasonable. There is a link for humans between reproduction and sexuality at the level of the species. There is no essential connection between reproduction and sexuality for humans at the level of acts or relationships.

Third, the bonding and procreative meanings of sexuality need not be inseparably connected in order for sexual activity to be morally good. The U.S. bishops have argued that "without its ordering toward the procreative, the unitive meaning of marriage is undermined."[17] I have been married over thirty-nine years, and while these purposes have been connected on several occasions, for the most part, they were not. Their separation did not undermine our ability to make love or erode our fidelity or mutual respect.[18] Nor did the practice lead us down a sexually libertine path, as church officials predict will surely follow.

Our experience is no sure source of moral wisdom. Though personal, our interpretation of the practice of contraception within marriage is not unique. Over a decade ago, the Catholic moral theologian Cristina H. L. Traina wrote an article similarly comparing her experience of "marital realities" with official church teaching prohibiting birth control.[19] Addressing the scene among U.S. Catholics, it was recently noted that the church's "prohibition against the use of artificial birth control, for example, is rejected by perhaps 90 percent of Catholic married couples."[20] Of course, two couples do not make for a significant sample, but undoubtedly it will come as no surprise that most heterosexual Catholics in the U.S. practice birth control. Currently, only 2 percent of Catholic women rely on natural family planning; 68 percent use highly effective methods of contraception.[21] This is not just a U.S. phenomenon. In 2008, *The Tablet*, a Catholic weekly published in Britain, surveyed 1,500 regular Mass-goers in England and Wales about their contraceptive practices. This study found that the teaching against so-called artificial forms of birth control was ignored by the great majority of these Catholics, many of whom regularly used the contraceptive pill and/or condoms.[22]

Of course, just because "everybody" is doing something does not make it right! Despite clear consciences and ongoing communion, all of these Catholics could be wrong. Alternatively, the Spirit could be leading the people of God deeper into the truth. Certainly the bishops' teaching about the inseparable connection between the unitive and procreative meanings of sexual activity has not been well received. It does not enjoy what theologians call the "sense of the faithful."[23] Yet according to Catholic doctrine such reception is an important sign of sound teaching. Perhaps the bishops need to pay more attention to the experience of all faithful Catholics, straight and gay.

Homosexual Activity Can Be Genuinely Complementary

In response to the distress expressed by thousands of Catholics when the condemnation of contraception was reiterated by Paul VI, some bishops' conferences across the globe—including the U.S. Conference of Catholic

Bishops—took the occasion to remind Catholic confessors and lay people alike of the absolute priority of the faithful Catholic's conscience in this matter. It has long been a matter of Catholic doctrine that each person has an obligation both to form their conscience well and to follow its dictates (even if mistaken).

In a set of pastoral guidelines that focus on contraception, the Vatican recommends that confessors "inspire all, in a gradual way, to embrace the path of holiness,"[24] to recognize that "frequent relapse into sins of contraception does not in itself constitute a motive for denying absolution,"[25] and to "let penitents remain in good faith . . . whenever it is foreseen that the penitent, although oriented towards living within the bounds of a life of faith, would not be prepared to change his own conduct."[26]

Yet the church has not publicly treated gay couples distressed by these teachings similarly. It may well be that the best confessors respond with pastoral respect to both heterosexual and homosexual couples who in good conscience have wrestled with but reject this emphasis on procreativity. But the Magisterium has neither publicly announced this priority of conscience to distressed gay and lesbian Catholics nor offered analogous pastoral guidelines to confessors regarding same-sex activity. Furthermore, while the "contraceptive mentality" is still decried in official teachings, it is rarely attacked in the public arena in the United States. There has been no recent, serious effort to ban the sale and distribution of contraceptives nor any lobbying effort to advocate that marriage licenses be withheld from straight couples who plan to be childfree. (While the U.S. bishops adamantly rejected in the spring of 2012 the Affordable Care Act mandate that contraception coverage be made available to employees of some Catholic institutions, it is important to note that they did so on the ground that this requirement threatened religious freedom, not on the basis of an argument about the [im]morality of contraception.)

Church officials might respond: we must pick political battles we can win, and "the horse has left the barn" with regard to both the morality of divorce and contraception in countries that border the North Atlantic. It seems, however, that in practice church officials have singled out gay couples for special condemnation in regard to their teaching about the exclusively normative nature of coitus.

The moral weight given to heterogenital complementarity is the reason why. A comparative newcomer, the concept of complementarity only recently became foundational to Catholic sexual ethics.[27] In their fine book, Salzman and Lawler define complementarity as the notion that "certain realities belong together and produce a whole that neither produces alone."[28] Catholic officials presume that while persons are complete as individuals, insofar as humans are made to form intimate sexual partnerships, we are incomplete and need to partner with someone who complements us. Apart from such complementarity, no truly unitive relationship of mutual assistance can be established. Furthermore, there is a relationship between the body and the person such that genuine sexual complementarity between persons can be possible only if their embodiment is taken seriously. Dualistic accounts of sexuality are inadequate.

So far, so good, but here's the rub: the Magisterium teaches further that the only normatively natural, human orientation is heterosexual, so only partners of the opposite sex can be complementary. This means that the only form of normatively natural complementarity is heterogenital. Heterogenital complementarity is the sine qua non of complementarity in official church teachings.[29] This is why the bishops believe continued political efforts to curtail homosexual behavior are warranted. Yet doesn't this beg the very question under consideration?

Alternatively, if diversity in sexual orientation is presumed to be normatively natural, then genital complementarity would vary in accord with the orientation of an individual's desire. In this framework, heterogenital difference would not be requisite.[30] Genuine affective and sexual complementarity would not necessarily require a partner of the opposite sex but rather one of the *apposite* sex. *Apt* for what? Apt for the task of making love and forging bonds through the mutual sharing of sexual delights. Only in relationship with someone of the *apposite* sex is it possible to establish the mutual vulnerability and the trust that opens us to God's healing. Complementarity remains significant, but the factors relevant to it are expanded so as to include people's sexual orientation. This is a more comprehensive—a "holistic"—account of complementarity.[31] Only in such relationships is there the potential for recognizing ourselves and each other as beloved—at the deepest level by God. Rowan Williams has described the ache that fuels our sexual attraction to others as the desire to know ourselves as desired and as occasions of joy. This is "the body's grace."[32] But doesn't this presumption beg the question as well?

The decisive issue, then: who bears the burden of proof in this regard? God clearly delights in and treasures diversity. Presuming difference in sexual orientation to be part of God's good design, and not a disorder in it, makes the best sense. There is no compelling evidence to the contrary. Without such documentation, it is an offense against the Creator to think otherwise. For decades now, scientists have challenged rigid accounts of heterosexuality that suggest complementarity is possible only between the sexes, detailing the tremendous range of physical and psychological variability within each gender and the huge overlapping similarities between the sexes. Social scientific studies of committed same-sex relationships indicate that they evidence emotional qualities, such as stability and satisfaction rates, similar to long-term heterosexual relationships.[33] A few differences have surfaced. Same-sex relationships currently evidence more equity in the distribution of household labor, greater skill at conflict resolution, and greater relationship support from friends (though less from families).[34] Straight couples might have important lessons to learn from gay couples. Still, the weight of evidence suggests *both* heterosexual and homosexual partnerships can be complementary. This requires an account of complementarity more "holistic"[35] than the heterosexist version adopted by the bishops.

Homosexual Acts Can Be Natural in the Normative Sense

Church officials teach that humans have the intellectual capacity to grasp at least some of the aspects of our nature that cross cultures and run through the ages. We can know something of this "natural law," even if our insights into it are partial, subject to distortion, and hence in need of constant testing and reformation. The Vatican also teaches that sexuality "is a fundamental component of personality"[36] and that its orientation is deeply seated and relatively stable. (This is largely true, though while sexual orientation is fairly stable in men, it appears to be more fluid in women and may vary over time in some.) Sexual orientation is one of the few human traits that is probably bimodal, rather than distributed along a bell curve. Like handedness, most people are strongly inclined in one sexual direction or another. Estimates about sexual orientation vary considerably. David G. Myers and Letha Dawson Scanzoni conservatively estimate that about 3 to 4 percent of men and 1 to 2 percent of women are basically homosexual in orientation, while about 1 percent are bisexual and another 1 percent are asexual.[37] Most agree that sexuality cannot be reoriented. Like an individual's temperament, it is neither chosen nor intentionally changeable. Everyone party to this debate agrees that people can both resist their sexual desires and act against them. It does not follow from this that any one or more particular sexual orientation is (un)natural in a normative sense.

Yet church officials teach that homosexual acts are unnatural. Why? Because they are (1) biologically closed to the possibility of procreativity and (2) presumed not to be genuinely complementary. I have already refuted these two lines of argument, noting the capacity of committed same-sex relationships to serve both life and love. Still, I would raise a concern about the bishops' unwarranted use of the label "unnatural." This label sanctifies the internalization of profoundly negative self-understandings by LGBTQ persons as well as hateful attitudes in the wider community toward them. While Rome and U.S. bishops teach it is not a sin to be gay, they describe this "inclination" as intrinsically and gravely disordered. Stephen Pope has argued that describing such a deep-seated aspect of a person "as 'intrinsically disordered' is inherently stigmatizing and at least tacitly, if not overtly, supportive of the unjust discrimination that the Church has repeatedly condemned."[38] As he so sharply puts it, no one wants "to live next door to, or work with, someone who is 'gravely disordered.'" I would only add: who would want to be "gravely disordered?" To employ such language without justification is morally irresponsible.

In light of the language they employ, it should not have come as a surprise to the bishops when in November 2011 the policy advisor for marriage and family at the United States Conference of Catholic Bishops, Daniel Avila, suggested that "Satan" might be responsible for same-sex attraction. Bryan Cones, the managing editor of *U.S. Catholic*, rightly declared Avila's language to be "spiritually violent." Even though Avila published an apology, distinguishing his view from that of the bishops, and within the week resigned his position, the bishops themselves remain silent on the point and are ultimately morally responsible for such spiritual harm because of their irresponsible use of terms like "gravely disordered" and "unnatural."

Official Catholic Teaching on Marriage Equality

According to the 1983 Code of Canon Law, a marriage can be consummated only by sexual activity that is "apt for the generation of offspring" and that is truly human in the integrated sense discussed earlier.[39] Consequently, the church is presently unwilling to bless or recognize the sacramental character of same-sex marriages. It takes the same stance toward divorced heterosexual couples who seek to remarry without a declaration of annulment.[40] Yet the U.S. bishops do not lobby against or politically oppose the civil licensing of multiple remarriages for divorced heterosexual people. Given that the church refuses to bless both practices, why are its legislative recommendations regarding marriage equality so different? This seems especially curious given that the bishops teach that a person's sexual orientation is irrelevant to his or her intrinsic human dignity and, consequently, to the fundamental human rights that are a corollary of that dignity.[41]

The contemporary case for such differential treatment was first articulated by the Vatican in 1992, when the CDF argued that in regard to adoption, foster care, military recruitment, the hiring of teachers and coaches, and even in regard to housing, people are morally required to lobby for public policies that discriminate against gays.[42] In 1997 the U.S. bishops confirmed that "in matters where sexual orientation has a clear relevance, the common good does justify it being taken into account."[43]

The Vatican first opposed domestic partnership legislation and the licensing of same-sex marriages in 2000.[44] This was followed three years later by the CDF's "Considerations Regarding Proposals to Give Legal Recognition to Unions Between Homosexual Persons." Then, in his 2005 New Year's Eve address—an occasion when pontiffs traditionally identify the greatest challenges facing humanity in the coming year—John Paul II identified challenges to an exclusively heterosexual structure of marriage and family as a threat to the sanctuary of life itself, the family. Though they presently enjoy a favorable reception among some Catholics living below the equator and in Asia, these instructions enjoy less of the *sensus fidelium* within countries that border the North Atlantic.[45] In 2009 the U.S. bishops identified the legal recognition of what they call same-sex unions as one of four threats to the nature and purpose of marriage. They discussed at length the basic reasons for their vehement opposition to marriage equality.[46] A careful examination of these claims follows, but let me sketch beforehand other Catholic perspectives on marriage equality.

The Variety of Catholic Perspectives on Marriage Equality

Here again, Catholics calling for marriage equality fall broadly into two camps. Some accept the normative sexual anthropology that presently frames church teaching but interpret this as an ideal that faithful Catholics are obliged to approximate insofar as possible. This enables them to recognize as morally tolerable some of what falls short of that ideal. They also frequently modify or reject—as neither logically required nor supported by empirical evidence—many of the public policy recommendations taught to be corollaries of this framework.

Consider an essay entitled "The Civil Rights of Homosexual People: Vatican Perspectives," written by Robert Nugent in 1994. In it, Nugent refuted the Vatican's arguments aimed at justifying discrimination against homosexual people in certain circumstances. Yet this was not an argument for immunity from discrimination because the question of who carries the burden of proof in this matter was not addressed. Important as this essay was, Nugent did not develop a rationale for either nondiscrimination or the civil endorsement of same-sex marriage.[47] In his 1996 book *Gay and Lesbian Rights: A Question: Sexual Ethics or Social Justice?*, Richard A. Peddicord OP noted that there was a conflict between the equal treatment commended by Catholic social justice traditions and the specific acts of discrimination commended by the church's official teachings in sexual ethics. He concluded that since there was no evidence to support the claim that homosexual relations per se would harm the common good, the church's emphasis on justice should prevail.[48]

While both arguments are important, it is crucial to recognize that neither establishes homosexual desire as an "occasion of grace" nor homosexual relationships as potentially worth civil promotion and ecclesial celebration. In contrast, others have argued that sexual diversity (not heterosexual uniformity) is natural in a normative sense and that the church's official sexual anthropology needs to recognize this. Distinctively Catholic versions of this line of argument emphasize the corporate—that is, the biological, evolutionary, and communal—significance of sexual diversity.

Here is a sampling of such reasoning. In an essay published in 1983, Daniel Maguire argued on the basis of an ethical theory known as probabilism that gay Catholics could in good conscience marry, since arguments about the morality and holiness of such covenants were as strong as those outlined against the practice.[49] In 1993 Ralph F. Smith and I mounted a case for the blessing of same-sex marriages.[50] In 1997 David Matzko McCarthy argued that gay marriages should be treated as anomalous, not deviant, like those of childless heterosexual couples.[51] New Ways Ministry published a pamphlet, *Marriage Equality: A Positive Catholic Approach*, authored by its executive director, Francis DeBernardo, in 2011. Attentive to the voices of bishops, theologians, and laity alike, DeBernardo tackles a dozen of the questions central to this debate.[52]

Given these arguments, why do the bishops continue to oppose the licensing of same-sex marriage? They believe that marriage equality will harm the institution of (heterosexual) marriage, harm the dignity of all persons, and harm children, as well as unduly violate the religious liberty of those who share their vision of marriage. Let us consider each of these claims in turn.

Marriage Equality Will Not Harm Marriage

It is true that marriage as an institution in North Atlantic countries is undergoing a tremendous transformation: fewer people in these countries are getting married, and more are getting divorced.[53] Church officials assert that marriage equality will contribute to the further deterioration of marriage as an institution, but they are not specific here.

One could hypothesize that perhaps marriage equality will contribute to a rise in divorce rates, but studies suggest not. The Centers for Disease Control has reported that all five of the states that allowed same-sex marriage in 2007 had divorce rates nearly 20 percent lower than the rest of the country.[54] This does not establish a causal relationship, but it is encouraging. A study of demographic data drawn from the eight countries that gave significant rights to legally registered same-sex couples between 1989 and 2000 is equally encouraging.[55] If in fact the "sky is going to fall" for the institution of heterosexual marriage when same-sex marriages are civilly recognized, then in these countries the rate for first marriages should have declined with changing public policies regarding marriage equality. Further, divorce, cohabitation and nonmarital birth rates should have climbed. But this did not happen. For the same reason, there should be notably different trends regarding the health of heterosexual marriage in countries that do not recognize same-sex marriage, but reviews of relevant demographic data indicate this is also not true.[56]

Marriage Equality Will Not Harm the Dignity of Persons

The U.S. bishops rightly argue that marriage protects and promotes the dignity of all. Any policy change that would harm our sense of the God-given nature of personal worth nurtured within marriage threatens human dignity. Since the bishops believe marriage equality will harm the institution of marriage, they conclude it will threaten human dignity. But since there is no evidence to support the former claim, there is no evidence to support the latter.

Marriage Equality Will Not Harm Children

It goes without saying that children are increasingly at risk today. Many U.S. children—41 percent overall and 53 percent of those with mothers in their twenties—are born outside marriage. Statistically, these children are at greater risk for poverty and emotional and behavioral problems than their counterparts born to married parents.[57] While in some North Atlantic countries cohabitation creates relationships as stable as marriage, in the United States cohabiting couples are twice as likely to split up. Two-thirds of those who cohabitate with children separate by the time their child is ten. Still, there is no evidence that marriage equality would harm children. On the contrary, there is evidence to suggest marriage equality could contribute to their flourishing.

Implicit in the Vatican's 1992 directives was the assumption that homosexual people are especially prone to seduce those who are young and vulnerable, to recruit those whose desires may "waver," or, worse, to be abusive sexual predators. I will not honor these claims except to say there is not a shred of evidence for such a vicious stereotype and to note that the church has dropped this line of argument.

Currently, Rome is making a more subtle claim, arguing that marriage equality will prove morally confusing. As the Vatican puts it, such a "scandalous" practice will give young people and others[58] "erroneous ideas about sexuality and marriage that would deprive them of their necessary defenses and contribute to the spread of the phenomenon."[59] It will "modify the younger generation's perception and evaluation of forms of behavior."[60] The U.S. bishops claim that the licensing of same-sex marriage "ignores the rights of children, who deserve from society clear guidance as they grow to sexual maturity."[61]

Of course the message sent by marriage equality is not confusing or unclear. The problem is that it sends a message that conflicts with church teaching. It makes sense to judge the pedagogical power of marriage equality harmful if you believe homosexuality is disordered. Civil law has a pedagogical function. The approval of same-sex marriage will be socially transformative. The licensing of same-sex marriages might lessen the social pressure on homosexual people to closet themselves. Far from being corrosive, when same-sex marriage is licensed, people will find it easier to live sexually authentic lives. Ironically, the U.S. bishops commended at least private forms of precisely such sexual integrity when they taught that we all need to integrate better our "thoughts, feelings and actions in the area of human sexuality in a way that values and respects one's own dignity and that of others" as children of God.[62] While the church's "worry" makes sense given its teachings on the (im)morality of homosexual acts, it begs the question of how to build a society that fosters the greater sexual integrity and authenticity called forth by its own teachings. Support for sexual authenticity via marriage equality will not harm children.

Neither will same-sex parenting harm children. The Vatican teaches that same-sex couples lack what has been aptly labeled "parental complementarity": "As experience has shown, the absence of sexual complementarity in these unions creates obstacles in the moral development of children who would be placed in the care of such parents. . . . Allowing children to be adopted by persons living in such unions would actually mean doing violence to these children."[63] However, despite the Vatican's assertion that its claim is based in experience, after more than twenty years of scrutiny, not a single research study suggests that children raised by same-sex parents fail to flourish. As early as 1999, reviews of the relevant literature had given clear evidence to the contrary.[64] From a longitudinal study of lesbian families completed a decade later, it was learned that while there were no significant differences on measures of social development and behavior, teens from lesbian homes scored higher than adolescents from straight families on some measures of self-esteem, did better academically, and had fewer behavioral problems.[65] A multiyear comparative study of 106 school-age children living in different parts of the United States found that children adopted by lesbian and gay couples are thriving and develop normally, including in regard to their gender identity.[66]

Marriage Equality Will Not Unduly Violate Religious Liberty

The U.S. bishops rightly note that "the legal protection of marriage as the union of one man and one woman also protects the religious freedom of those who adhere to that vision of marriage."[67] The bishops do *not* note that marriage *in*equality denies religious freedom to those who do *not* adhere to their vision of marriage. Still, though it is unlikely that states would force priests to officiate at same-sex marriage ceremonies, even with generous religious protections and exemptions, in some cases those who dissent from marriage equality may have to pay a price for their beliefs.[68] For example, Catholic universities that discriminate against gay spouses might lose federal or state funding for their married student housing if no reasonable alternative is available to those students. Those who live in democracies should always have good reasons for their public policies. I will detail those reasons below.

Moral Judgments, Civil Law, and the Burden of Proof

Before proceeding to that task, a brief word on Catholic thinking about the relationship of moral judgments to civil law is in order. The church has always recognized that *all* of what it judges immoral should not necessarily be prohibited by public policy, which aims to serve the more limited requirements of the public good. Traditionally, in developing its public policy recommendations, the church would begin with its moral teachings and then press for the civil prohibition of either only the most grievous offenses (if one had been trained Thomistically) or tolerate only those evils deemed prudentially necessary (if one had been schooled in Augustinian thought).

However, with its "Declaration on Religious Freedom" in 1965, the Second Vatican Council developed further the Catholic approach to civil law. It declared that the inviolable dignity of each and every person mandates that everyone should respect individual freedom of conscience. This freedom should be curtailed "only when and in so far as necessary."[69] Individual freedom of conscience itself was also officially recognized as an important constituent of the common good. While there remain limits to human liberty, note that the burden of proof shifts to those who would restrict freedom and discriminate.

In the older approach, church officials might propose civil legislation closely modeled on the church's moral teaching. They would then consider arguments against the strict embodiment of this teaching in civil law, such as whether it could be enforced or whether this was truly a grievous matter appropriate to codification. But in the newer approach approved at Vatican II, church officials should recommend the limitation of individual freedom, for instance in regard to the licensing of civil marriages, only to the extent necessary to preserve the public good. This is akin to what has become known in the secular press as the conservative case for gay marriage, which begins with equality, respect for individual liberty, and the concern to protect freedom from government interference. It is the withholding of the civil license to marry, not its granting, that requires powerful justification(s).

A careful review of the evidence suggests that in fact the civil recognition of same-sex marriages will not harm the institution of marriage, the dignity of persons, or children. Since those who would withhold marriage licenses bear the burden of proof, and since that burden has not been met, the bishops' teachings about civil legislation in this regard should be rejected. As the *Catechism* makes clear, only justified instances of differential treatment should ever be tolerated. Unwarranted discrimination is unjust. All unjust discrimination against homosexual people should be condemned.[70]

Promoting Marriage Equality

For the most part, the case for marriage equality is the same as the case for marriage in general: it is for life and love. Some marriages serve the common good by providing for the "succession of generations" and by providing a stable environment for the rearing of children. But the common good is served by marriage in a variety of ways beyond procreation, particularly by assisting spouses and children. It follows then that all of those called by God into love relationships and/or toward parenthood ought to marry or be open to the possibility.[71]

Marriage is good for most spouses most of the time. It is associated with reduced rates of drug abuse; longer life expectancy, especially for men; lower rates of domestic violence; less criminal activity; fewer sexually transmitted diseases; and other positive outcomes. Spouses are on average healthier, happier, and safer than their peers who are single.[72] Spouses often help each other cope with unemployment, accept loss, survive accidents and illnesses, live with chronic disease, negotiate life with disabilities, endure growing diminishment, age gracefully, enjoy retirement, and (in the case of one spouse) die well. All these forms of mutual assistance are as true for queer spouses as they are for straight ones. Because of such mutual assistance, the state does not view childless and/or childfree heterosexual marriages as invalid, nor does it consider them harmful to the commonwealth. On the contrary, the state promotes such marriages.

The state also encourages people to marry not only because it helps the spouses but also because it stretches them to think beyond their dyadic interests. Marriage connects spouses to children and other kin. Society encourages marriage because such expanded interests and commitments benefit our society as a whole. Again, this is just as true for gay marriage as it is for straight marriage.

The assistance spouses mutually offer each other, their children, and their extended families is foundational to the common good. It stabilizes lives that otherwise might be shattered by various crises. When people marry, they take on each other's "business," which enables spouses to support each other's paid and volunteer work in the world. Marriage weaves spouses into extended kin relations not established by blood, binding spouses to in-laws of all sorts and generations. The state encourages people to marry precisely because it does not serve just the individuals involved but stretches individuals to think beyond their private interests. Society encourages marriage because such expanded interests and commitments benefit our society as a whole. This is just as true for gay as it is for straight marriage.

One such societal benefit, for example, is that married parents, on average, are best able to create a stable environment for the nurture of children.[73] Married parents can provide support and respite for each other when the demands of childrearing becoming overwhelming. They can bring complementary, mutually enriching skills to the process. The promotion of same-sex marriage will help the children already being raised by gay parents by further stabilizing their partnerships. Recent U.S. Census data included a count of same-sex households and their children. According to an analysis of this data done by the Williams Institute, a UCLA School of Law think tank, there are at least six hundred thousand households headed by same-sex couples, and though this varies by gender and state by state, roughly one-fourth of them are raising children.[74] Presumably a significant number of these same-sex parents would marry, if given a chance, to further strengthen their households. This would enable the children from many of these 150,000 households to receive automatically *all* the medical and dental care benefits; *all* the social security benefits, hospital visitation, and inheritance rights; and educational benefits for which they would become eligible upon their parents' marriage. The state promotes marriage by associating this estate with a broad array of economic and legal benefits for both spouses and children. These cannot be accessed any other way.[75]

In the United States, some "rights and benefits accrue only to family members as such—e.g., some workplace benefits, joint income tax status, the right to make medical decisions in the absence of written instructions."[76] At the national level and in several state chapters, the American Medical Association has called for recognition of same-sex marriage because of the way it will increase access by spouses and children in gay households to the health care, health insurance, and survivor benefits to which they have a right.

There are additional rationales for promoting marriage equality. It may reduce the social stigma and internalized shame associated with being gay,[77] improve gay men's health,[78] and even reduce hate crimes.[79] When marriage equality is normalized, it is reasonable to expect both the homophobia and heterosexism reinforced by arguments against same-sex marriage to begin to wither, and with that, to expect a decline in the stigma, shame, and crimes that spew from such views.

In sum, we should promote marriage equality for the same reasons that we promote marriage in general. It serves spouses, children, and other kin across generations, gay and straight alike. Additionally, it may serve the common good by reducing the stigma, shame, and crimes associated with heterosexism. Because we have these several good reasons to promote marriage equality and little reason to see its curtailment as "necessary," the religious liberty of those who do not share this vision will not be unduly constrained. Further, because homosexual behavior can be morally good and because same-sex marriage serves the commonweal, like the psalmist we are grateful that "God sets the lonely in families."

Response to Patricia Beattie Jung

JOAN M. MARTIN

Episcopal Divinity School

Although I am a mature voice on sexual diversity, this is the first opportunity I have had to address same-sex marriage and the Catholic Church. I come with a different voice, particularly one from the Protestant tradition, the African American tradition within it, and the Commonwealth of Massachusetts, the first state to legalize marriage equality. Dr. Patricia Beattie Jung and I come from two different traditions, with distinct histories of social thought on marriage, procreation, and homosexuality. We are ourselves of different sexual orientations. We will, of course, have nuanced divergences in our thinking. It is important to say, however, that there is in fact a new and growing ecumenical consensus arising, and I am glad to be a part of this consensus along with laypersons, selected clergy, and scholars from the Roman Catholic Church. So let me address just a few issues in Jung's essay in order to expand upon or to put in my own words some particular issues that I think are important.

In the first section of Jung's paper, she speaks to the question about the morality of homosexuality and writes that in the doctrine of the Catholic Church, homosexuality and homosexual acts in particular have always been and are still considered immoral. The question that emerges from this may be put this way: is homosexual activity closed to God's gift of life?[1] That's my rendering from the statement of Pope Paul VI that "each and every marriage act must remain open to the transmission of life."[2] Jung talks about what that statement means in terms of coital activities for heterosexual couples in marriage and for expressions of openness to God's gift of life for those who do not participate in that particular sexual expression of openness. For the latter, openness may be found in child adoption and care for those who are needy, disabled, or pushed to the margins of society and by support of and participation in the works of charity.

The underlying argument here is that theologically all heterosexual couples in marriage symbolize openness to the possibility of procreation.

But not all couples personally choose the possibility of procreation or are even biologically capable of procreation. Where would an older, lesbian woman, such as myself for example, fit in such procreation-oriented expressions of openness to life? Thus I think it is wonderful that the ecumenical consensus is growing that, in fact, there are all sorts of expressions of openness to life, and what I am intending to say with this is purposeful. I want to suggest that a way to separate these very significant issues of which Jung has written from the inseparability in the doctrine regarding coitus, reproductive sex, and the unitive purposes of marriage for heterosexuals is to reverse, on a variety of levels, the notions that the procreation of life is the primary purpose of marriage and that biological oneness of male and female sex organs constitutes the necessary unitive purpose.

Rather, as I have maintained for a number of years, and similar to the thinking of Kelly Brown Douglas in *Sexuality and the Sacred*,[3] we ought to think theologically that love of the other, not only of the individual other but of the other outside of self, is a generative principle of life, whether of children or of broader expressions of the transmission of life. That is to say that the meaning of life that I think Jung is most elegantly suggesting both in the Catholic tradition and in the larger Christian tradition is one that is not confined to the material creation of human beings per se as the offspring of heterosexual unions. More importantly, Jung is suggesting that the bringing into being of love, that is, the *Imago Dei*, and caring for those who are least likely to be loved in our contemporary world *is* the principle that God is love and life. Furthermore, when two persons of the same sex express God's love to each other and beyond themselves (including in the birthing and nurturing of children), they also express "God is life."

I understand that the first principle of the first creation story is that God's love was so overwhelming that God created something for God's love to have purpose. Or, as it is in the Gospel of John, "God so loved the world that God gave God's only Son" (3:16ff). The meaning of incarnation is that love is given through life but that love, at least God's love, exists before life. Later on in that same Gospel, as contentious as it is, it can rightly be interpreted that the life of Jesus means, "I came that they may have life [love], and have it abundantly" (10:10). Love precedes the creation and priority of life, particularly from God's perspective.

Jung argues very forcefully in response to the church's notion that reproduction is clearly sexual and essential to the flourishing of the species.

However, she goes on to say, "When we take *all* the natural, biological facts of human embodiment seriously, then it becomes clear that while there is a link between reproduction and sexuality at the level of the species, there is no essential connection at the level of acts or relationships." So next, let me say that eroticism is not limited to monthly cycles. My humor notwithstanding, I take seriously the underlying claim of the bishops and other marriage traditionalists (who also have their counterparts in Protestantism), a claim that I believe mistakes biological difference per se for social constructions of dual-gender complementarity that is hierarchical and essentialist.

Gender and complementarity, when one follows the claims of the marriage traditionalists, become more subtle forms of assumptions about sexual otherness, about what it means to be male and female, about the necessity for bonding, about social structuring in the family, and about the family in the economic sphere, the political and military spheres, and in the ecclesia. These assumptions oftentimes ruin that great and mystical metaphor of Christ and the church as the essence of the relationship between God and God's people. Rather than marriage traditionalists challenging their own Western assumptions about heteronormative monogamy as naturalized by dominant interpretive thought and discourse, feminist, womanist, LGBTQ justice liberationist perspectives are derided as destroying marriage, "the family," and society and therefore are labeled immoral. Yet these same perspectives actually promote not a destruction of family and society but a mutuality of caring and long-term commitment grounded not in sexual hierarchy but in legal, relational, economic, and social equality as well as the fullest possibilities for the moral agency of both partners for their relationship and for their life in the world. As an ethicist, the latter is the part that I think is most crucial.

Jung also notes that some reproductive organs, like the uterus, have no sexual function and that there are some sexual organs that have no reproductive function, like the clitoris. Clearly, Jung helps us see that there is no way to expand on that observation, let alone disagree with it. The fact of full moral or sexual embodiment—particularly female embodiment—seems to elude those who believe that sex is foremost for procreation and therefore only permissible within traditional heterosexual marriage. In the latter view, LGBTQ people are fundamentally defined not as persons. As an African American I come from a people who have known the existential experience of being defined as nonpersons for hundreds of years. So in that sense, women remain subtly defined and socially structured by male definitions of what human means, what sexuality means, and by male ownership and moral agency; they are not defined as women in their own right. What remains unspoken is that heterosexual men, too, are seen as lacking full mature, sexual, and moral agency and thus must be constrained in that great nineteenth-century Victorian sexuality (and republican morality with a small r), constrained within the boundary of compulsory hierarchical heterosexual marriage.

Jung also speaks of the homogenital behavior that has been documented in over 450 species, including primates. One of the things that I think is critically important is that she recognizes that evolution favors not just breeding but survival mechanisms, and survival requires forms of bonding for both mating and nonbreeding behaviors as necessary in ways we may not yet understand fully. To that point I have to offer my own witness: I had a goddaughter who was birthed by a crack mother in Texas and adopted by friends of mine. She is now "he" and is gender nonconforming, handsomely African American, and courageously transgendered. He has brought me to understand deeply and personally that phenomenon. I can only imagine that when one supports marriage equality, it is not just about gays and lesbians but about people like my godson as well. Therefore, what Jung has learned and remarked upon from the lesson of evolution is very, very crucial to this discussion.

I also want to raise just briefly, then, the issue that Jung addresses in her second full category: that homosexual activity can be genuinely complementary. It is fundamental to understand that our notions of the desire of persons for same-sex marriage, its intimacy, and its contributions to the common good befit natural law when the term "natural" becomes more in keeping with dynamic and evolving notions of "human being" and "human beingness." The absolute norm and necessity of heterosexual orientation as a prerequisite for the moral goods of marriage simply flies in the face of the church's affirmation of the unfathomable mystery of God's love and the finiteness of human reason. The church still contests its own affirmations rather than grasping the dynamic meaning of human beingness as a sense of ever-revealing personhood and species created by God. This is much like what the Episcopal historian Richard Norris was developing before his untimely death a number of years ago.

Norris perceived that the notion of "natural" in Thomistic law could be understood as morally neutral—neither morally good or morally bad in itself—and not related to the question of the physiological, but rather to the purposes of human well-being so as to bridge the divide between marriage traditionalists and their interpretation of the Bible and more liberal interpreters of the Bible. (Norris is a person whose writings the Catholic ethicist Margaret Farley took very seriously regarding these matters.)[4] Indeed, these notions yield a more dynamic and less static perspective. They may help us understand that the universalistic comes through understanding difference and particularity.

I do want to point to some particularly important questions that move us beyond even the focus on this question about marriage equality. My colleague and Presbyterian minister Marvin Ellison raises some very important considerations for us, particularly as ethicists, to think about, in the seventh chapter of his book *Same-Sex Marriage? A Christian Ethical Analysis.*[5] He reminds us that we are going to have to ask the hard questions about marriage as vocation and calling, something that we choose. Marriage as primarily for heterosexual procreation and as a reinforcement of traditional privatized nuclear families "against the world" is a box with very little choice, very little equality, and very little respect for the full human dignity of all its members, not to mention the "other" in society. I cannot count the number of women in the churches who have had to make a false choice to get married because they wanted to have children, or who have suffered physical, emotional, and sexual abuse at the hands of their spouses; nor can I count the numbers of women who have suffered spiritual abuse when told by their pastors or priests to remain in abusive relationships. Though persons "choose" it, hierarchical and socially defined roles continue to infuse marriage with unequal power and dominant/subordinate role expectations.

Both the church and society have the opportunity to participate in remaking marriage for the human fulfillment of gays, lesbians, bisexuals, and transgendered persons—and also heterosexual persons. The fundamental issue behind that statement is one of justice making in marriage on the basis of equality and dignity in gender and sexual orientation for both parties in such an intimate relationship. Now it seems to me we have to do better at understanding marriage as vocation and understand it as a more elaborate, complex, institution of free choice, equality, and dignity, theologically and ethically.

In 2011, I participated in a panel discussion in Washington, D.C., at the Metropolitan Community Church—euphemistically known as the "gay church"—with the Christian feminist ethicist Tracy West, who spoke about how violence has "come home to roost" in the church, vis-à-vis the clergy sexual scandals prominently coming to the fore in the last decade. Several participants who attended our panel raised the question about multiple partners in the constructs of marriage equality for LGBT folks. Now, that's not saying that LGBT folks should not have the civil right to marriage, but we will need to ask ourselves very shortly as ethicists questions unthinkable twenty years ago: Should marriage be limited to two and only two persons, or should it include those persons who have been sent to the margins of our society because they must put together other forms of human sexualities and other pairings or partnerships in order to survive with a matter of dignity? Should we not address the matter of other forms of intimate relationships and whether or not they will be protected? I am reminded of my transgendered godson. I also think about a married gay male couple in Boston who have two children conceived with a lesbian couple. How do I as a Christian social ethicist understand them as family?

Then there are the relationships like that of my friends Alex and Rhonda[6] on the west coast. Rhonda was once a practicing lesbian and still says she identifies as such even now that she is married to Alex, who says he is bisexual. Wow! As a former pastor and now a theological ethicist, my head often spins with the perplexities of relationships and self-identifications such as these. Why does the sex or sexual orientation of intimate partners matter? We're going to have to address questions like these very soon, whether or not we like it, because LGBTQ persons and others with emerging gender identification realities come to the church for inclusion, spiritual nurture, and a yearning to serve others. What shall we say and do?

Finally, I would like to consider the tennis player who was once Dr. Richard Raskind and who in the 1970s became Renée Richards. Richards had to legally fight the United States Tennis Association to be in one of the U.S. Open tennis tournaments and compete as a woman. When we consider issues about not only gays, lesbians, and transgendered persons but also transsexual, gender-identified persons and people with other forms of human sexualities, we will once again and continually have to come to grips with questions about traditional and essentialist, dualistic, sex-gender paradigms that reduce complex questions to what makes us comfortable. Because Christian ethical reflection in and for the church is my vocation—indeed, it is a basic element of my vocation as a Christian—reflection on Jung's essay suggests that the foundational question is not necessarily whether procreation is the highest moral good of marriage. Instead, the question seems to be: What constitutes an ethical marriage and ethical family, and who has the authority in the church to define and determine these matters? Of course, the struggle to reflect upon and answer these questions will differ according to our traditions, polities, and notions of justice making. I do not necessarily look forward to these questions, but they are the questions I believe that God and the human condition have placed and will place before us whether or not we are ready or want to ask and answer them.

7   Same-Sex Marriage and Catholicism

Dialogue, Learning, and Change

LISA SOWLE CAHILL

Boston College

This paper and the volume in which it appears were inspired in part by the 2008 decision of the Connecticut Supreme Court, in a 4–3 vote, to recognize same-sex marriage. The Connecticut Catholic Conference, claiming to represent the bishops, clergy, and laity of the state, condemned this decision, citing the dissenting opinion of Justice Peter Zarella: "The ancient definition of marriage as the union of one man and one woman has its basis in biology, not bigotry."[1] On similar grounds, the United States Conference of Catholic Bishops has advocated for the Defense of Marriage Act against the federal administration of President Barack Obama.[2] The Vatican construes gay marriage as a threat to traditional marriage, the family, and society. In 2003, the Congregation for the Doctrine of the Faith (CDF) asserted that

> there are absolutely no grounds for considering homosexual unions to be in any way similar or even remotely analogous to God's plan for marriage and family. Marriage is holy, while homosexual acts go against the natural moral law. Homosexual acts "close the sexual act to the gift of life. They do not proceed from a genuine affective and sexual complementarity. Under no circumstances can they be approved."[3]

Gay couples, lacking "sexual complementarity," cannot guide the "normal development" of children. Indeed, allowing adoption by gay couples "would mean actually doing violence to these children."[4]

Dialogue of Mutual Learning?

Do episcopal condemnations and alarm tactics represent the authentic, exclusive, and authoritative voice of "Catholicism" as a whole? In thinking about homosexuality and "the Catholic Church," it is important to realize that "the church" is not constituted only or even primarily by its formal ecclesial institutions and offices or by the body of formal magisterial teaching. In an essay on Catholic identity, Tim Muldoon notes that Christian spirituality has passed through five phases, the first four of which are the apostolic, the monastic, the mendicant, and the missionary. The fifth is "a lay-led movement of engagement with the secular world."[5] Insofar as "spirituality" refers to an encompassing religious worldview in which humans and all creation are understood in relation to God, the dialogue in the church today over gay identity and unions is part and parcel of the spirituality of engagement. According to the Second Vatican Council's document on the church, *Lumen Gentium*, the pastors of the church should "recognize and promote the dignity and responsibility of the laity in the Church." Pastors and official teachers should "consider attentively in Christ initial moves, suggestions and desires proposed by the laity," and "respect and recognize the liberty which belongs to all in the terrestrial city."[6] Presumably the "terrestrial city" includes the realms of law and policy and possibly also those spheres of human historical existence where Christians live out their identities in cooperation for the common good. Marriage and family would be among those spheres.

Carolyn Weir Herman adds that, since the Holy Spirit bestows a sense of faith on all followers of Christ, it is incumbent on the ecclesial hierarchy to "engage in 'holy conversation' with the laity and lay associations . . . in order to discern the *sensus fidelium*," making decisions that "reflect a prayerful, Spirit-guided consensus."[7] All the faithful are both teachers and learners. Thus,

> the hierarchy must learn from the laity's faith and experience of formulating doctrines, and the laity must continue to receive and be educated by magisterial teaching. For this reason, there must be collaboration and co-responsibility among all the faithful in discerning and naming new and deeper understandings of the Christian faith.[8]

If the episcopacy were to dialogue with "all the faithful" on homosexuality, what could be learned? Recent research shows that, among the U.S. population of self-identified Catholics, nearly three-quarters support legal recognition of same-sex unions, with 43 percent supporting gay marriage. If marriage is defined in explicitly civil terms—a wedding at city hall—Catholic support for gay marriage jumps to 71 percent. In fact, *Catholics are more supportive of legalizing gay unions than other Christians and more supportive than Americans overall.* Moreover, 60 percent favor allowing gay couples to adopt children.[9]

These progressive attitudes are backed by data from the Census Bureau and the Centers for Disease Control, showing that of the ten states with the lowest divorce rates, five are among the nine that also permit same-sex marriage.[10] This does not mean that the legalization of same-sex marriage causes a lower divorce rate, but it does show that the two can coexist. The argument that same-sex marriage undermines heterosexual unions and family stability has no demonstrable foundation in reality. In addition, research indicates that children raised by same-sex parents show few differences from those with heterosexual parents, in terms of achievement, mental health, and social functioning. And homosexual parents are more likely to give permanent homes to hard-to-place children from the foster care system. More than half of those with special needs are adopted by gays and lesbians. A bonus of being raised by gays may be more openness and tolerance later in life.[11]

Complementing the developing perspective on gay unions among the Catholic faithful in general, there is also "more than a monologue" going on among Catholic theologians.[12] Theologians have weighed in on both sides of the issue of gay marriage. Two works among many—by Todd Salzman and Michael Lawler and by Margaret Farley—will be discussed below. The debate about homosexuality is taking shape at different sites of Catholic identity, such as lay and ordained ecclesial ministries, Catholic health care, higher education, and the academy, including scholarship in theology, the other humanities, the social and natural sciences, and the professional disciplines, such as social work, nursing, medicine, and law. The initiative of Catholics to engage critically with "official" church teaching, public opinion, and perspectives from a variety of disciplines of knowledge has increased since the Second Vatican Council (1962–1965).

Natural Law and Sexual Ethics

Engagement and dialogue do not mean relativism. They mean participatory discernment of the *objective reality* and moral significance of human sexual diversity. In the Catholic moral tradition, morality is not based on revelation or on church authority alone but on what has been known as "natural law." To some, this term has the probably well-deserved connotation of a rigid and legalistic system of general principles that are applied deductively to moral cases. It is true that this would be an apt characterization of approaches that prevailed in the "moral theology" of the late nineteenth and early twentieth centuries, still reflected in pronouncements such as that of the CDF in 2003. For example, a commonly used seminary textbook of the 1940s simply announces, with no explanatory rationale, that the Sixth Commandment against adultery entails that "all actions contrary to the orderly propagation of the race are implicitly forbidden."[13] In other words, the "propagation of the race" is the primary purpose of sex, and an indispensable one. The only framework in which to accomplish this purpose morally is marriage. Every sexual ("venereal") thought, feeling, desire, or act "has an essential relation . . . to the complete sexual act which is legitimately exercised in marriage," and any deliberately sought sexual pleasure outside of marriage "destroys that relation" and is gravely sinful.[14] It goes without saying that by "marriage" is meant a union of one man and one woman, and the material in the book actually covering homosexuality and other egregious offenses is written in Latin, so as not to titillate the beginning seminarian.

Vatican II, however, brought in an understanding of the moral life that was more personalistic, more biblical, more consultative, and more open to the integrity of every person's conscience. More fundamentally, the deductive method so typical of neoscholasticism was not shared by the primary formulator of the Catholic natural law tradition, Thomas Aquinas. For Aquinas, moral values and norms are not known deductively but practically—by the practical reason engaged with the world and human relationships, discerning what does and does not lead to human fulfillment and to the enjoyment of the goods "natural" to humans. To know the natural law through the exercise of practical reason is to know God's design for human happiness.

As a man of the thirteenth century, Aquinas did believe that procreation is the primary purpose of sex and that heterosexual, permanent marriage establishes sex's moral framework. But he also knew that the relation between general moral principles, guides to concrete action, and solutions to specific moral dilemmas is not deductive. "Although there is necessity in the general principles, the more we descend to matters of detail, the more frequently we encounter defects," that is, departures from what the general principle seems on the face of it to demand.[15] Revelation is given to help clarify the demands of the natural law, but revelation does not take away the need for practical moral reasoning. Therefore the essential natural law tradition encourages progressive reflection on the natural law, gradual refinement of its moral requirements, occasional revision of past conclusions, and even the expectation that some of its supposed provisions can change.

In a 2009 document meant to reinvigorate interest in the natural law as the basis of a common morality in a time of global problems and global communication, the International Theological Commission (ITC) proposes that reflection on "common ethical values" is a "planetary responsibility" and one that depends on "the reflection of academics and of scientists concerning the cultural, political, economic, moral and religious dimensions of our social existence."[16] The ITC continues, "the idea of a natural law is justified primarily on the basis of the reflective observation of the anthropological constants that characterize a successful humanization of the person and a harmonious social life."[17]

This reflective process of observation and consensus building is invoked to find solutions to problems like global poverty, war, and dangers to the environment. Yet that process is short-circuited in the case of human sexuality, concerning which the ITC states that "sins against nature" are those sexual practices that "are directly opposed to the finality inscribed in the human sexual body," that is, the purpose of heterosexual union and procreation. These unnatural practices—certainly including homosexuality—then necessarily and inherently "also contradict the interpersonal values that should promote a responsible and fully human sexual life."[18] The *Catechism of the Catholic Church* makes the exclusion of homosexual relations explicit. "Tradition has always declared that 'homosexual acts are intrinsically disordered.' They are contrary to the gift of life. They do not proceed from a genuine affective complementarity. Under no circumstances can they be approved."[19]

Need for Dialogue: Three Examples

The consensus emerging from the experience of the laity—also a realm of the Spirit's enlightenment and empowerment—is that questions should be raised about precisely these points. Do homosexual acts betray "the gift of life"? Is it true that homosexual partners cannot manifest "genuine affective complementarity"? These questions are not receiving a hearing from the "official" Magisterium of the church, at least not publicly.

In an incisive diagnosis of the problem, Patrick McCormick notes that for decades the chasm between "official teachings" on sexuality and the beliefs and practices of the majority of Catholics, including priests, theologians, and "an unknown number" of bishops, has been widening. This reality has been met by the silence of "the Catholic episcopal hierarchy." As a result, most bishops are afraid to express their true views; pastors are mute or covert on sexual matters; the voices of lay women are ignored, while "dissenting" religious women are reprimanded; and theologians are investigated, sanctioned, and restricted. The upshot is that the views propounded by the Magisterium have become increasingly incredible, while Catholics, especially Catholic young people, have been deprived of "a useful and persuasive sexual ethic."[20] Catholics, at least those in the United States, are left to seek out alternative guidance in a culture of "hook-ups," a 50 percent divorce rate, and the use of sex to market products, entertainment, and celebrities.

The silence to which McCormick refers is primarily a silencing of open discussion of possible revision of teachings in the past seen as adequate to the human sexual reality. Instead of discussion, there has simply been a reiteration of positions that were originally derived within different cultural contexts, different social realities, and different states of knowledge about human sexuality. While these positions grasp certain aspects of human sexual "nature," they will inevitably incorporate cultural limits and biases. This will necessarily be true of all Christian perspectives on human nature and human goods, from biblical ones to our own. It is not that the Magisterium has been totally silent, nor does it produce a true "monologue." But it has attempted to silence critical discussion of the evolution of Catholic sexual teaching.

Let me offer three examples of the need for dialogue about homosexual unions. In 2012, the Vatican Congregation for the Doctrine of the Faith issued a "Notification" concerning the work of Margaret Farley RSM, targeting her 2006 book *Just Love*. According to Farley, opposition to same-sex love "can bring deep and unnecessary suffering to the lives of homosexual persons and partnerships." She maintains that such relationships are in fact conducive to "human flourishing"; experience shows that "homosexuality can be a way of embodying responsible human love and sustaining human and Christian friendship."[21] Any and all sexual relationships must meet the test of "just love": equal respect for the dignity of all persons and for the good of the other, understood in terms of his or her concrete reality.

The CDF does not reply substantively to Farley's claim that homosexuality serves rather than undermines human goods and well-being. (Nor does it attempt any disciplinary action against her. Farley is professor emerita at Yale University and a member of a women's religious congregation.) Instead, the CDF simply asserts, "This opinion is not acceptable," then repeats the condemnation of the *Catechism*, cited above.[22] This intervention is a good example of the "silence" discerned by McCormick regarding contentious sexual issues.

A different case is presented by the interaction of the U.S. bishops with Todd Salzman and Michael Lawler, two lay theologians teaching at a Jesuit university (Creighton, in Omaha, Nebraska) who authored the 2008 revision of Catholic sexual ethics, *The Sexual Person*. They agree with Farley that experience is a foundational source of Christian ethics, though not the only one. Experience can be wrong and should not be accepted uncritically as a moral guide. Nevertheless, they take from *Gaudium et Spes* a "foundational" principle for all ethics and sexual ethics: morality must be judged in light of "the human person adequately considered."[23] This principle refers back to the Catholic natural law tradition of morality based on human ends and goods. Yet it also implies that "adequate" consideration of the human reality must be grounded in reliable empirical evidence and in concrete human experiences and must take into account contextual factors requiring that morality be nuanced to specific situations and responsibilities.

For Salzman and Lawler, the overarching "formal" norm that applies in all contexts is: "For any sexual act to be truly human, it must exhibit holistic complementarity, equality between the partners, equal freedom for both partners, free mutuality between the partners, and the mutual commitment of both partners."[24] For Christians all these qualities are informed and transformed by love of God and neighbor as revealed in Jesus Christ. Therefore both heterosexual and homosexual acts and relationships are moral if they exhibit holistic complementarity, equality, freedom, mutuality, and commitment. Christian unions will also love and serve the neighbor as a form of love of God.

Salzman and Lawler find a "disconnect" between "unsubstantiated magisterial claims," on the one side, and the views of the majority of Catholic people and empirical evidence about the experiences of homosexual couples and parents, on the other.[25] The U.S. bishops' Committee on Doctrine does in fact enter into what could be called a "dialogue" in that the committee engages with the specific arguments put forward by Salzman and Lawler. Yet they are not open to the modification of any current teachings on the basis of such arguments. The Committee on Doctrine takes issue particularly with the ideas that experience can be a source of moral norms alongside Scripture, reason, and church tradition and that dialogue between experience and the other sources might result in criticism of traditional authorities. They reject Salzman and Lawler's conclusion that on homosexuality, experience is the primary and determining source.[26]

More fundamentally, the bishops dispute the arguments that Scripture and natural law are historically conditioned and that the human mind cannot know the divine law certainly and definitively in the area of morals. "The root of the problem here is philosophical, an epistemology distorted by skepticism," leading inevitably to relativism.[27] To the contrary, they claim, the teachings of the Catholic Church about human sexuality are known certainly, on the basis of natural law and Scripture. Despite the reality of different times and cultures, human sexual nature does not vary. Sexual morality can and must be guided by absolute norms that can judge the morality of specific sexual acts like contraception, premarital sex, and homosexual acts. These norms are objective and universal and do not change with "experience."

A different instance of "dialogue" between the Magisterium and contemporary sexual experience is "Always Our Children: A Pastoral Message to Parents of Homosexual Children," published in 1997 by the U.S. bishops' Committee on Marriage and Family.[28] This document was an attempt to respond to the pain experienced by families with gay members, especially children, whom they perceived to be condemned and rejected by their faith community. These Catholics "experience a tension between loving [their] child as God's precious creation and not wanting to endorse any behavior [they] know the Church teaches is wrong."[29] The bishops reassure them that "it is through the community of his faithful that Jesus offers you hope, help and healing."[30] Catholicism does not regard the orientation itself as wrong, although it is "disordered" insofar as it orients the person to a sexual end that is not a true or authentic end of human sexuality. The dialogue with gay persons and their families leads the bishops pastorally to call gay people to a celibate life, while affirming that the church welcomes gay persons with respect and compassion and rejects all forms of injustice, discrimination, and violence against them.[31]

As one religious educator responds, not all parents today experience pain and confusion when met with the news that their child is gay, nor should they. The bishops' dialogue partners have not been adequately heard. Intending pastoral compassion, "Always Our Children" communicates a not-so-subtle negativity about those whom it addresses that is "'out of synch'" with the experiences of Catholics today. In fact, high school and college students may even consider homosexuality "to be almost a non-issue," asking instead why the bishops didn't write about sexual harassment or date rape.[32] In "Always Our Children," the episcopacy does attempt to appreciate and accommodate to the experiences of gay Catholics and their families, seeing them as relevant to its pastoral mission. But it is stymied by the necessity to retain the condemnatory teaching that is the source of the problem in the first place and remains the specific point of contention between them and their audiences. Yet "Always Our Children" does serve as an overture and reminder that the rejection and abuse gay people do still meet from fellow Catholics are unacceptable.

Two Moral Models in Tension

Behind these three examples is a changing Catholic interpretation of sex and marriage, and this bears closer examination. Historically and in most cultures globally even today, the purposes of sex and marriage have not been seen in terms of interpersonal love as much as in terms of formation of generational kinship networks organized around procreative alliances of men and women from different kin groups.[33] Marriage as a social institution assures control over reproduction (especially women's reproductive capacity), certainty of parentage, responsibility for the upbringing and education of children, and transmission of property to heirs.

Of course, sex has always been both experienced and interpreted as a source of pleasure (though primarily male pleasure). Sex as the consummation of love or desire for another is an age-old theme of literature and art.

Mutual and permanent commitment, however, has been associated more with marriage than with sex as such, the point being the domestic stability necessary to raise children and to provide for women after their child-bearing years. Marriage has been patriarchal as well. The choice to enter or end sexual and marital relationships has been more a male than female prerogative, with elder men arranging the marriages of youth and men being more able to obtain prostitutes or concubines, to take male or female lovers, and to divorce spouses. Worldwide, our North American and European portrayal of marriage primarily in terms of love, romance, finding a soulmate, a lifetime partner, has been and is still definitely a minority position.

Until recently the Catholic tradition on marriage reflected the dominant patriarchal model of marriage. But there have also been equalizing modifications. In the twelfth century, Pope Alexander III decreed that the consent of both parties (not sexual intercourse) establishes a valid and binding marriage, which functioned to protect young people and women against forced marriages and divorces. The 1917 Code of Canon Law defined marriage as a contract in which each party gives and accepts a perpetual and exclusive right over the body for acts that are themselves suitable for the generation of children. This definition assumes basic equality, though it also focuses on procreation; love is not considered a necessary part of marital union. The 1930 encyclical of Pius XI, *Casti Connubii (On Christian Marriage)* is a landmark in elevating love as a purpose of marriage. Pius XI still regarded procreation as the primary purpose of sex and saw wives as subordinate to husbands. Yet he also said that "mutual love can in a very real sense be said to be the chief reason and purpose of marriage, if marriage is seen more widely as the blending of life as a whole and the mutual interchange and sharing thereof."[34]

The Second Vatican Council's *Gaudium et Spes (Pastoral Constitution on the Church in the Modern World)* describes marriage as a "communion of love" and an "intimate partnership of life and love." Marriage is founded in "a conjugal covenant of irrevocable personal consent."[35] Marriage and marital love are still said to be ordained for the procreation of children, but "that does not make the other ends of marriage of less account," and marriage "is not instituted solely for procreation."[36] The 1983 Code of Canon Law redefines marriage not as a contract but a "covenant," "by which a man and a woman establish between themselves a partnership of the whole of life, which is ordered by its nature to the good of spouses [mentioned first] and the procreation and education of offspring."[37]

Paul VI's encyclical *Humanae Vitae* is notorious for banning artificial birth control. One of the important yet often overlooked aspects of this encyclical, an aspect that leads directly into John Paul II's "theology of the body," is its escalating emphasis on the love of the couple as providing the moral meaning of sex. Both Paul VI and John Paul II see marriage and especially sex as a "mutual self-gift." According to *Humanae Vitae*, marriage involves "the reciprocal personal gift of self," by which the spouses "tend toward the communion of their beings."[38] In fact, "this love is *total* . . . a very special form of personal friendship, in which husband and wife generously share everything, loving their partners for themselves, and bestowing on each other the 'gift of self.'"[39] Sexual intercourse is the sign and culmination of this relationship (at least according to the papal idealization), and sex does not require procreation or even its possibility to be moral.

Yet morality does require that sex be "open to the transmission of life," meaning the preservation of the "natural" structure of the act of sex. This provision means of course that the total, personal, mutual self-gift of sexual love is meant for heterosexual couples, not gay men or lesbians. Moreover, the "natural" structure of sex excludes "artificial" means of contraception—even though sex is permitted between infertile persons or those who are making use of periodic female infertility to avoid procreation.[40] In this teaching, the so-called unitive and procreative meanings of sex are joined.[41] Yet one might argue that even in papal teaching, love is beginning to take precedence over procreation as the defining and indispensable meaning of both marriage and sex, especially as *Humanae Vitae* justifies deliberate avoidance of procreation by loving married couples, under the aegis of "responsible procreation."[42]

In my view this shift in official teaching, as responsive to changing cultural norms and expectations of sex and love, is at least partly responsible for the emergent Catholic perception that gay unions are as acceptable as straight ones if they are mutual, generous, loving, and permanent. The changing face of Catholic teaching may actually be a factor in the greater favorability of Catholics toward gay unions, as compared to other Christians, the largest subset of whom in the United States is evangelical.[43]

John Paul II carries forward this perspective on the meaning of sex under the rubric of his "theology of the body."[44] The pope brings together the key themes of this theology in the Apostolic Exhortation he composed in response to the 1980 Synod on the Family:

> sexuality by means of which man and woman give themselves to one another through the acts which are proper and exclusive to spouses, is by no means something purely biological, but concerns the innermost being of the human person as such. It is realized in a truly human way only if it is an integral part of the love by which a man and a woman commit themselves totally to one another until death. The total physical self-giving would be a lie if it were not the sign and fruit of a total personal self-giving, in which the whole person, including the temporal dimension, is present: If the person were to withhold something . . . by this very fact he or she would not be giving totally.[45]

Once again we find a primary emphasis on total, committed, self-giving love. It is this intense interpersonal relation that sustains the structure or institution of marriage. Yet gay persons are excluded from this form of personal self-gift. Heterosexual "complementarity" and procreation are somewhat awkwardly retained as norms for marriage by stipulating that total self-giving requires complementarity, both physical and psychological, and that complementarity requires one male and one female. According to the theology of the body, full and total self-gift occurs only if it respects and represents the bodily meaning of sex as male-female and as "structurally" if not literally procreative.

This theology has enjoyed significant popularity among a minority of young Catholics who find in it an attractive alternative to the often baffling and alienating sexual culture around them. One reason for its appeal is that it grounds an inspiring and demanding sexual discipline not in the Bible, "revelation," or mere authority but in human sexual reality itself. The body has a communicative meaning, and the body's natural "language" is what sex is about. Sex is for relationships and commitment and even for building a family—not for unsatisfying casual encounters or impermanent relationships after whose breakup one partner feels used and exploited by the other.[46] At the anecdotal level I can attest that there are Boston College undergraduates who embrace the theology of the body and its ideal of chastity—but who are willing to see its implied norm of committed monogamous marriage as covering their gay peers in faithful relationships.

Learning from Both Models

In sum, there has been in Catholicism, as in Western cultures generally, a development as well as an ambivalence concerning what marriage really is, as focusing around two different though not necessarily opposed purposes. One is procreation and the organization of intergenerational kinship networks. The other is a union of two deeply committed individuals tied by their love and the public recognition of that love.

In the popular Catholic imagination, as in cultural images generally, the priority of love and romance over childbearing and family has become increasingly pronounced. Yet this idealization of romantic sexual love coexists in our culture with the hook-up culture; heterosexual infidelity, especially male infidelity; an ethos of no-fault divorce; serial monogamy; and in many cases the lack of sustained commitment of one or both parents, especially fathers, to the children for whose existence they are responsible.

I would not want to go back to condemnation of divorce or the stigmatizing of all those who divorce, but most Catholics would agree that a 50 percent national divorce rate is a problem.[47] The same applies to the fact that in 2010, 40 percent of all births in the United States were to unmarried parents.[48] These worrisome statistics are undoubtedly related to rising economic insecurity. They have little or nothing to do with gay people, except in as much as they too are affected by them. Gay couples seem to be getting divorced at about half the rate as straight ones, but that may be due to the fact that at this point in time, more gays are marrying partners with whom they have a longstanding relationship than are straight people.[49]

A one-sided view of sex as primarily about "true love" and romance encourages the expectation that a "perfect" partner will be able to fulfill one's needs in the same way over the lifespan, and if one's real partner fails, one is entitled to and should sever the relationship. The "natural" connection of heterosexual sex to pregnancy, birth, and faithful family building has become a marginal moral consideration, in comparison to the personal fulfillment of the lovers, spouses, or parents.

Procreative sexual responsibility does not apply to all marriages or apply in the same way (for example, gay versus straight, young versus old). This is the point the teaching church needs to learn from its married members. On the other side, those who advocate for homosexual love and marriage should not uncritically buy into a marriage ideal in which one-to-one "total" relationship connects barely if at all with the larger parental, familial, and social responsibilities of couples. The Magisterium has played into a truncated marriage model by promoting an image of marital love as total self-gift without showing realistically and persuasively what procreation and children actually have to do with it. Tying these important dimensions of sexual meaning to the supposedly universal and normative "complementary" structure of male-female sex acts does not connect to the sexual and parental experiences of most people and is not credible.

Yet, according to Julie Hanlon Rubio, echoing other Catholic scholars who are "married, with children,"[50] marriage is more than a personal relationship. It is a "communion" of love and discipleship that includes children and opens out to the larger community in service to the common good. Rubio is a strong critic of divorce. The sacramental value of marriage lies not in the "total" quality of the sex act but in the personal and communal commitment marriage constitutes and that is faithful even as ordinary and extraordinary difficulties emerge and romance fades or at least changes.[51] Not deductively or rigidly but inductively and pastorally, such authors are making a case for the procreative, familial side of sex as well as for its interpersonal "self-gift" potential. In general (as a species phenomenon), sex is "about" *both* procreation and intergenerational family building *and* the lasting devotion of two partners who love each other.

It is widely recognized among most Catholics today that gay persons are capable of "marital" love and that the quality of interpersonal love between gay spouses is in no way inferior to that of straight ones. One reason for gay marriage is to respect the dignity, rights, and personal commitments of both gay and straight persons. But the case for gay marriage should also be made on the basis of the enduring value in the older, more procreation- and family-focused understanding of marriage. The value I see in this model is its social view of sex and marriage, in which individuals are accountable not only to themselves but to families and society. It is to the good of society and the public order to extend the social ethos of permanency in marriage and family. An ethos of responsibility for spouse, children if any, larger family, and community should be communicated to as many participants in these institutions as possible, whether or not they are male-female or literally procreative. Therefore same-sex marriages and the children that may be raised within those marriages should come under the protection of the law and be expected to meet the responsibilities of married couples under the law. It is to the disadvantage of both church and society to deprive such unions of legal recognition and ecclesial respect.

8   Embracing the Stranger

Reflections on the Ambivalent Hospitality of LGBTIQ Catholics

MICHAEL SEPIDOZA CAMPOS

Emerging Queer Asian / Pacific Island Religion Scholars

Strange Homecomings

> You are no longer strangers and aliens, but . . . citizens with the saints and also members of the household of God.
>
> *Paul's Letter to the Ephesians 2:19*

The stranger has long haunted Christian life. Paul's assurance to the faithful at Ephesus—"You are no longer strangers . . . but citizens"— illuminates a kind of community that moves from alienation to belonging. Citizenship is fluid, secured not through documentation but relationship. The ambiguity of the stranger's location—as one standing outside, peering in—is resolved by a community's embrace. Rather than a problematic presence, the stranger defines the boundaries at which belonging *begins* and *ends*.

As a first-generation Filipino American, I resonate with the figure of the stranger. Simultaneously straddling two nations, multiple cultures, and languages, I convey an ambivalence that makes it difficult for many to take me at face value. Something as simple as speaking English—a language with which I grew up—requires constant idiomatic translation, given the language's diverse iterations in colonial contexts. My identity as a gay man committed to queer ministry while teaching in Catholic institutions further complicates my location. Constantly negotiating relationships, I re-shift comportment, speech, citizenship, and numerous other identity markers to secure an awkward assimilation. It is a dance that never ends, leaving me grasping for an elusive rest. But in some obscure way, the specter of the stranger lends stability to my narrative as well. Standing at the edge of belonging, I am "made real" by my very inability to fully fit in.

In my work with lesbian, gay, bisexual, transgender, intersex, and queer (LGBTIQ) people of faith, the figure of the stranger relentlessly haunts, shapes, and informs our scholarship and activism.[1] Before institutional churches, our attempts to "theologize" from the perspective of queer life is often met with suspicion; our ministries forced to conformity and at times, silencing. With increasing demand for full civic participation, particularly the push for marriage equality, questions of belonging have forced much-needed discussions around theological anthropology, morality, and ecclesial participation. Nonetheless, drawn as we are by the promise of full integration, we recognize too that we will forever grapple with otherness, tottering always at the edge of expulsion.

In this reflection, I revisit the "stranger" as a critical springboard to reconsider the relationship of LGBTIQ Catholics with church. Often described as exceptions to sexual/moral normativity, LGBTIQ Catholics endure an ambivalent relationship with church, especially if definitions of "church" were reduced to institutional membership. We are unruly exiles, straddling an ecclesial belonging that both accepts the inherent goodness of our persons *and* rejects the actions that arise from our sexual orientation.[2] Standing at the margins, we are estranged from the believing corpus. More than a reflection on LGBTIQ life, this essay attempts to broaden ecclesial discourse, breaking open the pervading "monologue" that suffocates contemporary Catholic life.

I wield the term "catholic" loosely; it is less an ecclesiological category and more a phenomenon of normativity that forms, incorporates, and integrates bodies. Relying on the theologian Leo Rudloff's reading of monastic hospitality and stability, I trace the ways LGBTIQ faithful navigate tenuous belonging in a church that purports to welcome all. I suggest that LGBTIQ Catholics model a practice of belonging akin to monastic loving, one that allows for contradictory discourses to thrive. Breaking through the monologue, queer narratives broaden the scope of ecclesial language, blurring distinctions between truth/untruth, familiar/strange. Thus, what is "queer" refers not so much to LGBTIQ individuals themselves as to a church that constantly reorients lines of belonging in order to both welcome *and* hold strangers at bay.[3]

As corollary frameworks, "stranger" and "catholic" herald a porous boundary that illuminates what the late Argentinean theologian Marcella Althaus-Reid describes as "the transient, contingent relationship of God with humanity, through processes of mobility and change."[4] It is a boundary grounded in the complexity and abundance of encounter. To the extent that this "transient, contingent relationship" subverts the heteronormative fetish for stability, the church's welcome to the stranger is ambivalent, impossible, and queer.

From Ambivalent Hospitality to Stability

All guests to the monastery should be welcomed as Christ, because He will say, "I was a stranger, and you took me in."
Matthew 25:35

Show them every courtesy, especially servants of God and pilgrims. . . .
For it is Christ who is really being received.
Benedict of Nursia, The Rule of St. Benedict, *sec. 53*

During a brief foray into monastic life, I learned much about hospitality as encounters rife with graciousness and apprehension. Having already spent a month of my summer break with a monastic community, I extended my stay to complete a year-long period of postulancy.[5] I was, in a sense, a visitor who never quite left. Among these monks, we welcomed visitors to dine, pray, and work with us. At each encounter, I found myself constantly negotiating boundaries: should one relate to guests in ways that mirror the intimacy of monastic fraternity? How deeply should one invest in friendships beyond the enclosure? Often, boundaries became hazy, with relationships devolving to messiness. Yet the brothers remained committed to hospitality as a core practice of monastic life. In a sense, a posture of ambivalent welcome buoyed our common stability.

Benedictine practice accords special honor to the stranger who stands before the gates. The Rule of St. Benedict behooves a monk to welcome each guest "as Christ." But this hospitality is ambivalent to the extent that it situates the monk in a dual posture of welcome and caution. The act of renaming the unknown implies fear of the other, discomfort with mystery. This ambivalence echoes Jacques Derrida's reading of the host as "almost the hostage of the one invited, of the guest [*hôte*], the hostage of the one he receives, the one who keeps him *at home*."[6] There prevails in welcome an implicit hostility to the stranger.

For Rudloff, hospitality undergirds the practice of monastic stability. Informed by his own experience as a German-born abbot of the international Abbey of the Dormition in Jerusalem, Rudloff lived a life between nations, cultures, and languages, an ironic situation for one committed to *stabilitas loci*.[7] Fostering fraternity among monks divided by place, politics, and worldviews, Rudloff spent much of his abbatial ministry nurturing a spirit of welcome. For him, stability begins, first and foremost, in friendship. Stability arises out of each monk's welcome to the unpredictability of her/his fellow monastic. Evoking an unwieldy hospitality, stability stands in tension between the familiarity of one's fellow monk and the disruptive mystery that comes with her/his otherness.

In monastic communities, the vow of stability bears a practical purpose: it compels one to secure the life, resources, and security of the monastery. By it, "a monk promised to remain until death in the community that had accepted [her/his] profession. Thus, stability ensured the permanence of the monastic foundation itself as well as the relative fixity of its population."[8] For Rudloff, however, stability goes further. It is "akin to the commitment people enter into in matrimony. It is a life commitment. Only such a commitment to stability can help us toward *true* character, freedom, maturity, and wholesomeness."[9] Implicit in stability is the understanding that monks reach fullness in friendship with one another. Monasteries therefore mold individual gifts toward the collective, a site where "disciplines of the body and the regulations of the population constitute the two poles around which the organization of power over life is deployed."[10]

In reorienting stability toward the relational, Rudloff envisions a community that is necessarily messy and complex. Integration molds individual will, gently reorienting one's desire to nurture the common life.[11] But to the extent that individual impulses buttress community, these too subvert the regularity, order, and discipline of the collective. One remains a perennial stranger *in* community. The monk bears the potential to destabilize the community as much from *within* as beyond the enclosure. Individual agency thus "constantly escapes" the disciplinary mechanisms of the monastic rhythm.[12] Rather than guarantee, the vow of stability *betrays* the consistency of monastic friendship. It exacerbates—rather than diminishes—paranoia around an impossible community.[13]

Wielding hospitality and stability in tandem, monks are both *host* and *guest* to one another, bridging the known with the unknown, controlling the impulse of another's mystery. It is telling that Benedictine Rule should prescribe the renaming of the stranger "as Christ," a familiarizing strategy among diverse individuals with distinct experiences of God. More than a devotional claim, this gesture reveals and relieves the anxiety that individual other/strangeness bears on the monastic enclosure. The monk relates not to what is known but to what is strange. It is in the intruder that one apprehends mystery, the promise of abundance that Christ heralds. The practice of hospitality—as an *outreach* of sorts—unfolds to a gesture of profound *in-reaching* into the mystery of community.

An All-Embracing Welcome: A Catholic and Queer Impulse

> In many ecclesiologies . . . no mention is made of the negative side of the empirical churches, which in the language of faith are called the "community of God" . . .
>
> *Edward Schillebeeckx,* Church: The Human Story of God

For many LGBTIQ Catholics, engagement with the institutional church often leaves one feeling alienated, even diminished. Yet there prevail in local faith communities equally numerous instances of welcome. Indeed, I will always be grateful for the Paulists, Jesuits, Benedictines, Sisters of Saint Joseph, Sisters of Mercy, and diocesan clergy who ministered with LGBTIQ Catholics during my years of graduate study. Not only did they embrace the strangeness of my sexuality, they provided comfort to a Filipino-in-exile who found home in the familiar practices of his religious upbringing.

For many unaccustomed to Catholic life, this dual gesture of disavowal/welcome invites confusion. But as I have traced through Rudloff's reflections, this seemingly contradictory welcome is not altogether foreign—nor even new—to Catholic life. It is an unspoken ambivalence that is inherent to community, one that illuminates an all-embracing, truly catholic, sense of belonging. This ambivalent hospitality exposes that which Edward Schillebeeckx describes as the "negative side" of church, a community consolidated by shared suffering and empathy. This turn to the negative expands not only the locus of ministry but bears the potential to reorient the starting point of theological imagination as well.[14]

Amid such developments, however, contemporary LGBTIQ Catholic discourse is still often limited to discussions of theological anthropology and its application to sexual/gendered morality. But sexuality is not the sole basis of one's ecclesial belonging.[15] Neither is pastoral nor theological uniformity a guarantee of magisterial fidelity.[16] Addressing the "magisterial monologue" only through the language of official teaching deadens theological imagination. By drawing from Rudloff's reflections on monastic life, I attempt to expand Catholic discourse on belonging, insights that I claim to be latent and *already present* within church practice and thought. Indeed, nowhere is this more elegantly apparent than in the church's Pastoral Constitution, *Gaudium et Spes*, which describes conscience as emerging from the encounter of self with God:

> In the depths of his conscience, man detects a law which he does not impose upon himself, but which holds him to obedience. Always summoning him to love good and avoid evil, the voice of conscience when necessary speaks to his heart: do this, shun that. For man has in his heart a law written by God; to obey it is the very dignity of man; according to it he will be judged. Conscience is the most secret core and sanctuary of a man. There he is alone with God, Whose voice echoes in his depths.[17]

Within this relational framework, one apprehends Truth out of openness to the otherness of God. This encounter with Transcendence exposes one to what the theologian Mayra Rivera Rivera describes as "the manifestation of the intrinsic transcendence of creatures"—of the multiple communities that constitute one's existence.[18] In such encounters, otherness emerges as a source of richness. The (non-normative) experiences of women, ethnic minorities, the poor, and LGBTIQ people of faith interrupt the stark linearity of discourse, adding layer and complexity to existing theological monologue. Thus the stranger blurs the location of those who stand *inside* and *outside* of church, dismantling the imagined divide that distinguishes host from guest. This welcome to the strange fosters a kind of community where "Christians [are then able to join] with the rest of men in the search for truth, and for the genuine solution to the numerous problems which arise in the life of individuals from social relationships."[19] In touching God's transcendence, one is rent open to the mystery of others and of one's world.

In this dance between the familiar and strange, Truth emerges out of dynamic encounters. Neither stable nor ideological, Truth demands hospitality. To be a conscientious believer is, in a sense, to expose one's self before the other's mystery. The "disorientation" that inevitably follows renders such encounters rife with possibility, illuminating strange-/queerness as itself a gift.[20] The monologue breaks open, therefore, allowing both host and stranger to claim mystery as the currency of mutual convers(at)ion.

By defining conscience as a practice of encounter, the church retrieves the stranger and the queer as inherent to the consolidation of community. The church reanimates tradition over and again—"[disassembling] enclosed bowers, enclosures, fences"—courageously open to the abundance of God.[21] Embracing the paradox of welcome/alienation, the church unfolds itself to mystery.

The Stranger's Welcome

In the years since my "coming out," the Catholic Church has become more home for me than the ephemeral gay community of my supposed belonging. I have become a teacher of religion, a minister of young adults, a seminary professor, a queer and postcolonial theologian, truly a "professional Catholic." Among my queer friends, there is profound—and perhaps painful—irony in this. Jettisoning the singular trajectory of LGBTIQ activism, I have chosen to immerse myself in an institution infamous for its strategic silencing of queer voices. I embrace the church as the home of my undeniably queer body, hewn upon devotional practices and theological articulations that have buttressed the instability of my exile. I have come to realize that it is *this* church—with its tenacious homophobia— that has given me the moral impetus and accompanying strategies to practice hospitality. In choosing to *welcome* the church to the specificity of my own location, I reorient boundaries of belonging, multiply locations of conversation, and blur the illusory delineation of center and periphery.

More than a recipient of hospitality, the stranger *welcomes* those within the enclosure, reminding the community of its own mystery. Openness to the stranger is necessary for church "membership." Even more importantly, one must risk becoming "hostage to the one invited"—to channel Derrida. And so, Rudloff was right to discern an ambivalent hospitality in the practice of stability: by welcoming the stranger, one blurs the line between the one who welcomes and the one who receives hospitality. Rendered vulnerable, both host and guest break open boundaries of belonging.

LGBTIQ Catholics will never leave the church. Religious practices may cease; ecclesial rules may effectively silence our voices. But the strangeness we herald will always haunt the seemingly immovable stability of church. The stranger will forever remind the institution of its arbitrariness and prod it toward abundance. The initiative of hospitality rests, therefore, on the very bodies of strangers—LGBTIQ bodies—who cannot but remind the church of its own instability, the porousness of its boundaries, its inherent queerness. It is these strangers who beckon to those within: "*You* are strangers no longer." Reaching inward, we calm the fears and apprehensions of those who remain blind to their own strangeness, our very queerness proffering assurance and possibility. Indeed, there is something to be said about standing toe to toe before one another's incomprehensibility. Confronted by the otherness of the stranger, we become attuned to the abundance of our *own* mystery. And so, we move from pusillanimity to magnanimity, from fear to graciousness, in an ambivalent gesture of welcome.

9   *Domine, Non Sum Dignus*

Theological Bullying and the Roman Catholic Church

PATRICK S. CHENG

Episcopal Divinity School

Much has been written recently about the classroom bullying of lesbian, gay, bisexual, and transgender (LGBT) youth. Since the fall of 2010, the press has reported a number of horrific suicides, most often those of young teenagers who killed themselves after being bullied repeatedly by their classmates for their actual or perceived sexual orientation or gender identity.[1] The syndicated columnist Dan Savage and his husband Terry Miller founded the "It Gets Better" project in late 2010 as a response to these suicides.[2]

Sadly, as of the summer of 2012, the series of bullying-related suicides by gay youth has continued unabated. On April 15, 2012, fourteen-year-old Kenneth Weishuhn killed himself in Iowa after coming out; allegedly, he had received death threats on his cell phone and was targeted by a Facebook hate group.[3] Just a week later, on April 22, seventeen-year-old Jack Denton Reese killed himself in Utah after experiencing antigay bullying in school.[4] On May 6, seventeen-year-old Jay "Corey" Jones jumped to his death from a bridge in Minnesota after suffering years of bullying for being gay.[5] And on June 2, sixteen-year-old Brandon Elizares killed himself in Texas after allegedly receiving a threatening text message about his sexuality from a classmate.[6]

This essay will focus on a related—and arguably even more harmful—form of bullying: *theological bullying.*[7] In particular, it examines the ways in which the Roman Catholic hierarchy engages in theological bullying against those priests, members of religious orders, and lay people who dissent from the Roman Catholic Church's official teaching about homosexuality (that is, that people who engage in such acts are "intrinsically disordered" and the acts themselves are of "grave depravity").[8]

The first part of this essay will focus on the parallels between classroom bullying and theological bullying. The second part will focus on why we must all resist—and stop—the harmful cycle of theological bullying by the bishops of the Roman Catholic Church. The final part will focus on some hopeful ways in which LGBT theologies are developing inside and outside the Roman Catholic Church, even in the face of theological bullying.

Theological Bullying

Bullying is defined as a situation in which a stronger person (the "bully") singles out a less powerful person (the "victim") and targets the victim with behaviors intended to harm her or him, often repeatedly over time.[9] Barbara Coloroso, an expert on classroom bullying, has identified five characteristics of bullying in her book *The Bully, the Bullied, and the Bystander*.[10] According to Coloroso, (1) bullying is intentional, (2) bullying is ongoing, (3) bullying uses terror, (4) bullying is marked by an imbalance of power, and (5) bullying arises out of contempt for the "other."[11] Each of these five marks of bullying can be seen in how the Roman Catholic hierarchy treats those who dissent from its teachings about same-sex acts.

First, theological bullying is *intentional*. The targeting of individuals who disagree with the Roman Catholic Church's teachings on same-sex acts is not an accidental matter. Rather, it is very much an intentional act that is intended to shut down any debate. In 1986, the Congregation for the Doctrine of the Faith (CDF)—headed by then-Cardinal Joseph Ratzinger—issued its infamous "Halloween Letter," the "Letter to the Bishops of the Catholic Church on the Pastoral Care of Homosexual Persons," in which the CDF emphasized that same-sex acts were "in no case to be approved of" and are never "a morally acceptable option."[12]

Since 1986, the bishops of the Roman Catholic Church have relied upon the language and reasoning of the CDF's Halloween Letter as part of an intentional and coordinated campaign to silence dissenting voices on this topic. In April 2012, for example, the CDF appointed an archbishop-delegate to oversee the affairs of the Leadership Conference of Women Religious (LCWR). The CDF's doctrinal assessment expressly cited the LCWR's alleged opposition to the Vatican's "correct pastoral approach to ministry to homosexual persons."[13] Further evidence of this intentionality can be seen in the active role that the Roman Catholic Church has played in supporting anti-marriage-equality state constitutional amendments such as California Proposition 8 in 2008 and North Carolina Amendment 1 in 2012.[14]

Second, theological bullying is *ongoing.* The Roman Catholic Church's targeting of individuals who disagree with its teaching on same-sex acts is systematic and has occurred for decades (and, arguably, for centuries).[15] This can be traced at least as far back as the silencing of Father John McNeill in 1977, following the publication of his book *The Church and the Homosexual,* as well as his subsequent expulsion from the Jesuit order in 1987.[16] Father McNeill's silencing was followed in 1999 by the CDF's cease-and-desist order to Sister Jeannine Gramick and Father Robert Nugent with respect to their ministries to lesbians and gay men and their silencing in 2000.[17] Over a decade after Gramick and Nugent's silencing, the CDF has continued its ongoing campaign against dissenting individuals by its actions with respect to the LCWR. In sum, these acts of theological bullying by the Roman Catholic hierarchy are not one-time or isolated events; they have been occurring for many decades.

Third, theological bullying uses *terror.* The Roman Catholic hierarchy uses spiritual terror—as well as economic and political terror—to achieve its ends. By designating same-sex acts as mortal sins, the Roman Catholic Church teaches that noncelibate LGBT people are eternally damned unless they repent and seek absolution from the church. Furthermore, the Roman Catholic hierarchy uses economic terror by directing most of its condemnations against priests and members of religious orders. That is, such individuals make promises or vows of poverty and thus are entirely dependent upon the church for their economic livelihood.

In addition to spiritual and economic terror, the hierarchy also uses veiled political threats, as in the case of then-Archbishop Timothy Dolan's letter to President Barack Obama on September 20, 2011, in which Dolan claimed that the administration's refusal to enforce the Defense of Marriage Act (DOMA) could "precipitate a national conflict between Church and State of enormous proportions."[18] On May 9, 2012, Cardinal Dolan issued a statement that followed President Obama's nationally televised comments in support of same-sex marriage. In that statement, Dolan criticized Obama's position as eroding and ignoring "the true meaning of marriage" and urged all Roman Catholics to "promote and protect marriage."[19]

Fourth, theological bullying is marked by an *imbalance of power.* Under Roman Catholic canon law, the hierarchy holds virtually all of the ecclesial power within the Roman Catholic Church. It has no need to consult with those who hold alternative views. Those who are silenced have no realistic means of appealing the findings against them. The late English theologian Gareth Moore, a Roman Catholic priest and member of the Dominican order, argued in his book *A Matter of Truth: Christianity and Homosexuality* that "the church teaches badly."[20] That is, instead of testing the truth or falsity of its claims about homosexuality (which, ironically, would be more faithful to the scholastic methods of noted theologians such as Thomas Aquinas), the Roman Catholic Church actually "produces no good arguments to assent to."[21] That is, it uses power and not reason to support its views.[22] Another example of this imbalance of power can be seen in the May 2012 decision by the United States Conference of Catholic Bishops to initiate an inquiry into the Girl Scouts of America following the Girl Scouts' decision to allow transgender girls to participate in its programs.[23] As the Roman Catholic lesbian theologian Mary E. Hunt has put it, the bishops are having a *"Saturday Night Live* moment," employing their vast resources in order to intimidate the Girl Scouts but ending up searching "in vain for condoms in the cookie boxes."[24]

Fifth, theological bullying is marked by *contempt for the "other."* The Roman Catholic bishops refuse to respond to anyone who disagrees with their teachings. More often than not, these individuals are summarily dismissed and ignored. This can be seen in a number of situations in which the "other" is treated without any sense of basic dignity. For example, Dominic Sheahan-Stahl, an alumnus of a Roman Catholic high school in Michigan, was summarily disinvited from speaking at his alma mater's graduation ceremonies simply because he had posted pictures of his engagement to another man on Facebook.[25] Similarly, Cardinal Dolan has refused to meet with or even acknowledge the existence of LGBT homeless youth in New York City, which led Joseph Amodeo, an openly gay member of the junior board of Catholic Charities of the Archdiocese of New York, to resign his position.[26] These are just some of the many ways in which the Roman Catholic bishops exhibit a fundamental contempt for the "other."

Stopping the Cycle

Why should we care about theological bullying? Why is this not simply an internal matter of discipline between the Roman Catholic Church and its members? One reason is that bullies are formed and *not* "born that way."

That is, bullies are shaped by households—or organizations—with dysfunctional dynamics. Left unchecked, these dynamics perpetuate themselves in future generations.

Classroom bullies learn how to bully from their families and from their churches. According to Coloroso, bullies often come from what she calls "brick-wall" families that have the following nine characteristics: (1) a parent who has "absolute authority, who enforces order, and who always wins"; (2) a parent who rigidly enforces the rules "by means of actual, threatened, or imagined violence"; (3) a parent who attempts to "break the child's will and spirit with fear and punishment"; (4) a parent who uses humiliation; (5) a parent who uses threats and bribes; (6) a parent who relies heavily upon competition; (7) a parent who creates an "atmosphere of fear" with respect to learning; (8) a parent who shows "love" that is "highly conditional"; and (9) a parent who teaches a child "what to think, not *how* to think."[27]

It is no accident that the Roman Catholic hierarchy and its defenders exhibit many—if not all—of these "brick-wall" family characteristics. Personally, I experienced these dynamics first hand in the spring of 2011, when my book *Radical Love: An Introduction to Queer Theology* was published.[28] In March 2011, I wrote an article for the *Huffington Post* on why I believe Christianity is, at heart, a queer religion.[29] That is, I argued that Christianity, like queerness, is about a radical love so strong that it dissolves the boundaries that separate us.

Shortly after my article was published, the Catholic League for Religious and Civil Rights issued a press release that mocked my article.[30] Even though the Roman Catholic Church was not mentioned in my article, Bill Donahue, the president of the Catholic League, said that I needed a "reality check" and asked whether I had read the Book of Leviticus (which specifies the death penalty for certain same-sex acts).[31] Donahue's attempt to humiliate and silence me is indicative of the kind of "brick-wall" family dynamics described by Coloroso above. Donahue reacted in a similarly uncharitable and dismissive manner when he e-mailed Rabbi Arthur Waskow in June 2012 after Waskow had criticized the Roman Catholic Church's response to the nuns and the LCWR. Donahue told Waskow that not only was he "clueless" about the situation (and that he had "stuck [his] nose" where it didn't belong) but that "Jews had better not make enemies of their Catholic friends since they have so few of them."[32]

What, then, can we do to stop the destructive cycle of theological bullying? Coloroso, in her book on bullying, proposes a solution that involves the important role of the *bystander*. According to Coloroso, there are always three players in any bullying situation: (1) the bully, (2) the victim, and (3) the bystander. According to Coloroso, the bully counts on silence and on the failure of the bystander to speak up against such bullying. Given the important role of the bystander, anybody who witnesses theological bullying must speak up against such bullying.[33] We simply cannot afford to turn a blind eye to any act of bullying, theological or otherwise.

Given the five marks of bullying that are described above, we can—and we must—challenge the theological bullying of the Roman Catholic Church. As bystanders, we must confront the Roman Catholic hierarchy about its intentional targeting and humiliation of those who question church teachings about same-sex acts. Regardless of the imbalance of canonical power between the hierarchy and the laity, we must question and challenge the ongoing punishment of such individuals and not turn a blind eye to this bullying behavior. We must help create safe spaces— economic and otherwise—for those who experience terror from this targeting. We must correct the imbalance of power by supporting prophetic organizations such as New Ways Ministry[34] and the Women's Alliance for Theology, Ethics, and Ritual (WATER).[35] And we must demand that *all* people are treated with respect and dignity as beings who are created in the image and likeness of God.[36]

Voices of Hope

Notwithstanding the existence of widespread theological bullying by the hierarchy of the Roman Catholic Church, the good news is that LGBT theologies have continued to develop—and even flourish—inside and outside of the church. In this section, I will discuss a few hopeful trends with respect to queer theology and the Roman Catholic Church.[37]

First, we have seen the flowering of queer theology outside of the church. In fact, many of the foundational voices of queer theology have been—and continue to be—former Roman Catholics. These voices include not only John McNeill[38] but also Robert Shore-Goss (author of *Jesus Acted Up* and *Queering Christ*),[39] Elizabeth Stuart (author of *Just Good Friends* and *Gay and Lesbian Theologies*),[40] Mark Jordan (author of *Silence of Sodom* and *Telling Truths in Church*),[41] Donald Boisvert (author of *Out on Holy Ground* and *Sanctity and Male Desire*),[42] and myself.[43] Indeed, it is fair to say that the academic discipline of queer theology would not exist without the groundbreaking work of queer theologians who were raised in the Roman Catholic Church.

Second, we have witnessed the amazing grace of queer theologians who have stayed within the Roman Catholic Church as a result of safe spaces and/or economic freedom. These individuals include Mary Hunt, the Catholic lesbian theologian who co-founded WATER, a world-renowned feminist theological think tank that has operated for nearly thirty years. Hunt is the author and editor of many feminist theological works, including *Fierce Tenderness* and *New Feminist Christianity*.[44] She is also a prolific writer and blogger. Hunt has sharply criticized the Roman Catholic hierarchy for its bullying and intimidation of the LCWR. She has also criticized the CDF's censure of Sister Margaret A. Farley's *Just Love: A Framework for Christian Sexual Ethics* as "the intellectually embarrassing and morally tawdry work of a group that obviously needs a permanent vacation."[45]

Another theologian who has stayed within the Roman Catholic Church is James Alison, a gay priest who has described himself as an ecclesiastical "nonperson" who nevertheless survives "deep in enemy territory," at least from the perspective of the current Roman Catholic hierarchy.[46] Alison's many books include *Faith Beyond Resentment* and *Broken Hearts and New Creations*.[47] In a powerful essay entitled "Letter to a Young Gay Catholic," Alison encourages young LGBT Roman Catholics to persevere in their vocations despite the fact that they are developing ministries "without any public backing from Church authority." One day, Alison writes, there may be a "thaw in the ecclesiastical permafrost," and "talk will get much, much easier." Until then, he assures them that "you are not alone."[48]

Third, we have seen the emergence of LGBT Catholic theologians of color and their allies. For example, we have seen the development of a queer Latino/a Catholic theology by Orlando O. Espín in his book *Grace and Humanness* as well as in his work with the Latino/a roundtable of the Center for Gay and Lesbian Studies in Religion and Ministry at the Pacific School of Religion in Berkeley, California.[49] Espín, a gay Latino professor of systematic theology at the University of San Diego, writes that Latino/a and black Catholic theologians "cannot ignore LGBT blacks and Latina/os in our theologies, because sexual orientation is an unavoidable real contextualization—as real and unavoidable as race, gender, ethnicity, or culture."[50]

We have also seen the development of queer Black Catholic theologies by scholars such as M. Shawn Copeland. Copeland, an African American professor of theology at Boston College, has argued in her book *Enfleshing Freedom: Body, Race, and Being* that we are all "made new in Christ" and thus must "abolish all claims to racial and cultural superiority" and also "contradict repressive codes of gender formation and sexual orientation." According to Copeland, the Body of Christ is the "only body capable of taking us *all* in as we are with all our different body marks—certainly including the mark of homosexuality."[51]

With respect to Asian and Asian American Catholic queer theologies, we have seen the creative cross-cultural work of Michael S. Campos, who holds a doctorate from the Graduate Theological Union, who has written about the effeminate gay Filipino man known as the *baklâ* and gendered religious performance in Filipino cultural spaces.[52] Other queer Asian Catholic theologies include the work of Lai-shan Yip, who has written about the experiences of Roman Catholic *nu-tongzhi*, or lesbians, in Hong Kong,[53] as well as the work of Joseph Goh, who has written about the doctrine of Mariology and *mak nyahs*, or male-to-female transsexuals, in Malaysia.[54] Campos, Yip, and Goh are all members of the international Emerging Queer Asian Religion Scholars (EQARS) theological collective, which meets monthly via teleconference.[55]

Fourth, we have seen an expansion of what constitutes a Roman Catholic "theologian." That is, in addition to the academic theologians described above, we have also seen the emergence of many Roman Catholics who engage in public theology through new and innovative media channels. These individuals include Marianne Duddy-Burke, the executive director of DignityUSA, the national affirming organization for LGBT Roman Catholics;[56] Diann Neu, the co-founder and co-director of WATER, as well as the co-editor of the *New Feminist Christianity* anthology;[57] Victoria Rue, a Roman Catholic Womanpriest who is also an author, professor, and playwright;[58] and Jamie L. Manson, an alumna of Yale Divinity School and blogger for the *National Catholic Reporter*.[59] By contrast with the more traditional academic theologians listed above, these individuals—all women—are redefining the role of what it means to be a "theologian" both inside and outside the Roman Catholic Church.

Fifth, we have seen an expansion of what constitutes Roman Catholic "theology." For example, there has been an explosion of LGBT lay Catholic theological reflections in recent years, including the contributions to the *Queer and Catholic* anthology edited by Amie M. Evans and Trebor Healey.[60] New genres of queer Catholic writings have also emerged, including autobiographies of gay Catholics,[61] autobiographies of gay bishops and priests,[62] histories of LGBT-welcoming parishes like Most Holy Redeemer Church in the Castro District of San Francisco,[63] collections of LGBT-affirming liturgies,[64] queer Catholic literary theory,[65] and writings by and for families of LGBT Catholics.[66]

So there is hope, even in the face of widespread theological bullying by the hierarchy of the Roman Catholic Church. To restate a popular saying from my childhood years: The more the Roman Catholic Church tightens its grip, the more queer theological voices will slip through its fingers.[67]

The ideas in this essay were originally presented during the fall of 2011 at the More than a Monologue conference held at Union Theological Seminary in New York City. The Union conference focused on the theme of antigay bullying and was entitled "Pro-Queer Life: The Youth Suicide Crisis, Catholic Education, and the Souls of LGBTQ People." The title of the panel on which I served was "Lord, I Am Not Worthy," or, in Latin, "*Domine, non sum dignus.*"[68] As all good Roman Catholics know, these are the words—more precisely, "Lord, I am not worthy that you should enter under my roof, but only say the word and my soul shall be healed"—that are said at Mass after the *Agnus Dei* and immediately before one goes up to receive Holy Communion.

What most Roman Catholics do not realize, however, is that "*Domine, non sum dignus*" was originally spoken by a Roman centurion who was begging Jesus to heal his beloved servant, or *pais* in the Greek, which could have denoted "a younger lover." As the New Testament scholar L. William Countryman has noted, "it is not intrinsically improbable that this was a case where the slave was the master's sexual companion."[69] Jesus, responding to the centurion's pleading, does in fact grant his request and heals the servant. Ironically, both the centurion and the servant would be denied Holy Communion at most Roman Catholic churches today.[70]

It is time for the Roman Catholic hierarchy to start acting more like Jesus and to follow his unconditional embrace of the centurion and the servant. In other words, the hierarchy should act less like theological bullies and more in accordance with *in persona Christi* (that is, "in the person of Christ").[71] They should welcome to the Eucharistic table all those who seek God's sacramental grace, regardless of whether they are in same-sex or opposite-sex relationships. And perhaps, in so doing, the souls of the Roman Catholic hierarchy might be healed.

10 Wild(e) Theology

On Choosing Love

FREDERICK S. RODEN

University of Connecticut

This essay began as a talk in a panel entitled "Lord, I Am Not Worthy to Receive You," words taken from the order of the mass. Thus I could not resist (in speech or in prose) beginning with a quotation from perhaps the most famous Catholic homosexual (if deathbed convert), Oscar Wilde. Imprisoned in 1895 for "gross indecency" (homosexual acts), Wilde writes Bosie Douglas—his former lover and his enemy—with praise and blame: "Love is a sacrament that should be taken kneeling, and *Domine, non sum dignus* [Lord, I am not worthy] should be on the lips and in the hearts of those who receive it."[1]

What does it mean to be worthy of receiving—and giving—love? What does it mean to be worthy of receiving and giving God—in the Eucharist and in our lives, in our connections with one another? Once we get beyond Wilde's salacious double-entendre, we are left with these questions in the relationship between the devout and their faith. The bodies *should* receive love not from their God alone but from *God's* Body, the church on earth.

The More than a Monologue series of conferences prompted us to consider moral and ethical imperatives in Catholic education and the responsibility of the church to give love to all of its members. I am particularly concerned with the teaching authority of the church with respect to its mission as a source of God's love in the world. During the past decade and a half, we have been exposed to gruesome details about "abuse," "abusers," and specifically "sexual abuse." There are many types of abuse and many different kinds of abusers. Failure to teach Jesus's gospel of love can be a form of abuse, even if it is a sin of omission rather than commission. This is true when religious authorities (teachers, clergy) do not use their office to show love. Unlike Wilde, I do not seek to praise or blame. But I do feel obliged to begin with a statement of the commandment to love others as we have been loved by God.

Clergy and pastoral ministers offer teachings *from* the pulpit and *for* the pulpit. I wish to provide a different perspective, one from the secular humanities academy. As a scholar who identifies as religious yet has always written and taught about religious subjects while affiliated with nonreligious institutions, the "spiritual direction" I share with my students and the "responsa" that I write with and to my colleagues show me that our questions apply independent of religion. Faiths have benefited and wounded many secular people. We who labor in other vineyards are allies to Catholic advocates. I mean that from an interfaith perspective as well. LGBTQ-affirming people from different religious traditions (and no religious traditions) must at least share *this* communion.

I had the privilege of a Catholic education, although I do not write today from a Catholic perspective. As a gay man, the love and acceptance I received from my Catholic father prompted me to learn about the surprisingly rich heritage of LGBTQ people within Catholicism and defined the beginning of my scholarly career and identity. I started graduate school in literature at a time when queer approaches to canonical authors were in vogue. Although I planned to write a doctoral dissertation in this mode, I did not expect to become a specialist in studies of religion and homosexuality, let alone gay Catholicism. I did not realize how deep my Catholic education and milieu, and particularly my relationship with my Catholic father, had shaped my consciousness. Even today as I may personally dissent from the "faith of my father," that religious difference is not based on my sexual orientation, for I have been welcomed in many Catholic spaces.

As a young graduate student struggling to define my own adult gay identity, I was surprised to find an intellectual home in Catholicism, a history of men of same-sex desire who also grappled with homosexuality and the religious tradition. I found a rich heritage that dates back at least to the modern Catholic discussion concerning homosexuality that developed among clergy and laity over a century ago. A man by the name of Marc-André Raffalovich, himself a Jewish convert to Catholicism—and an acquaintance of Oscar Wilde—helped initiate this conversation.[2] In a sexological text that I have called an *apologia* for homosexual orientation, Raffalovich argued that not only are homosexuals good Christians; they make the best priests.[3] Raffalovich takes a position that the twenty-first century church might advocate: he favors celibacy, but in a "homophilic" rather than homophobic argument. Following the teachings of *The Symposium*, sexual restraint preserves the cerebral beauties of friendship and enables the "invert" to deploy a wider compassion in a religious vocation, he maintains. Since Raffalovich's acceptance of late Victorian psychological notions of sexual inversion does not prevent him from placing homosexuals in the highest space in religious life, lapses from his Platonic ideal of sublimated intellectual love become minor offenses, not major catastrophes.

Raffalovich states that "In practice or in theory, every doctrine can favor homosexuality . . . it is not contrary to the sexual instinct nor to human intelligence. The Catholic Church . . . must be the depository of good returns for the education of homosexuals."[4] This was written in 1896 by a man who was patron to John Gray, a poet once called "Dorian Gray" in a letter from Oscar Wilde. Gray became a Catholic priest; Raffalovich paid for his education, built a church for him in Edinburgh, and established himself in a home several blocks away. These two men maintained their spiritual friendship over four decades. After their deaths in 1934, Raffalovich's fortune went to the Roman Catholic Dominican Order, which still owns his papers.[5]

Raffalovich was a great philanthropist for causes aiding youth. The occasion of a pastor's suggestion to the parish council that the local Boy Scouts publicly present Mr. Raffalovich with a bouquet of lilies for his generosity brought howls of laughter, given the benefactor's aesthetic flamboyance and the open secret of his homoerotic proclivities. But Catholic gay men's "ministry" to youth is not limited to the pederastic. Rather, the Roman Catholic cult of the saints—its adoration of the beautiful young male body, like devotion to the body of Jesus—has served as an impetus, rather than a stumbling block, to a Catholic social ethics of homosexuality. The ability of the man of same-sex desire to discern his love for male beauty opens the door to its wider realization in a love for all humanity. Here desire can serve to universalize love, extending it, while also committing one to the pursuit of social justice for the misunderstood and persecuted. Given Catholicism's incarnational and eucharistic theology, it is impossible for the devout Catholic to find Christ *except* in and through the bodies of others. The same conscience and belief that drove many of Raffalovich's contemporaries to Christian socialism must fuel a Catholicism of love for, not rejection of, LGBTQ youth today.

I have deliberately raised the painful topic of Catholic pedophilia because that subject shaped discussions of homosexuality a century ago. Clerical outreach to youth defended itself as containing "more . . . of Christ than Socrates," in the words of a 1918 poem anxious about "Greek love."[6] Can our own historical moment resurrect Catholicism from contemporary scandals manipulated by churchmen to further pathologize homosexuality and scapegoat homosexuals? The tragedy of this culture war is that a meaningful Catholic ministry to LGBTQ youth has been sidelined if not sidetracked while the church continues to affirm perspectives on "objective disorderedness" that distract from the commandment to realize love in the world—while professing human rights and nominally disavowing hate crimes. The failure to love is a hate crime, for the sin of omission turns to one of commission once theology is deployed in pastoral practice.

If Victorian discourses of homosexuality were deeply confused with pedophilia—consider the notorious story "The Priest and the Acolyte" by John Francis Bloxam, later ordained Father Bloxam—twenty-first-century ones need not be. In this gothic tale, the love of an Anglo-Catholic priest for his acolyte comes to a tragic end. The two die in a double suicide, by poison drunk from a chalice in a parody of the mass. The transubstantiation becomes an act of sacrifice for love that portrays the "invert" as sacrificial victim. Despite the sensational and absurd narrative, Bloxam's priest articulates a gripping *apologia* for same-sex love and essential difference. He argues that it would have been a sin for him to have married a woman, that it would have gone against his nature. Conversations about LGBTQ moral theology are always informed by history. A variety of turn-of-the-century LGBTQ writers read the religious past. Raffalovich and his friend Father Gray were preoccupied with the devotional homoerotics of John of the Cross, who, they felt, named their own spiritual longings. Raffalovich even located John in his sexological work as an invert; Gray translated his poetry and wrote poems about him. Both men found in the past a means to read their own present: a sublimation of their same-sex desire and friendship into love of God.

When we read Bloxam's story, which blurs a moral argument for homosexual rights with reality-show level sexual scandal, we miss the former point on account of the latter. This reality is especially true today, given both the tragedies and sensationalism surrounding church sexual abuse scandals. Even as we are always reading the past in some way, we need not remain, in ecclesiastical discussions of homosexual ethics, trapped where they were trapped *about* the past. When in 1907 Pope Pius X issued his encyclical condemning Modernism, he silenced dissident Catholic voices on sexual ethics into our millennium. The church's refusal to acknowledge new understandings of sexuality has ensured there can effectively be no new official moral theologies pertaining to homosexual behavior. For even in the historical moment I am concerned with, there were those Roman Catholic theologians who spoke out about religion and same-sex desire. This century-old heritage includes the Irish Jesuit Modernist Father George Tyrrell (excommunicated in 1907), who corresponded with Raffalovich.[7] In an 1899 letter, the priest states that Raffalovich's study of homosexuality "deals with problems . . . [his] mind ha[d] long worked at."[8] "Moral theology scamps the whole question ludicrously," Tyrrell observes.[9] He himself had written a tract for Jesuits that suggests addressing sexual orientation. He tells Raffalovich, "The criminal folly of educators in this matter has been so much obtruded upon me . . . that I am determined to use any liberty I have in bringing it to light. . . . Many of our Jesuits and a great number outside the [Society of Jesus] feel that another line must be taken and that speedily. The confusion of ignorance with innocence is of all confusions the most disastrous."[10] Tyrrell's last sentiment in this 1899 letter could have been spoken in 1999 conversations about sexual abuse scandals and the church.

Tyrrell's 1897 *On the Catholic Doctrine of Purity* is among the earliest works written by a priest to address modern understandings of homosexuality seriously. Tyrrell suggests that most people have same-sex desires, which he attributes to developmental biology (following late Victorian rhetoric that understood the "invert" as having a "man's soul in a woman's body" or vice versa). While as a priest Tyrrell was more restricted in his public speech, with a hierarchy of superiors to report to, he encouraged Raffalovich, the independent layman, to pursue this inquiry further. He writes him in 1903: "The Church is blind and deaf and dumb in this matter. . . . You . . . might do more for souls . . . than all the confessors of Christendom will do in centuries."[11] In 1905 Tyrrell observes to Raffalovich that "the foundations of our traditional sex-morality are doomed . . . through their own unsoundness and implicit immorality . . . it is exactly what you maintain when you say, so rightly, that inversion is a normal phenomenon."[12] Many Christian theologians today would agree with this assertion, as well as Tyrrell's point that laity must claim their role as the Body of Christ to formulate new Catholic theologies of homosexuality.

To return to Oscar Wilde: although it may seem unusual to think of Wilde as a Catholic, let alone a lay theologian, he has much to offer Christian thought.[13] Wilde's first extended discussion of Christ occurs in his 1891 essay "The Soul of Man Under Socialism." Here Jesus is the supreme individualist. Wilde writes, "The message of Christ to man was simply 'Be Thyself.' . . . 'You have a wonderful personality. Develop it. . . . Your perfection is inside of you.'"[14] "He who would lead a Christlike life is he who is perfectly and absolutely himself. . . . It doesn't matter what he is, as long as he realizes the perfection of the soul that is within him."[15] Wilde develops a Christian theology that commands self- and soul-realization and presumes the diversity of human experience.[16]

If in the essay Wilde puts forth an ideal, it is one that faults Jesus for realizing his perfection through sorrow and suffering rather than through joy. By the time we get to Wilde's prison letter to Douglas (written just five years later), we find a broader view of Christ's message as well as a different attitude toward pain. This work, entitled "De Profundis" ("out of the depths"), was written after Wilde was tried and imprisoned for crimes of "gross indecency," that is, homosexual acts. He lost everything: family, career, possessions. Psalm 130 entreats, "Out of the depths have I cried unto thee, O Lord. Lord, hear my voice: let thine ears be attentive to the voice of my supplications. . . . I wait for the Lord, my soul doth wait, and in his word do I hope."[17] The souls of LGBTQ youth, who suffer when the church does not hear their cries, plead for this same mercy of God.

Christ in Wilde's "De Profundis" "realized in the entire sphere of human relations . . . imaginative sympathy": the ability to experience a feeling of oneness with the other who is different from the self.[18] As we likewise attempt in advocacy, activism, and education, Christ

> took the entire world of the inarticulate, the voiceless world of pain, as his kingdom, and made of himself its external mouthpiece. Those . . . who are dumb under oppression and "whose silence is heard only of God," he chose as his brothers. He sought to become eyes to the blind, ears to the deaf, and a cry in the lips of those whose tongues had been tied. His desire was to be to the myriads who had found no utterance a very trumpet through which they might call to heaven.[19]

For this Christ, Wilde says, "imagination was simply a form of love."[20] Can we fully imagine the pain of those who suffer in ways we do not? Can the Roman Catholic Church? For Wilde, Christ's "morality is all sympathy, just what morality should be."[21] Who will write such Catholic moral theology grounded in full identification with the other? In order for the church to offer radical welcome and acceptance—that is, love—to LGBTQ youth in pain, it must cultivate a fuller Christ-consciousness, which will require looking outside itself and even outside Christianity. In Wilde's words, Christ "does not really teach one anything, but by being brought into his presence one becomes something."[22]

I have sought here to provide some historical context for questions of homosexuality and Catholicism. I pray that the church may become worthy to receive all LGBTQ children in the spirit of love. John Bloxam's 1894 "The Priest and the Acolyte" concludes with the boy-loving priest joining his youth in a double suicide from the communion cup. May we work to create a church that can save itself and others, a church that honors a Christ who "came that they may have life, and have it abundantly."[23] Let us choose life.

Afterword

PAUL LAKELAND

Fairfield University

It is a striking truth that when religious reflection takes place at some point other than the power center of the church, wonderful things often happen. The two most notable instances of theology from the margins in recent times have been the ferment of thought associated in the first place with Latin American theology of liberation and the equally fruitful conversation between feminist, womanist, and *mujerista* theologies throughout the Americas. Both phenomena began as examples of previously marginalized voices insisting on having their day at center stage. As they developed from the 1960s onward, they also began to pay more attention to one another. Black, white, and Hispanic women's theologies have mutually critiqued and enriched one another, and each in its way has also stretched the imagination of other voices for liberation, so that today most contemporary theology is done self-consciously out of a particular context, and everyone tries to pay heed to everyone else. Remarkably, too, they have gone on to inspire theological method in general, to adopt more experiential and inductive approaches.

The development of LGBTQ theologies represents a third stage in wresting control of theological authority from the cathedrals, monasteries, and ivory towers of past ages. From the pioneering work of John McNeill, Robert Goss, Mary Daly, and others to the mainstream theological conversation of today, LGBTQ theologies are demanding that *their* voices be heard and at the same time enriching the perspective of other branches of the family of theologies because their particular social positioning makes them fertile sources of insights not so readily available to everyone. Like liberation and feminist theologies before them, their legitimacy comes from the rights of the marginalized to have voice, but— equally important—their fecundity lies in the ways they enrich the work of other laborers in the theological vineyard.

The More than a Monologue Project in Retrospect

The More than a Monologue (MtaM) project would not have been possible if the picture that I just painted were not true, but it must also be seen for its own particular importance, which is not reducible to any of the above. Of course, it is one example of claiming voice, and anyone who attended any of the four conferences can attest to the openness to new knowledge that was in the air and of which we have so much first-hand evidence in the papers that make up the body of this volume. Beyond all this, however, MtaM was an ecclesial event, not merely a sociological or even theological happening. As an ecclesial event, it certainly leaves space for sociological and theological commentary, but its first and fundamental importance lies in what it means for the Catholic Church. This will be the central concern of these few concluding words.

The first and most important thing about MtaM is that it happened. This was an unprecedented event in the life of the church, considered from a number of different angles. MtaM was a set of events that placed major Catholic institutions out in public as locations where neuralgic issues could be openly discussed. It demonstrated a unique collaboration of Catholic universities and nondenominational divinity schools. It gave time at the podium to people committed to broadening the range of voices that is usually heard in church circles on LGBTQ issues. It made fairly large numbers of Catholic gays and lesbians welcome on Catholic campuses as well as in the more familiarly supportive environments of the divinity schools. It set out neither to challenge nor to defend the official position of the Catholic Church on same-sex relations but instead addressed a whole range of issues that are real concerns in the church, whatever a person's perspective on the official teachings might be. And most importantly, it broadened the range of voices typically heard in the church to include those whom the official teaching of the church encourages to hide their true selves.

MtaM is fodder for any amount of rumination about the Catholic Church. First and foremost, that it took place at all is a signal that the energies in Catholic theological reflection no longer lie in the traditional locations. LGBTQ issues are one set of a considerable number of concerns where the official doctrinal position is sterile and moribund. This does not mean that any perspective that leans toward the more conservative end of the spectrum is ipso facto lifeless but rather that any position, left or right, which consists simply of the repetition of long-held positions is in danger of missing what the signs of the times have to say to the community of faith. We can certainly all legitimately argue about what the signs of the times are and how we should understand and respond to them. But we cannot pretend that attention to the signs of the times is not part of the project of being church in a credible way today.

A second matter upon which to ruminate is who exactly we ought to be imagining is included in the community of faith. The Second Vatican Council's *Lumen Gentium* was famously fuzzy in its preference for the term "the People of God" as its preferred image or model of the church. In fact, the council fathers announced that "everyone" is "included in or somehow related to" the People of God, thus reflecting the conviction that God offers salvation to all people, whatever their particular religious tradition or lack of it.[1] The MtaM conferences attracted people who were different in various ways. Inevitably, of course, the disproportionately large percentage of LGBTQ people drawn to the conferences were in large measure marginalized or perceived themselves to be. In the church or not, they could be hardly be said to be mainstream. Nor, for that matter, could the straight people present, since for the most part they were drawn to the events by the sense that what there is to be said about LGBTQ issues in the church is by no means exhausted by the official teaching. But what is even more striking is how so many of the speakers at the four events were people who see themselves as ex-Catholics yet who evidently retain a sense of attention to—if not always respect for—the tradition that had shaped their earlier years, for better or worse. In the present volume this is true of Mark Jordan, Kelby Harrison, Patrick Cheng, and Frederick Roden, but there are a number of others whose contributions appear in the companion volume, *Voices of Our Times*.

The situation in which almost all those who participated in the conferences stand is much as follows: in or out of the church, most everyone seemed to think that the church is doing a pretty poor job of celebrating the humanity of its LGBTQ members, but very few seem ready to give up on the possibility that this could change. Of course, the more accurate we take to be Mark Jordan's claim that the fundamental issue is one of power—and who is not persuaded by his analysis?—the harder it is to imagine that the church could one day make a volte-face. There is much more riding on such a decision than simply the place of LGBTQ people in the church or their right to marry, adopt, and so on. Nevertheless, in principle change might occur, and that is perhaps because while issues of power immensely complicate things, in the end there is no sound *theological* argument for the present position that the church maintains. Indeed, as I shortly hope to show, there are some excellent theological arguments for reversing the position of the church and, indeed, for celebrating the sacramental significance of same-sex marriage. In any confrontation between ecclesiastical power and the truth of the Gospel, Christian hope requires us to believe that the latter will eventually triumph, even if no date can be assigned to that event.

Thinking Theologically About Same-Sex Relationships: Preliminaries

Theological reflections on LGBTQ issues are too often oriented to addressing official church teaching about why same-sex relationships are "disordered" or about why same-sex marriage is unacceptable. Let us for a change ask a different question: is it indeed possible to make a case for treating same-sex sexual activity, partnership, and marriage exactly equally to that of heterosexual relationships? Moreover, we need to be clear that the question is placed within the context of the Catholic Church. It is surely beyond argument that the church has no legitimate role in attempting to impose its own understanding of same-sex relationships and marriage upon a pluralistic society, though that is certainly not always the impression one gets from the periodic efforts of the hierarchy to swing the community of faith behind the "Defense of Marriage Act" and various state and local antiequality initiatives. That kind of move is a species of the heresy of integrism, which we encounter whenever a religiously based position is employed as a kind of template for civil society. Faced with the fact that the church does seem to choose to be intrusive on the issue of same-sex civil marriage, some have argued that the best solution would be for the state to get out of the business of marriage, perform civil unions, and avoid the contentiousness of supposedly divine ordinances on the nature of marriage. Churches could then follow their own practices, though, as on the French model, church marriages would have no legal status if there were not already a civil contract in place.

To make the case for the sacramentality of same-sex marriage we find an unlikely but important ally in the mid-twentieth-century Canadian Jesuit theologian Bernard Lonergan. Lonergan never spoke or wrote about same-sex issues, and we cannot be sure how he would view them. However, in a remarkable series of essays written in the 1960s and published in *A Second Collection*,[2] he mapped out a transformation of Catholic theology that, if taken seriously, would lead to enormous changes in the way the church reflects religiously. The key to Lonergan's significance lies in his recasting of classical theology into a more distinctly modern format and in particular his argument that the understanding of the human person is now radically changed. The argument for the sacramentality of same-sex marriage begins, then, with anthropology.

The first essay in Lonergan's *A Second Collection* is entitled "Transition from a Classical World-View to Historical Mindedness." Here Lonergan suggests that as we think about things, the classical approach of looking for truths that somehow escape the historical process is not the only possible one or even the most advisable. We could also "begin from people as they are." The intentional acts out of which human beings construct their lives, he suggests, are "the hard-won fruit of man's [sic] advancing knowledge of nature." They are not a "stock of ideal forms subsistent in some Platonic heaven." This leads us to see humankind "as a concrete aggregate developing over time," enwrapped in historicity. It is "through this medium of changing meaning that divine revelation has entered the world and that the Church's witness is given to it."[3]

In this essay and in several others in this most important collection, Lonergan makes two points that bear directly upon the task of formulating a sacramental theology of same-sex relationships. The first is that notions of human nature are not fixed. There have certainly been times in which the church has thought so, especially as it developed an ahistorical version of scholastic philosophy and theology in order to shore up what it saw as the threat of historicity emerging in the Enlightenment. The true scholastics placed the philosophy of Aristotle into an encounter with their age, and Lonergan is clear that the return to inquiry "locked in an encounter with its age" is what distinguishes the newly historicist theology he is trying to identify. One result will be a dynamic understanding of human nature.

The second point of Lonergan's inquiry that is relevant to our concerns lies in the quest for certainty that marks an ahistorical approach. The anti-Enlightenment apologists for scholasticism, says Lonergan, turned from "the inquiry of the *quaestio*" to the "pedagogy of the thesis." In other words, instead of exploring a question, they defended a statement they had inherited. The dynamism of medieval scholasticism was thus rendered static, and so "demoted the quest of faith for understanding to a desirable but secondary, and indeed optional goal" and "gave basic and central significance to the certitudes of their faith, their presuppositions and their consequences."[4]

While Lonergan's depiction of the historical sophistication of contemporary theology is quite accurate, it is not the case that the pronouncements of the institutional church have always followed this example. It was over exactly this question that the modernist crisis of the early twentieth century came about, and it was not until midcentury that schools of thought such as that of *la nouvelle théologie* in Francophone Europe began to return to the question of history. The ground was thus prepared for the conclusions of Lonergan and the at least partial recognition of the importance of history in the documents of the Second Vatican Council (1962–1965). In the half-century since Vatican II, it is fair to say, the church has continued to show tensions between the "inquiry of the *quaestio*" and "the pedagogy of the thesis." In particular, especially during the pontificate of Benedict XVI, the truth that theology is always at the service of the church has often meant that theology has been understood as a species of catechetics, always at the service of the most recent pronouncements of the official teaching church. But what if those pronouncements are themselves committed to an ahistorical clinging to certitude?

If we have to some degree cleared the ground for our sacramental theology of same-sex relationships by the recognition of the historicity of notions of human nature and the problematic reduction of religious reflection to the repetition of dogmatic certitudes, the final act of preparation consists in reflection upon the Christian Gospel, and especially upon the nature of faith in an incarnate God that lies at its center. What does it mean to say that in Jesus Christ God was present in history, or that Jesus was God-made-human, or that God became human in the person of Jesus of Nazareth? It really does not matter whether one favors the so-called low Christology, in which the humanity of Jesus is the interpretive starting point, or the high Christology in which God comes down to earth in the person of Jesus Christ, the Son of God. Both of these are second-order reflections upon faith in Jesus Christ as the presence of God in history. And all christologies recognize the subjection of Jesus Christ to the conditions of human history. As St. Paul wrote in the Letter to the Philippians, "though he was in the form of God, [Jesus] did not regard equality with God something to be grasped. Rather, he emptied himself, taking the form of a slave, coming in human likeness; and found human in appearance, he humbled himself, becoming obedient to death, even death on a cross" (2:6–8). This is evidently a high Christology since it imagines Jesus Christ preexisting, determining his own *kenosis*, but the consequence is that in history he is, frankly, as historical as you or me. And if our Christian faith is certain that in Jesus Christ God entered history, it cannot be finally sure what this means for the community of faith or indeed for Jesus himself. We are all of us caught up in the dynamism of history, bringing our faith that Jesus was fully human into an encounter with the age of which we are a part, in which to say "fully human" is by no means to pronounce a dogmatic certitude, but rather to reassert "the inquiry of the *quaestio*."

A Sacramental Theology of Same-Sex Relationships

If we begin, as Lonergan proposed, from "people as they are," there can be no doubt that gays and lesbians demonstrate loving relationships in precisely similar ways to those of their heterosexual fellow human beings. They have siblings and parents and sometimes children. They have platonic friendships and romantic relationships. Sometimes these relationships grow into exclusive and extended acts of commitment to another person, often lifelong. Heterosexual and homosexual people are equally likely to be generous, passionate, selfish, altruistic, erotic, agapic, and on and on. All of us are as likely or unlikely as one another to be moved to sexual expression of at least some of these relationships. Aside from the fact of their sexual attractions being to the opposite sex or the same sex, they share the same tensions, fulfillments, joys, and griefs, and they need equally to be self-policing—no poaching, no use of power or psychological domination, no physical or emotional abuse, no giving in to attraction to children or minors.[5]

If it is true that we become the people we are through the choices we make, then we do so against the background of belief, in the Christian tradition, that we are created in the image and likeness of God. "People as they are" are people who are growing into the image and likeness of God the more they live their lives mirroring the generous love of the creator God and the utter gift of self that this God demonstrated in becoming human in Jesus Christ. Whatever the author of the Book of Genesis imagined when God is made to say, "let us make human being in our image and likeness" (Gen 1:26), it evidently does not refer to our animal nature but rather to the surplus that makes us human because we somehow mirror the divine. Indeed for Christians it is particularly complicated since it is in Jesus Christ that Christians first come to know God. But perhaps we can circumvent a lot of complex theological argument, while remaining true to the message of Scripture, by saying that human beings are created to love in the image of the God who creates out of love and to love in the manner of Jesus Christ, who gave himself up to the God of love out of love for others, even in the pain, suffering, and ambiguity that characterized the manner of his death. All human beings are created to love in the manner that Jesus Christ exemplified, and Christians are aware—through fortunate historical accident—of the nature and manner of this Christ who is the God of love and the love of God in history.

None of this is about sex. Love is much more all-embracing and complex than sex. The sexual instinct is something that human beings share with other creatures. But because we are human beings, the sexual act is transformed into an act of love. Procreation may but does not have to be the intention of the sexual act. Pleasure is intrinsic to the sexual act. But of itself sex exists in a human context neither solely for procreation nor pleasure but rather for the expression of love between two people. Sexual activity for the purpose of procreation may well be abusive and can sometimes be violent rape. Sexual activity solely for the purpose of pleasure can also be abusive and is frequently selfish, though there are times when it is legitimate giving and taking of pleasure. However, sexual relations are most fully human when they take place as part of a faithful, loving relationship, whether or not procreation is the intention. It is love, not the possibility of procreation or the likelihood of pleasure, that sanctifies the animal act of sex and makes it human, that is, makes it a reflection of the love of the God in whose image we are made.

If civil marriage is the ratification of a legal contract between two people, sacramental marriage is the recognition that the two people whose marriage is being celebrated truly reflect the love of God in the world. That Catholic marriage is not intrinsically about procreation but rather about love and faithfulness is apparent in the church's contentment with sanctifying marriage between older couples who cannot conceive or between couples one of whom is infertile. That it must have a sexual dimension is evident from the church's traditional insistence that a marriage is not complete until it is "consummated" and its refusal to marry a couple if the male partner is impotent. Putting these facts together, it would seem that for a marriage to be a sign or sacrament of the love of God, it must have a sexual dimension but need not be open to procreation. If marriage between an elderly heterosexual couple can be a sacrament of the love of God, then it is hard to explain why marriage between a homosexual couple cannot—unless we link marriage more to the animal act than to the love that transforms it into a human act and makes it a reflection of the divine.

While this understanding of marriage is not orthodox in one sense, in others it most certainly is. Obviously, the picture presented here does not correspond to the church's teaching on marriage, which restricts it to heterosexual couples, or to its insistence that sex is only moral when it takes place between a married heterosexual couple and when each sex act is "open" to the possibility of procreation. However, in other respects it is a high and indeed orthodox vision. It certainly conforms to Catholic teaching that sex outside of a loving and faithful relationship is not sacramental and is often sinful. It promotes sacramental marriage as the context for sexual activity that is fully human, that is, that reflects the love of God. And it subscribes to exactly the same sanctions against sinfulness in the sexual realm, whether the sin in question is abuse, adultery, or promiscuity. We are all of us, heterosexual or homosexual, sinful human beings in need of God's forgiveness, but we all have the right to move toward the love of God as fully embodied human beings, and that means that we have the right to have our sexual selves embraced within the love of God. When the church says that some of its children may not express their love bodily, it is creating a stumbling block for them on their way to holiness. Those of us who do not possess the gift of celibacy are invited to seek holiness as sexual creatures in and through the love of another human being.

The most subtle of all the temptations involved in intimate relationships is that they are just about themselves. Indeed, the biggest weakness of a romantic relationship that has become sexually active but has no commitment attached is that it becomes some form of narcissism or codependency. The church recognizes this fact in the very institution of marriage, with its public nature, and it is central to the third pillar of sacramental marriage, fruitfulness. It is a misunderstanding of fruitfulness to think that it is necessarily about children, though there is no doubt that children are the most concrete example, perhaps "the sacrament," of fruitfulness. For those who cannot or do not wish to have children, the challenge is to make the love between the couple into something with a surplus that spills over into the good of the community or, indeed, the love of the world God has given us. Christian sacramental marriage is a marvelous device for encouraging a movement outward beyond the couple to the wider world and its needs and challenges, all of which draw on love and build the capacity to love in ways that a romantic liaison alone, however genuine, can never experience.

It is considerations like this that make the church's inclination to see same-sex marriage, as well as civil unions, as threats to heterosexual marriage so difficult to understand. The sacrament of marriage is an aid to loving that goes beyond mutual satisfaction and can build a better world. Once we uncouple the idea of marriage from the injunction that all sexual expression must follow the "natural" biological processes, it becomes immediately apparent that marriage within the church is a desirable thing not only for each and every couple but for the church itself. The God who is love wills stable loving relationships, and marriage is their best defense— heterosexual or same-sex.

Moving Forward

There are at least two "next steps" for LGBTQ Catholics and their supporters in the years after the More than a Monologue conferences. The first is to promote open conversations about the challenges of being an LGBTQ Catholic, or an ally, parent, or friend, within the larger community of faith. In this respect our conferences did not succeed as well as we would have liked, because the attendance did not reflect the full breadth of church membership. This was unfortunate, particularly given the well-publicized fact that the Catholic community as a whole is more "gay-friendly" than any other American Christian group. So the biggest challenge is to figure out how to draw more widely on the Catholic community for conversations about the place of LGBTQ people in the church.

The principal experience of church for most Catholics occurs not in the widely publicized doings of bishops or the Vatican but in their regular participation in the life of the community of faith, and it for this reason that the parish is surely the best locale for continuing the conversations that began with More than a Monologue. Here is where people of any and every sexual orientation most naturally gather, for worship of God should be blind to these kinds of differentiation. Before God in Jesus Christ we are all equally members of the priesthood of all the baptized and all equally in need of God's grace to make us into less sinful and more loving members of the faith community. Any Catholic parish worthy of the name must be as welcoming to LGBTQ Catholics as it is to those who are racially or ethnically or socioeconomically different, or, in short, to the stranger in its midst.

It would be a wonderful thing for every parish to commit itself to a ceremony of renewal and welcome in which it articulates the openness that it must have to people of all varieties. It need not single out LGBTQ people any more than it need single out the divorced and remarried, but it must evidently include them. The Mass is a perfect vehicle for such an event, since it begins with a confession of our sinfulness, proceeds to listening to the word of God in Scripture, and culminates in the sacrament of unity with God and one another. Done correctly, it would also surely best be followed by some kind of social event in which people talked to one another and not just to their friends and family. If such an event were repeated annually and fortified by ongoing adult conversations about the challenges all of us face as people of faith, the vision of More than a Monologue would be well on the way to being realized.

The second step that would be enormously helpful would be for gay bishops and priests and gay and lesbian religious to come out of the closet. As long as the Roman Catholic Church remains committed to celibacy for its clergy and religious, we have an enormous resource for concretizing the teaching of the church that the homosexual individual is to be cherished as a child of God, made in the divine image. Clergy and religious with same-sex orientation are people striving to live up to their commitment to a celibate life in service of the people of God. How it would transform the face of the church into a more welcoming community, to have its ordained ministers be open about their sexual orientation, albeit in the context of celibacy! What role models of the struggle for holiness they would be to all of us, gay and straight alike! Instead, we have a church in which we know many of our clergy and religious have same-sex orientations but are required to hide their true selves. This may be "for the sake of the Gospel," but it cannot be in the spirit of the Gospel.

If this were to happen, it would not simply be a dramatic gesture. It would also be a wonderful teaching moment. It would show that while there may be a connection between ministerial priesthood and celibacy, there is no connection between sexual orientation and celibacy, and none between ministerial priesthood and heterosexuality (as if we have to be taught that!). It would be the public recognition on the part of our ordained ministers that they belong to the human race and live with the same challenges and need for love and growth as the rest of us. And it would be a much more natural way of expressing our incarnational faith, in which the enfleshment of God in Christ is at the center of our faith. In Jesus Christ we start with an embodied God. Full embodiment is open, not hidden. Coming out of the closet would be a wonderful gift to the church and, we must surely imagine, a great relief to people who feel they have to live their lives hiding their true selves from those they are called to serve.

Notes

Introduction

J. PATRICK HORNBECK II AND MICHAEL A. NORKO

1. Christine Firer Hinze and J. Patrick Hornbeck II, eds., *More than a Monologue: Sexual Diversity and the Catholic Church*, Vol. 1: *Voices of Our Times* (New York: Fordham University Press, 2014).

2. The conferences were attended by more than a thousand participants, with nearly fifty speakers in total. Descriptions of the conference series and its components and background, as well as video of most of the conference presentations, are available at http://www.morethanamonologue.org.

3. *Gaudium et Spes*, in *The Basic Sixteen Documents: Vatican Council II Constitutions, Decrees, Declarations*, ed. Austin Flannery, OP (Northport, N.Y.: Costello, 1996), no. 62, p. 240. Available online at http://www.vatican.va/archive/hist _councils/ii_vatican_council/documents/vat-ii_const_19651207_gaudium-et -spes_en.html.

4. Ibid.

5. Ibid., no. 4, p. 165.

6. Ibid., no. 62, p. 240.

7. Pope Benedict XVI, *Caritas in veritate*, http://www.vatican.va/holy_father/ benedict_xvi/encyclicals/documents/hf_ben-xvi_enc_20090629_caritas-in -veritate_en.html.

8. Suicide attempts and ideation in this population are two to three times more common than among straight peers, with very high rates of victimization (verbal abuse and physical attacks). See American Association of Suicidology, "Suicidal Behavior Among Lesbian, Gay, Bisexual, and Transgender Youth Fact Sheet," http://www.suicidology.org/c/document_library/get_file?folderId=232 &name=DLFE-334.pdf. It is also worth noting that Catholics are aware of this heightened suicide risk ratio, as well as that "seven-in-ten Catholics say that messages from America's places of worship contribute a lot (33%) or a little (37%) to higher rates of suicide among gay and lesbian youth." See Robert P. Jones and Daniel Cox, "Catholic Attitudes on Gay and Lesbian Issues: A Comprehensive Portrait from Recent Research," Public Religion Research Institute (March 22,

2011), 12, http://publicreligion.org/site/wp-content/uploads/2011/06/Catholics
-and-LGBT-Issues-Survey-Report.pdf.

9. United States Conference of Catholic Bishops, *Catholic Information Project*,
http://old.usccb.org/comm/cip.shtml#toc7.

10. United States Conference of Catholic Bishops, "Always Our Children: A
Pastoral Message to Parents of Homosexual Children and Suggestions for Pastoral Ministers" (October 1, 1997), http://old.usccb.org/laity/always.shtml.

11. Connecticut Catholic Public Affairs Conference, "Connecticut Catholic
Conference, on behalf of the Catholic bishops, clergy, religious, and laity of the
State of Connecticut, condemns today's Connecticut Supreme Court decision on
same-sex 'marriage'; calls for a 'Yes' vote on a Constitutional Convention" (October 10, 2008), http://www.ctcatholic.org/Statement-of-Bishops-on-Court-Same
-sex.php. The case was *Kerrigan v. Commissioner of Public Health*, 957 A.2d 407
(Conn 2008).

12. *Gaudium et Spes*, no. 44.

13. The study of homosexuality in premodern Christianity took a significant
step forward with the publication of John Boswell's now classic study *Christianity, Social Tolerance, and Homosexuality: Gay People in Western Europe from the
Beginning of the Christian Era to the Fourteenth Century* (Chicago: University of
Chicago Press, 1980). Responses to Boswell, both appreciative and otherwise,
are too numerous to list here, but for some recent assessments and reassess-
ments, see Matthew Kuefler, ed., *The Boswell Thesis: Essays on Christianity, Social
Tolerance, and Homosexuality* (Chicago: University of Chicago Press, 2006).

14. http://www.morethanamonologue.org.

15. Congregation for Catholic Education (CCE), "Educational Guidance in
Human Love" (November 1, 1983), no. 101, http://www.vatican.va/roman_curia/
congregations/ccatheduc/documents/rc_con_ccatheduc_doc_19831101_sexual
-education_en.html; Congregation for the Doctrine of the Faith (CDF), "Letter
to the Bishops of the Catholic Church on the Pastoral Care of Homosexual Persons" (*Homosexualitatis problema*) (October 1, 1986), http://www.vatican.va/roman
_curia/congregations/cfaith/documents/rc_con_cfaith_doc_19861001_homo-
sexual-persons_en.html; Richard McCormick, *The Critical Calling: Reflections on
Moral Dilemmas Since Vatican II* (Washington, D.C.: Georgetown University
Press, 1989), chap. 17.

16. *Toward a Quaker View of Sex: An Essay by a Group of Friends* (London:
Quaker Home Service, 1963), 26; Patricia Beattie Jung, "The Call to Wed: A
Catholic Argument for Same-Sex Marriage," *Liturgy* 20, no. 3 (2005): 31.

17. For "same-sex attraction," see, for instance, Andrew R. Baker, "Ordination
and Same-Sex Attraction," *America* (September 30, 2002), http://www.america
magazine.org/content/article.cfm?article_id=2513.

18. On the development of twentieth-century Christian discourse about homosexuality, see Mark D. Jordan, *Recruiting Young Love: How Christians Talk About Homosexuality* (Chicago: University of Chicago Press, 2011).

19. For the latter possibility, see especially Patricia Beattie Jung and Ralph F. Smith, *Heterosexism: An Ethical Challenge* (Albany, N.Y.: SUNY Press, 1993); and Marvin M. Ellison and Judith Plaskow, *Heterosexism in Contemporary World Religion: Problem and Prospect* (Cleveland, Ohio: Pilgrim, 2007).

20. Many examples of the contested use of these and other terms could be offered, but several especially stand out. On "orientation," there are differences in usage even among Vatican documents: CDF, "Declaration on Certain Questions Concerning Sexual Ethics" (*Persona humana*) (December 29, 1975), no. 8, mentions only "some kind of innate instinct or a pathological constitution judged to be incurable"; CDF, *Homosexualitatis problema*, no. 11, does use the phrase "homosexual orientation"; and CCE, "Instruction Concerning the Criteria for the Discernment of Vocations with Regard to Persons with Homosexual Tendencies in View of Their Admission to the Seminary and to Holy Orders" (November 4, 2005), no. 2, speaks of "deep-seated homosexual *tendencies*," emphasis in the original. This last document also puts in scare quotes the phrase " 'gay culture,' " the promotion of which disqualifies a man from entering the seminary or taking holy orders (no. 2). Scare quotes are also often used for the verb *to marry* and the noun *marriage* in many church documents. For instance, the U.S. bishops teach in their 2009 pastoral "Marriage: Love and Life in the Divine Plan" that "One of the most troubling developments in contemporary culture is the proposition that persons of the same sex can 'marry' " (22). Finally, a number of so-called new natural lawyers have recently taken the position that the word "intercourse" should be reserved for vaginal heterosexual intercourse, in the absence of which they believe "no real unity has been effected" between persons having sex; all other activities, these writers strongly imply, fall into the category of "sodomitical acts." See, for instance, Patrick Lee and Robert P. George, *Body-Self Dualism in Contemporary Ethics and Politics* (Cambridge: Cambridge University Press, 2007), 194–195.

21. The phrase first appears in CDF, *Homosexualitatis problema*, no. 3, and is cited in most related Vatican and U.S. bishops' documents; the earlier document *Persona humana* declared that "homosexual acts are intrinsically disordered" (no. 8). For critiques of this language, see, among many others, Bruce Williams, "Homosexuality: The New Vatican Statement," *Theological Studies* 48 (1987): 263–265; many of the essays in Jeannine Gramick and Pat Furey, eds., *The Vatican and Homosexuality: Reactions to the "Letter to the Bishops of the Catholic Church on the Pastoral Care of Homosexual Persons"* (New York: Crossroad, 1988); and more recently Margaret Farley, *Just Love: A Framework for Christian Sexual Ethics* (New York: Continuum, 2006).

22. This paragraph does not claim to offer an exhaustive list of church documents about homosexuality and same-sex marriage. Indeed, in addition to Vatican and U.S. bishops' conference documents, several early texts issued by a number of episcopal conferences around the world contained somewhat less condemnatory stances on homosexuality. See, for instance, Netherlands Catholic Council for Church and Society, *Homosexual People in Society* (1979); England and Wales Catholic Social Welfare Commission, *An Introduction to the Pastoral Care of Homosexual People* (1979); and Washington State Catholic Conference, *Prejudice Against Homosexuals and the Ministry of the Church* (1983), all cited in Gramick and Furey, introduction to *The Vatican and Homosexuality*, xiv–xvi.

23. The CDF documents are *Persona humana*, *Homosexualitatis problema*, "Some Considerations Concerning the Response to Legislative Proposals on the Non-Discrimination of Homosexual Persons" (June 24, 1992), and "Considerations Regarding Proposals to Give Legal Recognition to Unions Between Homosexual Persons" (June 3, 2003). The CCE documents are "Educational Guidance" and "Instruction Concerning the Criteria," and the Pontifical Council for the Family document is "Family, Marriage and 'De Facto' Unions" (July 26, 2000). The description of the CDF's mission appears on its webpage: http://www.doctrinafidei.va/documents/rc_con_cfaith_pro_14071997_en.html.

24. These three documents are "Always Our Children: A Pastoral Message to Parents of Homosexual Children and Suggestions for Pastoral Ministers" (October 1, 1997), "Ministry to Persons with a Homosexual Inclination: Guidelines for Pastoral Care" (November 14, 2006), and "Marriage: Love and Life in the Divine Plan." "Always Our Children" was later amended "in consultation with the [Vatican] Congregation for the Doctrine of the Faith" and reissued on June 26, 2008. See "U.S. Bishops' Committee on Marriage and Family Modifies, Reissues 'Always Our Children: A Pastoral Message to Parents of Homosexual Children and Suggestions for Pastoral Ministers,'" *Origins* 28, no. 7 (July 2, 1998).

25. John McNeill, "The Christian Male Homosexual," *Homiletic and Pastoral Review* 70 (1970): 831. McNeill later developed his reflections in his now classic work *The Church and the Homosexual* (Kansas City, Kan.: Sheed, Andrews, and McMeel, 1976).

26. Charles Curran, "Dialogue with the Homophile Movement: The Morality of Homosexuality," in *Catholic Moral Theology in Dialogue* (Notre Dame, Ind.: Fides, 1972), 196, 216–217.

27. CDF, *Persona humana*, no. 8.

28. David Hollenbach, *The Common Good and Christian Ethics* (Cambridge: Cambridge University Press, 2002), 138. We are grateful to Charles Camosy for this reference.

29. See, for instance, Mark Jordan, *The Silence of Sodom: Homosexuality in Modern Catholicism* (Chicago: University of Chicago Press, 2000).

30. Ibid., and "Talking About Homosexuality by the (Church) Rules," Chapter 2 in this volume; James P. Hanigan, *Homosexuality: The Test Case for Christian Sexual Ethics* (New York: Paulist Press, 1988); and Anthony E. Giampietro, "Marriage and the Public Good," *Christian Bioethics* 13 (2007): 221.

31. Jung and Smith, *Heterosexism*, 23–30.

32. Andrew Sullivan, *Virtually Normal: An Argument About Homosexuality* (New York: Alfred A. Knopf, 1995), 95.

33. For one such bibliography of works published through 2003, see James F. Keenan, "The Open Debate: Moral Theology and the Lives of Gay and Lesbian Persons," *Theological Studies* 64 (2003): 127–150.

34. For the "Theology of the Body," see especially John Paul II, *The Theology of the Body: Human Love in the Divine Plan* (Boston: Pauline Books, 1997). Influential commentators have been Christopher West and George Weigel, *Theology of the Body Explained: A Commentary on John Paul II's "Gospel of the Body"* (Boston: Pauline Books, 2003); and Christopher West, *Good News about Sex and Marriage* (Cincinnati: Servant Books, 2004).

35. David Matzko McCarthy, "Homosexuality and the Practices of Marriage," *Modern Theology* 13, no. 3 (1997): 382.

36. Todd A. Salzman and Michael G. Lawler, "Catholic Sexual Ethics: Complementarity and the Truly Human," *Theological Studies* 67 (2006): 629.

37. Patrick Lee and Robert P. George, "What Male-Female Complementarity Makes Possible: Marriage as a Two-in-One-Flesh Union," *Theological Studies* 69 (2008): 641–662. On "intercourse," see n. 20 above.

38. Salzman and Lawler, "Catholic Sexual Ethics," 646; Lee and George, "Male-Female Complementarity," 655.

39. A number of social scientific and practical theological studies have sought to ask self-identified gay and lesbian Christians and Catholics about their perspectives on sexual diversity. For some such research, see Andrew K. T. Yip, "Dare to Differ: Gay and Lesbian Catholics' Assessment of Official Catholic Positions on Homosexuality," *Sociology of Religion* 58 (1997): 165–180; and many of Yip's other publications. Various forms of ethnographic analysis have also sought to trace the dynamics of LGBTQ persons' belonging within Catholic communities: see, for instance, several of the essays collected in Scott Thumma and Edward R. Gray, eds., *Gay Religion* (Walnut Creek, Calif.: AltaMira, 2005); and Donal Godfrey, *Gays and Grays: The Story of the Inclusion of the Gay Community at Most Holy Redeemer Parish in San Francisco* (Lanham, Md.: Lexington, 2007).

40. David Matzko McCarthy, "The Relationship of Bodies: A Nuptial Hermeneutic of Same-Sex Unions," *Theology and Sexuality* 8 (1998): 97; emphasis in the original.

41. Robert P. George, "What Marriage Is—and What It Isn't," *First Things* 195 (2009): 36.

42. See, for instance, CDF, "Considerations Regarding Proposals," esp. nos. 4–9; USCCB, "Marriage: Love and Life in the Divine Plan"; Giampietro, "Marriage and the Public Good."

43. See Salzman and Lawler, "Catholic Sexual Ethics"; and *The Sexual Person: Toward a Renewed Catholic Anthropology* (Washington: Georgetown University Press, 2008); Jung, "Call to Wed"; Stephen Pope, "The Magisterium's Arguments Against 'Same-Sex Marriage': An Ethical Analysis and Critique," *Theological Studies* 65 (2004): 530–565; and Francis DeBernardo, *Marriage Equality: A Positive Catholic Approach* (Mt. Rainier, Md.: New Ways Ministry, 2011).

44. See, for instance, "Statement of the Holy See Delegation at the 63rd Session of the General Assembly of the United Nations on the Declaration on Human Rights, Sexual Orientation and Gender Identity" (December 18, 2008), http://www.vatican.va/roman_curia/secretariat_state/2008/documents/rc_seg -st_20081218_statement-sexual-orientation_en.html.

45. While this and the following paragraphs deal specifically with the ministry of gay priests, Catholic ministry to LGBT persons remains controversial as well. See, for instance, Brian Roewe, "Gay Ministry Group Refuses to Sign Oath," *National Catholic Reporter* (June 25, 2012).

46. Jordan, *Silence of Sodom*, 8.

47. For the quotation, see n. 23 above. Given that the Roman Catholic Church does not ordain women to the diaconate, priesthood, or episcopacy, few Catholic conversations about sexual diversity among church ministers have explicitly involved lesbians. Some writers, such as Jordan, have (e.g., in *Silence of Sodom*) intentionally focused only on male-male homosexuality, since they see it as most central to the maintenance of systems of ecclesiastical power. Jeannine Gramick's essay in this volume (Chapter 3) amalgamates and expands upon the limited existing research on lesbian nuns.

48. For instance, the Catholic League for Religious and Civil Rights, in an advertisement in the *New York Times* on June 7, 2006, argued that most victims of clerical sexual abuse were "post-pubescent" young adult males. Catholic League president Bill Donohue was quoted by Fox News as saying that "Too many sexually active gays have been in the priesthood, and it's about time they were routed out." See *National Catholic Reporter*, "Spin Without End in Abuse Scandal" (June 16, 2006), http://natcath.org/NCR_Online/archives2/2006b/ 061606/061606w.htm.

49. On this point, see especially Patricia Beattie Jung, "Sexual Diversity and Ordained Ministry," *Union Seminary Quarterly Review* 57, no. 1–2 (2003): 67–87.

50. Ibid., 77.

51. See Baker, "Ordination and Same-Sex Attraction," emphasis in the original.

52. Thomas Gumbleton, "Yes, Gay Men Should Be Ordained," *America* (September 30, 2002), http://www.americamagazine.org/content/article.cfm?article_id=2508.

53. Dugan McGinley, *Acts of Faith, Acts of Love: Gay Catholic Autobiographies as Sacred Texts* (New York: Continuum, 2004), 99.

54. Jeffrey J. Kripal, "Heroic Heretical Heterosexuality," *Crosscurrents* (Fall 2004): 89.

55. Mary Hunt, "Duplicity Writ Large: A Response to *The Silence of Sodom*," *Theology and Sexuality* 9, no. 1 (2002): 13–14.

56. James A. Coriden, "The Canonical Doctrine of Reception," http://www.arcc-catholic-rights.net/doctrine_of_reception.htm.

57. Mark Massa, "Frederick R. McManus, *Worship*, and the Reception of Vatican II in the United States," *Worship* 81, no. 2 (2007): 121–141. In illustrating the principle of reception, Massa notes that within five years of the Council, more than 85 percent of practicing Catholics preferred the new liturgy to the former Roman Missal. This reception was the "mirror image" of the "non-reception" of the condemnation of artificial birth control in the 1968 encyclical *Humanae Vitae* (122–123). On the latter point, a 2012 Gallup poll found that 82 percent of Catholics perceived birth control as morally acceptable: http://www.gallup.com/poll/154799/americans-including-catholics-say-birth-control-morally.aspx.

58. Jean-Marie Tillard, "Reception-Communion," *One in Christ* 28, no. 4 (1992): 307.

59. *Lumen Gentium* (Dogmatic Constitution on the Church), no. 35, http://www.vatican.va/archive/hist_councils/ii_vatican_council/documents/vat-ii_const_19641121_lumen-gentium_en.html.

60. Tillard, "Reception-Communion," 319.

61. McGinley, *Acts of Faith, Acts of Love*.

62. Pew Forum on Religion and Public Life, *U.S. Religious Landscape Survey* (2008), 92, http://religions.pewforum.org/reports/#.

63. Pew Forum on Religion and Public Life, "'Nones' on the Rise: One-in-Five Adults Have No Religious Affiliation," 70, http://www.pewforum.org/uploaded Files/Topics/Religious_Affiliation/Unaffiliated/NonesOnTheRise-full.pdf.

64. Public Religion Research Institute, "Catholic Attitudes on Gay and Lesbian Issues," appendix B.

65. Lydia Saad, "Americans' Acceptance of Gay Relations Crosses 50% Threshold," http://www.gallup.com/poll/135764/Americans-Acceptance-Gay-Relations-Crosses-Threshold.aspx.

66. Public Religion Research Institute, "Roman Catholics and LGBT Justice Issues" (August 2008), 6, http://www.publicreligion.org. (This document is no longer available at this website but can be obtained from the editors.)

67. Ibid., 8.

68. ABC News: "Support for Gay Marriage Reaches a Milestone," http://abc news.go.com/Politics/support-gay-marriage-reaches-milestone-half-americans -support/story?id=13159608. Additional data from the poll was obtained from Gary Langer of Langer Associates, which conducted the poll. http://blog.fairfield .edu/morethanamonologue/?page_id=84.

69. ABC News/*Washington Post* poll: "Gay Marriage," http://abcnews.go.com/ images/Politics/1121a6%20Gay%20Marriage.pdf.

70. Public Religion Research Institute, "Religion News Survey, March 2012," http://publicreligion.org/research/2012/05/research-note-evolution-of-american -opinion-on-same-sex-marriage/.

71. Pew Forum on Religion and Public Life, " 'Nones' on the Rise," 70.

72. *Washington Post*/ABC Poll March 2013, "Same-Sex Marriage," http:// www.washingtonpost.com/page/2010-2019/WashingtonPost/2013/03/18 /National-Politics/Polling/question_10009.xml?uuid=qPNlgI_1EeKRc3 -Hzac7SQ#.

73. Public Religion Research Institute, "Catholic Attitudes on Gay and Lesbian Issues," 17.

74. Public Religion Research Institute, "Roman Catholics and LGBT Justice Issues," 9.

75. Center for American Values, *American Values Survey* (2006), 24, http:// media.pfaw.org/pdf/cav/AVSReport.pdf.

76. Public Religion Research Institute, "Catholic Attitudes on Gay and Lesbian Issues," 17.

77. Ibid., 8–9.

78. Ibid., 17.

79. http://pewresearch.org/pubs/1755/poll-gay-marriage-gains-acceptance -gays-in-the-military.

80. Public Religion Research Institute, "Catholic Attitudes on Gay and Lesbian Issues," 17.

81. Ibid., 13.

82. Ibid., 12.

83. *Gaudium et Spes*, no. 44.

1. Learning to Speak

KELBY HARRISON

1. Sexual subjectivity denotes one's sense of desires, attractions, and identity— as well as the continuously developing self-regard of those aspects of self. Most often this sexual subjectivity is internalized through social and cultural messaging and often has aspects that remain unconscious and seem natural although they are in fact highly scripted—particularly the emotive regard of self and the

desires and attractions that are self-experienced. Normative claims of sexual "shoulds" and "should nots" often leave lasting emotional impact.

2. My insertion of a "/" between LGBT and Q is intentional and meant to represent the current intellectual and cultural debates that live between the social understanding of lesbian, gay, bisexual, and transgender identities as fairly stable identifiers of different social locations and minority perspectives and the multiple understandings of queer as a sexual identity, as a refusal to employ a sexual identity, and as a community unifier of LGBT persons.

3. For example, in 2002, the Vatican instructed all bishops of the Roman Catholic Church that they should refuse to alter the gender of any individual in official church records. The Vatican determined that gender reassignment surgery only superficially (i.e., physically) changes the gender of an individual; the soul of the individual remains unchanged. Members of the transgender community have declared that this renders them nonexistent in the eyes of the church. The instruction in question was written in 2000 by the Congregation of the Doctrine of the Faith and sent *sub secretum* (under secrecy) to papal representatives in each country and then sent to the bishops in 2002. John Norton, *Catholic News Source*, http://ai.eecs.umich.edu/people/conway/TS/CatholicTSDe cision.html. The Metropolitan Community Church has made a formal response by transgendered people and on behalf of them, http://groups.yahoo.com/group/ transgendernews/message/2218. An additional resource on transgender theology is Justin Edward Tanis, *Trans-Gendered: Theology, Ministry, and Communities of Faith* (Cleveland: Pilgrim Press, 2003).

4. By "new" discourse, I am referring to one of the more contemporary versions of articulating sexual identity. In practical terms, in contemporary society this often means identities such as "lesbian," "gay," "bisexual," or even "BDSM" (bondage, discipline, sadism, masochism). The church, and religion more broadly, has had a strong influence in determining the contours of what it means to be a heterosexual, giving it moral priority and authority. To seek both the good and also an authentic expression of self—when it is clear that self is something other than heterosexual—creates a conundrum of discursive adaptation. Namely, the church provides one trajectory of what sexual morality means, and the newly defined sexual identities that are no more than 150 years old must find new ways of articulating what sexual morality means within new confines of identity commitments. This attempt to express and define oneself as a moral agent, though failing by one of the major measurers of moral value, leaves the individual both competing with the church and in opposition to it. This internal struggle is often the source of great distress.

5. The word "heterosexual" made its public debut in Germany in 1880 in a work defending homosexuality. In 1892 it appeared for the first time in the United States in an article by Chicagoan Dr. James G. Kiernan. Kiernan origi-

nally used the term to mean a kind of "psychical hermaphroditism": a mental condition where a patient exhibited both male erotic attractions to females and female erotic attractions to males (what we would now think of as bisexuality). After a bit of time and some debate, the word settled into its modern-day meaning of opposite-sex sexual desire. Jonathan Katz, *The Invention of Heterosexuality* (Chicago: University of Chicago Press, 2007), 22; Anne Fausto-Sterling, "Dueling Dualisms," in *Gender, Sex and Sexuality*, ed. Abby Ferber et al. (New York: Oxford University Press, 2009), 13.

6. The word "homosexuality" made its first public appearance in Germany in 1869 in a pamphlet against antisodomy laws published anonymously by Karl-Maria Kerbeny. Fausto-Sterling, "Dueling Dualisms," 13. Historians of sexual identity are quick to note that the identity of homosexuality was invented *before* the identity of heterosexuality. Prior to the late 1800s, the dominant thought surrounding sexual behavior privileged reproductive behavior as moral, with all other types of behavior as immoral. After the invention of homosexuality as an identity and the significant efforts of sexology to understand the contours of sexuality, opposite-sex sexual desire that privileged—but did not exclusively expect—procreation became the definition of natural sexual development. In addition, the types of persons who developed these opposite-sex sexual urges began to be understood as the healthiest of citizens, those who are natural and worthy of moral and psychological respect. See Katz, *The Invention of Heterosexuality*; Michel Foucault, *The History of Sexuality*, vol. 1, trans. Robert Hurley (New York: Vintage, 1990).

7. The term "queer" can be employed in contemporary sexual identity discourse in at least four disparate ways: (1) as a political umbrella term that covers lesbian, gay, bisexual, and sometimes BDSM sexual identities; (2) as a term that destabilizes the binary of straight or gay in one's sexual location; (3) as a term that refuses lesbian, gay, and bisexual identity markers; and (4) as a reference to an academic notion of "queer" that is established by "queer theory"—an exploration of sexual identity that seeks to rupture the usual categories of sexuality.

8. Take, for example, the 1968 encyclical *Humanae Vitae*, which prohibits all forms of artificial birth control, a teaching that is sometimes cited as being followed by as few as 2 percent of faithful Catholics. See Paul VI, encyclical letter, *Humanae Vitae*, A.A.S. 60 (1968): 481–503. According to a 2011 study by the Guttmacher Institute, a sexual and reproductive health nonprofit, 98 percent of Catholic women, including married women, have used some form of birth control other than natural family planning. http://www.guttmacher.org/media/in thenews/2012/02/15/index.html.

9. "Post-Catholic" is a term gaining popularity (a quick Google search on "post-Catholic" will yield hits to numerous blog projects) in describing a religious location that was formulated in childhood through the cultural or familial influ-

ence of Catholicism yet has moved forward from those Catholic roots while yet retaining the importance of that history and religious-spiritual formation. I identify as "post-Catholic."

10. This is an abstract articulation of LGBT subjectivity under Catholic influence. But this abstraction derives from my own soul, my own experience, my own pain of feeling outside a sacred system—rejected by default—rather than feeling inside, spoken to, ministered to. In this attempt to use twentieth-century postmodern thinking to articulate this process of subjectification, I hope that others will recognize their own experience and struggles. Like many LGBT/Q people, I have gone through—and still go through—the daily recognition that religion is too often on the side of the oppressor. Alongside that recognition is the dual self-deception that I do not need to experience that oppression if I walk away from the church and that I do not need the church. But I do. We all do—at least insofar as a pro-LGBT Catholic Church will make for more thoroughly pro-LGBT global cultures.

11. Michel Foucault, *The History of Sexuality*, vol. 1, 17.

12. Ibid., 33.

13. Ibid.

14. Michel Foucault, *Power/Knowledge*, ed. Colin Gordon (New York: Vintage, 1980), 131.

15. Michel Foucault, "Truth and Power," in *Power*, ed. J. Fabion, trans. R. Hurley (New York City: The New Press, 2001), 73.

16. Foucault, *Power/Knowledge*, 119.

17. Cited from "Sexuality and Power," in Mark Jordan, *The Ethics of Sex* (Malden, Mass.: Blackwell, 2002), 136.

18. Foucault, "Truth and Power," 111–133.

19. Michel Foucault, *Discipline and Punish*, trans. Alan Sheridan (New York: Vintage, 1995), 136.

20. Ibid., 136–137.

21. Ibid., 138.

22. Ibid., 187.

23. For example, this internalization becomes readily visible in the noticeable moment of humorous mockery that occurs when the words "queerly forward" or even just "forward" are substituted in giving physical directions to an LGBT/Q person to "go straight."

24. Congregation for the Doctrine of the Faith, "On the Pastoral Care of Homosexual Persons" (October 1, 1986), no. 10, http://www.vatican.va/roman _curia/congregations/cfaith/documents/rc_con_cfaith_doc_19861001_homo sexual-persons_en.html.

25. United States Conference of Catholic Bishops, "Ministry to Persons with a Homosexual Inclination: Guidelines for Pastoral Care" (November 14, 2006),

http://www.usccb.org/issues-and-action/human-life-and-dignity/homosexuality
/upload/minstry-persons-homosexual-inclination-2006.pdf.

26. Sara Ahmed, *Queer Phenomenology: Orientations, Objects, Others* (Durham, N.C.: Duke University Press, 2006), 67.

27. Ibid., 91. Emphasis in the original.

28. Ibid., 100.

29. Ibid., 67, citing Fabio Cleto, "Introduction: Queering the Camp," in *Camp: Queer Aesthetics and the Performing Subject* (Ann Arbor: University of Michigan Press, 1999), 13.

30. Ibid., 78.

31. Charles Taylor, *Sources of the Self: The Making of Modern Identity* (Cambridge, Mass.: Harvard University Press, 1992), 28.

32. Ibid., 47.

33. A healthy amount of philosophical skepticism arises for me on this point as a generalizable principle. As an ethicist, this rings true for me. I suspect there are certain other professions, as well, for whom this would not seem to be far from the literal mark of daily activity: workers for social justice and global peace, clergy. It is easy to question the obvious counterexamples (career criminals, sociopaths, etc.), but I am also wondering it if holds true for humanity as a whole, i.e., for the ordinary expanse of the population.

34. Kwame Anthony Appiah, *Ethics of Identity* (Princeton, N.J.: Princeton University Press, 2007).

35. See, for example, Jürgen Habermas, "Struggles for Recognition in a Democratic Constitutional State," in *Multiculturalism*, ed. Amy Gutmann, trans. Shierry Weber Nicholsen (Princeton, N.J.: Princeton University Press, 1994), 107–148.

2. Talking About Homosexuality by the (Church) Rules
MARK D. JORDAN

1. Mark Jordan, *The Silence of Sodom: Homosexuality in Modern Catholicism* (Chicago: University of Chicago Press, 2000), 1–2.

2. Together these authors have produced a small library of important books on Catholicism and sexuality. Readers in search of complete bibliographies can find them by the usual means. Some of the particular books I had present to mind as I wrote in the late 1990s were John McNeill, *The Church and the Homosexual* (Kansas City, Kan.: Sheed, Andrews, and McMeel, 1976); John Boswell, *Christianity, Social Tolerance, and Homosexuality: Gay People in Western Europe from the Beginning of the Christian Era to the Fourteenth Century* (Chicago: University of Chicago Press, 1980); Richard Woods, *Another Kind of Love: Homosexuality and Spirituality* (Chicago: Thomas More Press, 1977); Mary Hunt, *Fierce Tender-*

ness: A Feminist Theology of Friendship (New York: Crossroad, 1991); Elizabeth Stuart, *Just Good Friends: Towards a Lesbian and Gay Theology of Relationships* (London: Mowbray, 1995); and James Alison, *The Joy of Being Wrong: Original Sin Through Easter Eyes* (New York: Crossroad, 1998).

3. John McNeill, "The Christian Male Homosexual," *Homiletic and Pastoral Review* 70, no. 9 (June 1970): 667–677; 70, no. 10 (July 1970): 747–758; 70, no. 11 (August 1970): 828–836.

4. I put quotation marks around the word "conservative" as a triple warning about the deceptions of that word in church debates. First, self-styled "Catholic conservatives" are not in fact conserving a complex tradition. They are enforcing a thoroughly modern caricature of traditions. So, second, they are not "conservatives" in anything like Edmund Burke's sense—or even in the sense of the Oxford Movement at its most hopeful. Third, I want to resist and decry our habit of using the tags of political parties to describe church life. Or I want to note that a church faction that describes itself principally in such political terms has misunderstood what a church is called to be.

5. Michel Foucault, *Histoire de la sexualité* 1: *La volonté de savoir* (Paris: NRF/Gallimard, 1976), 113.

6. I here present a highly abbreviated version of what is a complicated and still poorly known story. I tell a slightly longer version in *Recruiting Young Love: How Christians Talk About Homosexuality* (Chicago: University of Chicago Press, 2011), 52–58. But Bailey deserves much more, from theologians as well as historians.

7. Church of England, Moral Welfare Council, *The Problem of Homosexuality: An Interim Report* (London: Church Information Board, 1954), 4, in the foreword by Michael, Bishop of St. Albans.

8. Ibid., 7.

9. Ibid., 11, italics in original.

10. Derrick Sherwin Bailey, "The Problem of Sexual Inversion," *Theology* 55, no. 380 (February 1952): 49.

11. Church of England, Moral Welfare Council, *Problem of Homosexuality*, 15, 13.

12. Ibid., 14, italics in original.

13. Congregation for the Doctrine of the Faith, *Persona humana* [Declaration on Certain Questions Pertaining to Sexual Ethics, December 29, 1975]. *Acta Apostolicae Sedis* 68 (1976): 77–96, no. 5.

14. Ibid., no. 8.

15. Ibid.

16. Ibid.: "non sine causa fieri videtur."

17. Ibid.

18. General Convention, *Journal of the General Convention of . . . the Episcopal Church, Minneapolis 1976* (New York: General Convention, 1977), C-109.

19. Congregation for the Doctrine of the Faith, *Homosexualitatis problema* [October 1, 1986], *Acta Apostolicae Sedis* 79 (1987): 543–554, nos. 3 (for the correction), 17 (for the expulsion), 9 (for the allusion to AIDS), and 10 (for understandably violent reactions).

20. Congregation for the Doctrine of the Faith, "Some Considerations Concerning the Response to Legislative Proposals on the Non-Discrimination of Homosexual Persons" (July 23, 1992), http://www.vatican.va/roman_curia/congregations/cfaith/documents/rc_con_cfaith_doc_20030731_homosexual-unions_en.html, esp. nos. 10–12. This document has not been published in *AAS*, but it is available online at the Vatican's official website, and it has appeared in various official or semiofficial publications, including *Documenti e Studi* 11: *Cura pastorale delle persone omosessuali, Lettera e commenti* (Vatican City: Libreria Editrice Vaticana, 1995). This text was released by the CDF after an earlier version, circulated to the Roman Catholic bishops, had been leaked to the press.

21. "Pastoral Message to Parents of Homosexual Children and Suggestions for Pastoral Ministers," *Origins* 27, no. 17 (October 9, 1997): 285, 287–291; "U.S. Bishops' Committee Modifies, Reissues Message," *Origins* 28, no. 7 (July 2, 1998): 97, 99–102.

22. "Notification Regarding Sister Jeannine Gramick, SSND, and Father Robert Nugent, SDS" (May 31, 1999), *Acta Apostolicae Sedis* 91 (1999): 821–825.

23. One of the most striking examples remains a comment by (then) Bishop Wilton Gregory in the midst of the heaviest reporting on pedophilia cases. Gregory spoke at a news conference during the urgent visit of American prelates to the Vatican. On April 23, 2002, the Associated Press quoted him as saying, "It is an ongoing struggle to make sure that the Catholic priesthood is not dominated by homosexual men." CNN carried a very similar quotation. In other contexts, this would have been an astonishing admission. In this context, Gregory's remark pointed to gay men as scapegoats.

24. Congregation for Catholic Education, "Instruction Concerning the Criteria for the Discernment of Vocations with Regard to Persons with Homosexual Tendencies in View of Their Admission to the Seminary and to Holy Orders" (November 4, 2005), http://www.vatican.va/roman_curia/congregations/ccatheduc/documents/rc_con_ccatheduc_doc_20051104_istruzione_en.html, no. 2.

25. Michel Foucault, *Les anormaux: Cours au Collège de France. 1974–1975*, dir. François Ewald and Alessandro Fontana, ed. Valerio Marchetti and Antonella Salomoni (Paris: Gallimard/Le Seuil, 1999), 187.

26. Ibid., 189.

27. Ibid., 157.

Response to Mark D. Jordan

ELIZABETH DREYER

1. Joan Chittister, "Lack of Women Will Irreversibly Harm the Church," National Catholic Reporter (October 16, 2011), http://ncronline.org/blogs/where-i-stand/lack-women-will-irreversibly-harm-church.

2. Michelle Dillon, "Can Catholic Women Revitalize the Church?" The Anne Drummey O'Callaghan Lecture on Women in the Church, Fairfield University, October 5, 2011.

3. Gregory Nazianzen, The Fifth Theological Oration. On the Holy Spirit, XXVI, XXVII, http://ww.newadvent.org/fathers/310231.htm.

4. Xavier J. Seubert, "The Sacramentality of Metaphors: Reflections on Homosexuality," Cross Currents 41 (1991): 52–58.

5. Jürgen Moltmann, The Spirit of Life: A Universal Affirmation, trans. Margaret Kohl (Minneapolis: Fortress, 1992), 8.

6. Revised Standard Edition (Nashville: Thomas Nelson, Inc., 1972).

7. For specific biblical references to these terms, see Luke Timothy Johnson, Religious Experience in Earliest Christianity (Minneapolis: Fortress, 1998), 6n12.

8. Bernard Loomer, "Two Kinds of Power," Process Studies 6 (1976): 5–32.

3. Lesbian Nuns: A Gift to the Church

JEANNINE GRAMICK

1. For a discussion of gender differences, including the numbers of gay priests and brothers compared to the numbers of lesbian sisters, see Jeannine Gramick, "Lesbian Nuns: Identity, Affirmation, and Gender Differences," in Homosexuality in the Priesthood and Religious Life, ed. Jeannine Gramick (New York: Crossroad, 1989), 219–236.

2. Judith Brown, Immodest Acts: The Life of a Lesbian Nun in Renaissance Italy (New York: Oxford University Press, 1986).

3. Frederika Randall, "Divine Visions, Diabolical Obsessions," New York Times (January 19, 1986).

4. Rosemary Curb and Nancy Manahan, eds., Lesbian Nuns: Breaking Silence (Tallahassee, Fla.: Naiad, 1985).

5. Joan Turner Beifuss, "Lesbian Silence-Breaking Makes Little Noise," National Catholic Reporter (May 17, 1985); reprinted in Bondings (Spring-Summer 1985): 7. Judith [no last name given], "Lesbian Nuns: Another Perspective," Sisters Today 59, no. 6 (February 1988): 344–348.

6. Gramick, ed., Homosexuality in the Priesthood and Religious Life.

7. Mary Louise St. John OSB, "Patient Weavers," in Gramick, ed., Homosexuality in the Priesthood and Religious Life, 113.

8. Sister Sharon Marie, "Recommended Reading," *Womanjourney Weavings* 1 (1991): 4.

9. Jeannine Gramick, "Our Lesbian Sisters," *PROBE* 7, no. 6 (March 1978): 5–6; "Gay and Celibate," *PROBE* 9, no. 4 (January 1980): 5–7.

10. Jeannine Gramick, "Cracks in the Convent Closets," *News/Views*, National Sisters Vocation Conference (November-December 1982): 1–7.

11. Jeannine Gramick, "Homosexuality, Religious Life, and Vocation Ministry," *Horizon* 14, no. 2 (Winter 1989): 18–21.

12. To connect with the listserv, e-mail lesters@iname.com.

13. I wish to acknowledge and thank these sisters and the countless lesbian sisters who have provided information and inspiration to me for more than thirty years.

14. Sister Mary, "The Lost Coin," in Gramick, ed., *Homosexuality in the Priesthood and Religious Life*, 59–70.

15. Ibid., 63.

16. Ibid.

17. Ibid., 64–65.

18. Cynthia Nordone, "Organization Surveys Lesbian Sisters," *Womanjourney Weavings* 10, no. 1 (2000): 1, 4.

19. Janet Rozzano RSM, *Out of Silence God Has Called Me: A Lesbian Religious Reflects on Her Experience* (Mt. Rainier, Md.: New Ways Ministry, 2008).

20. Gertrud Ayerle MMS, "Ritual: Coming Out–Coming Home," *Womanjourney Weavings* 6 (1996): 3–4.

21. Linda Taylor CSJ, "Prayers from the Closet," *Womanjourney Weavings* 2 (1992): 2, 4.

22. Mary Kay Hunyady, "The Navigation of Sexual Orientation Issues by Roman Catholic Women in Religious Orders: A Study of the Lives and Psychologies of Lesbian Nuns" (PsyD. diss., the Wright Institute, 2004), chap. 6, http://il.pro quest.com/products_umi/dissertations/disexpress.shtml, no. 3156914.

23. Congregation for Catholic Education, "Instruction for the Criteria for the Discernment of Vocations with Regard to Persons with Homosexual Tendencies in View of Their Admission to the Seminary and to Holy Orders" (November 4, 2005), http://www.vatican.va/roman_curia/congregations/ccatheduc/docu ments/rc_con_ccatheduc_doc_20051104_istruzione_en.html.

24. The Vatican's Congregation for the Doctrine of the Faith issued the results of its "Doctrinal Assessment" of the Leadership Conference of Women Religious on April 18, 2012. http://www.usccb.org/loader.cfm?csModule=security/getfile &pageid=55544. An accompanying statement by Cardinal William Levada, Prefect of the Congregation for the Doctrine of the Faith, is available at http://www.usccb.org/loader.cfm?csModule=security/getfile&pageid=55673.

25. Mary Ann Zollmann BVM, "Tending the Holy Through the Power of Sisterhood," Presidential Address, Leadership Conference of Women Religious Assembly (August 22, 2003).

The Prophetic Life of Lesbian Nuns: A Response to Jeannine Gramick

JAMIE MANSON

1. Christian de la Huerta, *Coming Out Spiritually: The Next Step* (New York: Tarcher/Putnam, 1999), 3.

2. Patrick S. Cheng, *Radical Love: An Introduction to Queer Theology* (New York: Church Publishing, 2011), 7.

3. See Margaret Farley, *Just Love: A Framework for Christian Sexual Ethics* (Continuum, 2006), 24–25, for a discussion of major changes in North American and Western European sexual practices and beliefs. Note her discussion of Edward Shorter's *The Making of the Modern Family*, which traces how families have "lost interest in traditional kinship, generational, and wider community interaction" and instead prefer "romantic love . . . and the close intimacy of the nuclear family." Note also her section on John D'Emilio and Estelle B. Freedman's *Intimate Matters*, in which the authors discuss how, in contemporary sexuality and marriage, "sexual relations are expected to provide personal identity and individual happiness, apart from reproduction" (xi–xii).

4. Nicole Sotelo, "Knights, Minnesota Archbishop Endanger Church Neutrality," *National Catholic Reporter* (September 30, 2010).

5. Alan Cooperman, "Communion Denied to Activists," *Washington Post* (June 5, 2006).

6. Tom Roberts, "Catholic Services in Adoptions Ends in Illinois," *National Catholic Reporter* (November 22, 2011).

7. Congregation for the Doctrine of the Faith, "Doctrinal Assessment for the Leadership Conference of Women Religious" (April 18, 2012), http://www.usccb .org/loader.cfm?csModule=security/getfile&pageid=55544.

8. Leadership Conference of Women Religious, "Leadership Conference of Women Religious Decides Next Steps in Responding to CDF Report" (August 10, 2012), https://lcwr.org/sites/default/files/media/files/lcwr_2012_assembly_press _releases_-_8-10-12.pdf.

9. Sandra Schneiders, "Religious Life as Prophetic Life Form," *National Catholic Reporter* (January 4, 2010), http://ncronline.org/news/women/religious-life -prophetic-life-form.

4. Seminary, Priesthood, and the Vatican's Homosexual Dilemma

GERARD JACOBITZ

1. That the great majority of priest sexual-abuse cases in the United States has involved homosexual abuse of adolescent males has led some conservative voices in the church to blame a small percentage of priests acting inappropriately *because* they are homosexual. More liberal voices attribute the high number of homosexual cases to a small percentage of a much larger minority (or even majority) of homosexual priests. See Peter Steinfels, *A People Adrift: The Crisis of the Roman Catholic Church in America* (New York: Simon and Schuster, 2003), 274–275, 323–325, on homosexuality and the priest sexual-abuse scandal, and 40–67 on the polarizing effect the scandal has had on the American church.

2. Richard McBrien brought the issue to wide attention in a 1987 *Commonweal* article, "Homosexuality and the Priesthood: Questions We Can't Keep in the Closet" (June 19, 1987): 380–383, in which he questioned whether the growing percentage of homosexual candidates for the Catholic priesthood has become so pronounced as to discourage heterosexual candidates from applying. Donald Cozzens, in *The Changing Face of the Priesthood* (Collegeville, Minn.: Liturgical Press, 2000), 98–99, cites several studies that would suggest a percentage upward of 50 percent, with even higher percentages for religious orders, and he wonders if the priesthood is not becoming a gay profession (107–109). Peter Steinfels (*A People Adrift*, 323) reports as of 2003 that a consensus would agree with the 50 percent figure, at least among current seminarians and the recently ordained.

3. Decree on Ecumenism, *Unitatis Redintegratio*, no. 11. The quotation is from Austin Flannery, ed., *Vatican Council II: Constitutions, Decrees, Declarations* (Northport, N.Y.: Costello, 1996), 511.

4. John W. O'Malley, *What Happened at Vatican II* (Cambridge, Mass.: Harvard University Press, 2008), 47–52, 306, 307. The traditional conciliar forms of canon and anathema were replaced at Vatican II by the epideictic or panegyric exhortation, a form derived from classical humanism. This marks a radical departure from the style of previous councils.

5. Congregation for the Doctrine of the Faith (CDF), "Declaration on Certain Questions of Sexual Ethics" (*Persona Humana*, 1975), no. 8, http://www.vatican .va/roman_curia/congregations/cfaith/documents/rc_con_cfaith_doc_19751229 _persona-humana_en.html. An even earlier and more positive development of doctrine on sexual orientation on the part of the U.S. Catholic bishops is documented by Vincent J. Genovesi, *In Pursuit of Love: Catholic Morality and Human Sexuality* (Collegeville, Minn.: Liturgical Press, 1996), 255: "As early as 1973 they wrote that 'it can be said safely that [a] man or woman does not will to become homosexual. At a certain point in life, the person discovers that he is homosex-

ual and usually suffers a certain amount of trauma' (National Conference of Catholic Bishops [NCCB], *Principles to Guide Confessors in Questions of Homosexuality* [Washington: United States Catholic Conference (USCC), 1973], p. 5). In 1976 the bishops wrote: 'Some people find themselves through no fault of their own to have a homosexual orientation' (NCCB, *To Live in Christ Jesus: A Pastoral Reflection on the Moral Life* [Washington: USCC, 1976], p. 19). Finally, in 1990 they affirmed that this orientation, 'because [it is] not freely chosen, is not sinful' (NCCB, *Human Sexuality: A Catholic Perspective for Education and Lifelong Learning* [Washington: USCC, 1991], p. 55)."

6. CDF, "Letter to the Bishops of the Catholic Church on the Pastoral Care of Homosexual Persons" (1986), no. 3: "Although the particular inclination of the homosexual person is not a sin, it is a more or less strong tendency ordered toward an intrinsic moral evil; and thus the inclination itself must be seen as an objective disorder." http://www.vatican.va/roman_curia/congregations/cfaith /documents/rc_con_cfaith_doc_19861001_homosexual-persons_en.html.

7. Ibid., no. 16.

8. CDF, "Some Considerations Concerning the Response to Legislative Proposals on the Non-Discrimination of Homosexual Persons" (1992), no. 14 (see nos. 10 and 13), http://www.vatican.va/roman_curia/congregations/cfaith/docu ments/rc_con_cfaith_doc_19920724_homosexual-persons_en.html.

9. Congregation for Catholic Education (CCE), "Instruction Concerning the Criteria of Vocational Discernment Regarding Persons with Homosexual Tendencies, Considering Their Admission to Seminary and Holy Orders" (2005), http://www.vatican.va/roman_curia/congregations/ccatheduc/documents/rc _con_ccatheduc_doc_20051104_istruzione_en.html.

10. Michael Himes and Kenneth Himes, *Fullness of Faith: The Public Significance of Theology* (Mahwah, N.J.: Paulist Press, 1993), 30, with documentation at 193n4–7.

11. *Thirty-Nine Articles*, Article 9, "Of Original or Birth Sin," as quoted on the Anglican Communion website, http://www.anglicancommunion.org/resources/ acis/docs/thirty_nine_articles.cfm/.

12. H. J. Schroeder, *Canons and Decrees of the Council of Trent* (Rockford, Ill.: TAN, 1978), Fifth Session on Original Sin, no. 1, p. 21. (Again, I am following Himes and Himes, *Fullness of Faith*, 32–33.)

13. Council of Trent, Sixth Session on Justification, chapter 1 (Schroeder, *Canons and Decrees*, 30).

14. Ibid., canon 7 (Schroeder, *Canons and Decrees*, 43).

15. Council of Trent, Fifth Session on Original Sin, no. 5 (Schroeder, *Canons and Decrees*, 23).

16. Ibid. The italicized portion of the quotation refers to the biblical verse.

17. Ibid. The italicized portion of the quotation refers to the biblical verse.

18. Himes and Himes, *Fullness of Faith*, 33.

19. Servais Pinckaers, "Aquinas on the Dignity of the Human Person," in *The Pinckaers Reader: Renewing Thomistic Moral Theology*, ed. John Berkman and Craig Steven Titus (Washington, D.C.: Catholic University Press, 2005), 144–163.

20. See William Sweet, ed., *Philosophical Theory and the Universal Declaration of Human Rights* (Ottawa: University of Ottawa Press, 2003), especially the essay by Bradley Munro, "The Universal Declaration of Human Rights, Maritain, and the Universality of Human Rights," 109–126.

21. See, for example, Pastoral Constitution on the Church in the Modern World, *Gaudium et Spes*, nos. 12, 27, 29, 30, 35, 38, and 43, in Flannery, ed., *Vatican Council II*, 174–175, 192–196, 200–201, 203–204, 211–214.

22. Andrew Sullivan, *Virtually Normal: An Argument About Homosexuality* (New York: Vintage, 1996), 36–37. The Vatican's strict avoidance of the term "homosexual person" in its most recent pronouncements is certainly not without significance.

23. CDF, "Letter," no. 3, emphasis mine.

24. This is precisely the teaching of the Council of Trent's Fifth Session on Original Sin, no. 5, quoted above. The point is driven home especially well by James Alison in an essay as remarkable for its insight as for its playfulness, "Nicodemus and the Boys in the Square," in his *Faith Beyond Resentment* (New York: Crossroad, 2001), 209–235.

25. CDF, "Letter," no. 3.

26. CDF, "Declaration," no. 8.

27. APA Task Force on Appropriate Therapeutic Responses to Sexual Orientation, *Report of the Task Force on Appropriate Therapeutic Responses to Sexual Orientation* (Washington, D.C.: American Psychological Association, 2009), 83. http://www.apa.org/pi/lgbt/resources/sexual-orientation.aspx. The final tally of the vote (125 for; 4 against) was reported in the *New York Times*, "Psychologists Reject Gay 'Therapy,'" (August 5, 2009).

28. Ibid., 3.

29. Ibid., 2.

30. See the American Psychological Association's website, http://www.apa .org/about/policy/diagnoses-homosexuality.aspx.

31. See *Archives of Sexual Behavior*, "Spitzer Reassesses His 2003 Study of Reparative Therapy," letter to the editor by Robert L. Spitzer (May 24, 2012), http:// www.springerlink.com/content/0018m8113517qp1x/fulltext.pdf.

32. CDF, "Letter," no. 2.

33. See Vatican II's *Gaudium et Spes*, no. 62, on the importance of integrating scientific knowledge with theological reflection: "Let the faithful incorporate the findings of new sciences and teachings and the understanding of the most

recent discoveries into christian morality and thought, so that their practice of religion and their moral behavior may keep abreast of their acquaintance with science and of the relentless progress of technology: in this way they will succeed in evaluating and interpreting everything with an authentically christian sense of values." Flannery, ed., *Vatican Council II*, 239–240.

34. Ibid., no. 6, in which Gen 19:1–11, Lev 18:22 and 20:13, 1 Cor 6:9, Rom 1:18–32, and 1 Tim 1:10 are cited as if they refer to a modern understanding of homosexual relations. The *Catechism of the Catholic Church* (New York: Doubleday, 1995), no. 2357, cites the same passages, with the exception of Leviticus (because it prescribes the death penalty?).

35. For a concise yet thorough critique of the Vatican's use of scripture in its treatment of homosexuality, see Vincent Smiles, "The Bible and Homosexuality: A Test Case in the Proper Use of the Bible," *The Saint John's Symposium* (Faculty Journal, Collegeville, Minn.: Saint John's University), no. 18: 72–81.

36. Sullivan, *Virtually Normal*, 125.

37. CDF, "Some Considerations," no. 14.

38. See http://www.pwc.com/us/en/about-us/diversity/pwc-glbt-inclusion .jhtml.

39. One is reminded of Chesterton's quip, "Tradition means giving votes to the most obscure of all classes, our ancestors. It is the democracy of the dead." *Orthodoxy* (Garden City, N.Y.: Doubleday, 1959), 48.

40. It should be noted that in the practical application of Catholic canon law, the modern psychological concept of sexual orientation is not only assumed; it is used as a basis of canonical judgments. See Paul K. Thomas, "Gay and Lesbian Ministry During Marital Breakdown and the Annulment Process," in *A Challenge to Love: Gay and Lesbian Catholics in the Church*, ed. Robert Nugent (New York: Crossroad, 1983), 223: "In investigating the possibility of annulment, ecclesiastical courts focus directly . . . on sexual orientation rather than on overt genital behavior in itself. Wherefore, when confirmed homosexual persons attempt a heterosexual union, the canonist reflects on their *lack of necessary discretion* in failing to perceive the true dimension of marriage as adverse to their own basic orientation." When official Catholic teaching on homosexual orientation is inconsistent with itself across contexts, it should come as no surprise that it is contradicts other, more fundamental doctrines.

41. Public Religion Research Institute, http://www.publicreligion.org/re search/published/?id=509.

42. See, for example, the recent case of Vienna Cardinal Christoph Schönborn's support of a gay parish council member whose election was contested by the parish pastor. Schönborn issued a statement of support, overriding the pastor, after meeting with the young man and his partner, as reported on the *Commonweal* blog, http://www.commonwealmagazine.org/blog/?p=18270.

43. CCE, "Instruction," no. 2, quoted in Gerald D. Coleman, *Catholic Priesthood: Formation and Human Development* (Missouri: Ligouri, 2006), 58.

44. Ibid.

45. CCE, "Instruction," no. 2.

46. Ibid.

47. Donald Cozzens, "Gay Ministry at the Crossroads: The Plight of Gay Clergy in the Catholic Church," presentation for the fourth conference, "The Care of Souls: Sexual Diversity, Celibacy, and Ministry," in the series More than a Monologue: Sexual Diversity and the Catholic Church, Fairfield University, October 29, 2011. Links to this and other talks in the series are available at the conference website, http://blog.fairfield.edu/morethanamonologue/.

48. Donald Cozzens compares the current plight of gay men in the Catholic priesthood with the military's "Don't Ask, Don't Tell" policy in his More than a Monologue paper, "Gay Ministry at the Crossroads: The Plight of Gay Clergy in the Catholic Church," in *More than a Monologue*, Vol. 1: *Voices of Our Times*, ed. Christine Firer Hinze and J. Patrick Hornbeck II (New York: Fordham University Press, 2014), chap. 7.

49. Paul Stanosz, *The Struggle for Celibacy: The Culture of Catholic Seminary Life* (New York: Crossroad, 2006). Note the second bullet point on stigmatization in the APA's resolution of 2009 above. See also Paul Stanosz, "Gay Seminarians: Is the Vatican Bigoted or Prudent?" *Commonweal* 132/22 (December 16, 2005): 8–10.

50. Stanosz, *The Struggle for Celibacy*, 20.

51. Laura Smart and Daniel M. Wegner, "The Hidden Costs of Hidden Stigma," in *Social Psychology of Stigma*, ed. T. F. Heatherton and R. E. Kleck (New York: Guilford, 2003), 238–239.

52. Donald Cozzens, *Freeing Celibacy* (Collegeville, Minn.: Liturgical Press, 2006).

53. Ibid., especially chap. 2, "Celibacy as Charism," 19–29; and chap. 9, "Freeing Celibacy," 95–105.

54. John O'Malley, *What Happened at Vatican II*, 9, with reference to Murray's "This Matter of Religious Freedom," *America* 112 (January 9, 1965): 43.

55. *Gaudium et Spes*, no. 4 (Flannery, ed., *Vatican Council II*, 165).

56. On the possibility of such change in church doctrine as well as some striking historical examples, see John Noonan, *A Church That Can and Cannot Change: The Development of Catholic Moral Teaching* (Notre Dame, Ind.: University of Notre Dame Press, 2005).

5. Same-Sex Marriage, the Right to Religious and Moral Freedom, and the Catholic Church

MICHAEL JOHN PERRY

1. International Covenant on Civil and Political Rights, adopted by United Nations General Assembly 16, December 1966, Article 18, http://www2.ohchr .org/english/law/ccpr.html#art18. Emphasis added throughout.

2. Human Rights Committee, General Comment 22, Article 18 (48th session, 1993), in Compilation of General Comments and General Recommendations Adopted by Human Rights Treaty Bodies, U.N. Doc. HRI/GEN/1/Rev.1 at 35 (1994), http://www.unhchr.ch/tbs/doc.nsf/%28Symbol%29/9a30112c27d1167cc12563 ed004d8f15?Opendocument.

3. On the idea of the "transcendent," see Charles Taylor, *A Secular Age* (Cambridge, Mass.: The Belknap Press of Harvard University Press, 2007); Michael Warner, Jonathan VanAntwerpen, and Craig Calhoun, eds., *Varieties of Secularism in a Secular Age* (Cambridge, Mass.: Harvard University Press, 2010).

4. Human Rights Committee, General Comment 22, n. 1.

5. Ibid.

6. Article 7 states: "No one shall be subjected to torture or to cruel, inhuman or degrading treatment or punishment. In particular, no one shall be subjected without his free consent to medical or scientific experimentation."

7. At a conference of international law experts in Siracusa, Italy, in 1984, a set of principles on the limitations and derogation of the ICCPR were developed and then published by the UN Commission on Human Rights as the "Siracusa Principles." Article 10 of the "general interpretative principles" in Part I of the document states: "10. Whenever a limitation is required in the terms of the Covenant to be 'necessary,' this term implies that the limitation: (a) is based on one of the grounds justifying limitations recognized by the relevant article of the covenant, . . . [and] (c) pursues a legitimate aim." See UN Commission on Human Rights, *The Siracusa Principles on the Limitation and Derogation Provisions in the International Covenant on Civil and Political Rights* (September 28, 1984), E/CN.4/1985/4, http://www.unhcr.org/refworld/ docid/4672bc122.html.

8. The Siracusa Principles state: "11. In applying a limitation, a state shall use no more restrictive means than are required for the achievement of the purpose of the limitation."

9. The Siracusa Principles state: "10. Whenever a limitation is required in the terms of the Covenant to be "necessary," this term implies that the limitation: . . . (b) responds to a pressing public or social need, . . . and (d) is proportionate to that aim."

10. For the Siracusa Principles, see note 7, above.

11. The Siracusa Principles state: "27. Since public morality varies over time and from one culture to another, a state which invokes public morality as a ground for restricting human rights, while enjoying a certain margin of discretion, shall demonstrate that the limitation in question is essential to the maintenance of respect for fundamental values of the community."

12. Human Rights Committee, General Comment 22, n. 1.

13. Sarah Joseph, Jenny Schultz, and Melissa Castan, eds., *The International Covenant on Civil and Political Rights* (New York: Oxford University Press, 2004), 510.

14. James Griffin, *On Human Rights* (New York: Oxford University Press, 2008), 168.

15. Ibid., pp. 163–164 (emphasis added).

16. If you are skeptical about my "no credible argument" claim, I recommend that you read this relatively recent to-and-fro: Maggie Gallagher, "Prepared Statement of Maggie Gallagher," *Drake Law Review* 58 (2010): 889; Andrew Koppelman, "Prepared Statement of Andrew Koppelman," *Drake Law Review* 58 (2010): 905; Discussion [among Maggie Gallagher, Andrew Koppelman, and others], *Drake Law Review* 58 (2010): 913. See also Andrew M. Francis, Hugo M. Mialon, and Handie Peng, "The Effects on Same-Sex Marriage Laws on Public Health and Welfare," http://emory.academia.edu/HandiePeng/Papers/430809/The_Effects_of_Same-Sex_Marriage_Laws_on_Public_Health_and_Welfare. It bears mention here that in his letter "to Congress on Litigation Involving the Defense of Marriage Act" (February 23, 2011), U.S. Attorney General Eric Holder stated: "As the [U.S.] Department [of Justice] has explained in numerous filings, since the enactment of DOMA, many leading medical, psychological, and social welfare organizations have concluded, based on numerous studies, that children raised by gay and lesbian parents are as likely to be well-adjusted as children raised by heterosexual parents." http://www.justice.gov/opa/pr/2011/February/11-ag-223.html.

17. "According to the 2010 census, one-quarter of same-sex households are raising children." Kenji Yoshino, "For Obama, It's About the Children," *New York Times* (May 12, 2012). See Sabrina Tavernise, "Adoptions Rise by Same-Sex Couples, Despite Legal Barriers," *New York Times* (June 13, 2011); Frank Bruni, "2 Dads, 2 Daughters, 1 Big Day," *New York Times* (June 21, 2011).

18. In his letter to Congress (see note 16) regarding the Defense of Marriage Act, U.S. Attorney General Eric Holder stated: "The legislative record underlying DOMA's passage contains . . . numerous expressions reflecting moral disapproval of gays and lesbians and their intimate and family relationships." In a note attached to that sentence—note vii—the Letter states:

> *See, e.g.,* H.R. Rep. at 15–16 (judgment [opposing same-sex marriage] entails both moral disapproval of homosexuality and a moral conviction that hetero-

sexuality better comports with traditional (especially Judeo-Christian) morality"); *id.* at 16 (same-sex marriage "legitimates a public union, a legal status that
most people . . . feel ought to be illegitimate" and "put[s] a stamp of approval . . .
on a union that many people . . . think is immoral"); *id.* at 15 ("Civil laws that
permit only heterosexual marriage reflect and honor a collective moral judgment
about human sexuality"); *id.* (reasons behind heterosexual marriage—
procreation and child-rearing—are "in accord with nature and hence have a
moral component"); *id.* at 31 (favorably citing the holding [of the U.S. Supreme
Court in *Bowers v. Hardwick*, 478 U.S. 186 (1986)] that an "anti-sodomy law served
the rational purpose of expressing the presumed belief . . . that homosexual sodomy is immoral and unacceptable"); *id.* at 17 n.56 (favorably citing statement in
dissenting opinion in *Romer [v. Evans*, 517 U.S. 620 (1996)] that "[t]his Court has
no business . . . pronouncing that 'animosity' toward homosexuality is evil").

19. Congregation for the Doctrine of the Faith, *Considerations Regarding Proposals to Give Legal Recognition to Unions Between Homosexual Persons* (2003),
http://www.vatican.va/roman_curia/congregations/cfaith/documents/rc_con
_cfaith_doc_20030731_homosexual-unions_en.html.

20. So said the Rev. Ron Johnson Jr. on September 28, 2008. See Peter Slevin,
"33 Pastors Flout Tax Law with Political Sermons," *Washington Post* (September
29, 2008). See also John Frank, "Churches Speak Up on Gay Marriage," *News &
Observer* (Charlotte, N.C.) (September 18, 2011).

For many Christians, even many evangelical Christians, the belief that same-
sex sexual conduct is contrary to the will of God is no longer credible. See, e.g.,
David G. Meyers and Letha Dawson Scanzoni, *What God Has Joined Together?
A Christian Case for Gay Marriage* (New York: HarperOne, 2005). See also Brian K.
Blount, "Reading and Understanding the New Testament on Homosexuality," in
Homosexuality and Christian Community, ed. Choon-Leong Seow (Louisville, Ky.:
Westminster John Knox, 1996); Victor Paul Furnish, "The Bible and Homosexual-
ity: Reading the Texts in Context," in *Homosexuality in the Church*, ed. Jeffrey S.
Siker (Louisville, Ky.: Westminster John Knox, 1994); Daniel A. Helminiak, "The
Bible on Homosexuality: Ethically Neutral," in *Same Sex: Debating the Ethics, Sci-
ence, and Culture of Homosexuality*, ed. John Corvino (Lanham, Md.: Rowman &
Littlefield, 1999); Patricia Beattie Jung and Ralph F. Smith, "The Bible and Hetero-
sexism," in *Heterosexism: An Ethical Challenge* (Albany, N.Y.: SUNY Press, 1993), 61;
Bruce J. Malina, "The New Testament and Homosexuality," in *Sexual Diversity and
Catholicism: Toward the Development of Moral Theology*, ed. Patricia Beattie Jung and
Joseph Andrew Coray (Collegeville, Minn.: The Liturgical Press, 2001), 150;
Choon-Leong Seow, "A Heterotextual Perspective," in *Homosexuality and Christian
Community*; Jeffrey S. Siker, "Homosexual Christians, the Bible, and Gentile Inclu-
sion: Confessions of a Repenting Heterosexist," in *Homosexuality in the Church*.

I have explained elsewhere why Christians, as Christians, have good reason to be wary about relying on this biblically based argument as a ground for supporting the exclusion policy. See Michael J. Perry, *Under God? Religious Faith and Liberal Democracy* (Cambridge: Cambridge University Press, 2003), 55–80. Cf. Nicholas D. Kristof, "Lovers Under the Skin," *New York Times* (December 3, 2003): "A 1958 poll found that 96 percent of whites disapproved of marriages between blacks and whites. . . . In 1959 a judge justified Virginia's ban on interracial marriage by declaring that 'Almighty God . . . did not intend for the races to mix.'"

21. It is not always clear which of two different positions one is espousing when one says that X is contrary to the will of God: (1) X is contrary to the will of God and *therefore* immoral. (2) X is contrary to the will of God *because* X is immoral. According to the first position, the reason for concluding that X is immoral is theological: "X is contrary to the will of God." But according to the second position, the reason for concluding that X is immoral is unstated and not necessarily theological, even though the "therefore"—"X is immoral and therefore contrary to the will of God"—is a theological claim.

22. USCCB Administrative Committee, "Promote, Protect, Preserve Marriage: Statement on Marriage and Homosexual Unions," *Origins* 33 (2003): 257, 259. The pope and bishops also insist that all human beings, gays and lesbians no less than others, are equally beloved children of God.

23. See Leslie Woodcock Tentler, *Catholics and Contraception: An American History* (Ithaca, N.Y.: Cornell University Press, 2004).

24. USCCB Administrative Committee, "Promote, Protect, Preserve Marriage," 259. See also CDF, "Considerations Regarding Proposals to Give Legal Recognition to Unions Between Homosexual Persons."

25. See note 19, above. See David Hollenbach SJ, "Religious Freedom and Law: John Courtney Murray Today," *Journal of Moral Theology* 1 (2012): 69, 75:

> The United States Catholic Bishops have adopted particularly pointed public advocacy positions on . . . resistance to gay marriage and public acceptance of the legitimacy of same sex relationships. The Bishops' 2007 statement *Forming Consciences for Faithful Citizenship* was a formal instruction by the U.S. hierarchy covering the full range of the public dimensions of the Church's moral concerns. In this document . . . echoing the affirmation by the Catechism of the Catholic Church that homosexual acts "are contrary to the natural law" and that "under no circumstances can they be approved," the bishops oppose[d] "same-sex unions or other distortions of marriage."

26. See, e.g., Stephen J. Pope, "The Magisterium's Arguments Against 'Same-Sex Marriage': An Ethical Analysis and Critique," *Theological Studies* 65 (2004): 530; Todd A. Salzman and Michael G. Lawler, "Catholic Sexual Ethics: Comple-

mentarity and the Truly Human," *Theological Studies* 67 (2006): 625; Patrick Lee and Robert P. George, "What Male-Female Complementarity Makes Possible: Marriage as a Two-in-One-Flesh Union," *Theological Studies* 69 (2008): 641; Todd A. Salzman and Michael G. Lawler, "Truly Human Sexual Acts: A Response to Patrick Lee and Robert George," *Theological Studies* 69 (2008): 663.

Moreover, "a report by the Washington-based Public Religion Research Institute found that 74 percent of Catholics favor legal recognition for same-sex relationships, either through civil unions (31 percent) or civil marriage (43 percent). That figure is higher than the 64 percent of all Americans, 67 percent of mainline Protestants, 48 percent of black Protestants and 40 percent of evangelicals." *National Catholic Reporter* (April 1, 2011): 16. "What's more, even among Catholics who attend services weekly or more, only about one-third (31%) say there should be no legal recognition for a gay couple's relationship, a view held by just 13% of those who attend once or twice a month and 16% of those who attend less often." "New Poll: Nuance on Same-Sex Unions Drives Up Catholic Support," http://blog.faithinpubliclife.org/2011/03/new_poll_highlights_catholic_s.html.

27. Cf. *Salazar v. Buono*, 130 S.Ct. 1803, 1828 (2010) (Stevens, J., joined by Ginsburg and Sotomayor, JJ., dissenting): "The Establishment Clause, if nothing else, prohibits government from specifying details upon which men and women who believe in a benevolent, omnipotent Creator and Ruler of the world are known to differ."

28. Michael W. McConnell, "The Problem of Singling Out Religion," *DePaul Law Review* 50 (2000): 1, 44. Locke wrote: "The one only narrow way which leads to Heaven is not better known to the Magistrate than to private persons, and therefore I cannot safely take him for my Guide, who may probably be as ignorant of the way as my self, and who certainly is less concerned for my Salvation than I my self am." John Locke, *Letter Concerning Toleration* (1689), translated (from a less familiar to a more familiar English) by William Popple, http://www.constitution.org/jl/tolerati.htm, at 10.

29. "Memo to Cardinal Cushing on Contraception Legislation" (n.d., mid-1960s), http://woodstock.georgetown.edu/library/murray/1965f.htm. See also John Courtney Murray SJ, Toledo Talk, delivered in Toledo, May 5, 1967, http://woodstock.georgetown.edu/library/murray/1965f.htm. Murray's influence on Boston's archbishop, Cardinal Richard Cushing, and Cushing's influence on the repeal of the Massachusetts ban on the sale of contraceptives is discussed in Seth Meehan, "Legal Aid," *Boston College Magazine* (Spring 2011), and in Joshua J. McElwee, "A Cardinal's Role in the End of a State's Ban on Contraception," *National Catholic Reporter* (March 2–15, 2012). For the larger context within which Father Murray wrote and spoke, see Tentler, *Catholics and Contraception*. For a recent reflection on Murray's work by one of his foremost intellectual heirs, see Hollenbach, "Religious Freedom and Law."

30. See Samuel G. Freedman, "How Clergy Helped a Same-Sex Marriage Law Pass," *New York Times* (June 16, 2011); Laurie Goodstein, "Unions That Divide: Churches Split Over Gay Marriage," *New York Times* (May 13, 2012). See also William N. Eskridge Jr., "Noah's Curse: How Religion Often Conflates Status, Belief, and Conduct to Resist Antidiscrimination Norms," *Georgia Law Review* 45 (2011): 657, 707–708:

> The most contentious issue has been recognition of lesbian and gay marriages. The Roman Catholic Church considers different-sex, procreative marriage to be the centerpiece of Christian doctrine relating to sexuality, gender, and the family, and for this reason in 2003, the Vatican's Congregation for the Doctrine of the Faith issued *Considerations Regarding Proposals to Give Legal Recognition to Unions Between Homosexual Persons.* Admonishing Catholics to oppose state recognition of same-sex "marriages," the statement also expressed skepticism about other forms of legal recognition: "Those who would move from tolerance to the legitimization of specific rights for cohabiting homosexual persons need to be reminded that the approval or legalization of evil is something far different from the toleration of evil." The Mormons and the Southern Baptists have also strongly opposed gay marriage. For all three denominations, the gay marriage issue has become the new Maginot Line for homosexuality, essentially superseding consensual sodomy laws and laws denying gay people civil rights. . . . In contrast, gay marriages are recognized by the United Assembly of Hebrew Congregations (the Reformed Jews), the Unitarian Universalist Church, the United Church of Christ, the Society of Friends (the Quakers), and most recently, in 2009, the Episcopal Church. The Presbyterian General Assembly in 2004–2005 endorsed the idea that the state should recognize lesbian and gay relationships as civil unions, but not as marriages. Likewise, the Churchwide Assembly of the Evangelical Lutheran Church of America voted in 2009 to find ways to "allow congregations that choose to do so to recognize, support and hold publicly accountable, lifelong, monogamous, same-gender relationships." Other denominations have engaged in intense discussions about same-sex marriages and unions but have not changed their doctrine on this matter.

6. God Sets the Lonely in Families

PATRICIA BEATTIE JUNG

1. The title of this essay is taken from Psalm 68:6a.

2. Congregation for the Doctrine of the Faith (hereafter CDF), *Persona Humana* (hereafter *PH*, also known as the "Declaration on Certain Questions Concerning Sexual Ethics"), 1975, no. 8.

3. Pope Paul VI, *Humanae Vitae* (hereafter *HV*), 1968, no. 12.

4. CDF, "Considerations Regarding Proposals to Give Legal Recognition to Unions Between Homosexual Persons" (hereafter CRP), 2003, no. 7, http://www .vatican.va/roman_curia/congregations/cfaith/documents/rc_con_cfaith_doc _20030731_homosexual-unions_en.html.

5. In the first track, see John J. McNeill SJ, "The Christian Male Homosexual," *Homiletic and Pastoral Review* 70 (1970): 828–836; Charles E. Curran, *Catholic Moral Theology in Dialogue* (Notre Dame, Ind.: Fides, 1972), 184–219; Lisa Sowle Cahill, *Sex, Gender, and Christian Ethics* (Cambridge: University of Cambridge, 1996). In the second track, see John J. McNeill, *The Church and the Homosexual* (Kansas City, Kan.: Sheed, Andrews, and McMeel, 1976); Patricia Beattie Jung and Ralph Smith, *Heterosexism: An Ethical Challenge* (Albany, N.Y.: SUNY Press, 1993); Margaret A. Farley, *Just Love: A Framework for Christian Sexual Ethics* (New York: Continuum, 2006); and Todd A. Salzman and Michael G. Lawler, *The Sexual Person: Toward a Renewed Catholic Anthropology* (Washington, D.C.: Georgetown University Press, 2008).

6. *Catechism of the Catholic Church* (hereafter *CCC*) (New York: Doubleday, 1997), no. 2357; CRP, no. 4.

7. *HV*, no. 11.

8. U.S. Bishops, "Marriage: Love and Life in the Divine Plan" (hereafter MLL), November 17, 2009. Published in *Origins* 39, no. 26 (December 3, 2009): 417–435.

9. Ibid., 421–422.

10. *CCC*, no. 2379.

11. James P. Hanigan, *Homosexuality: The Test Case for Christian Sexual Ethics* (New York: Paulist Press, 1988).

12. Gareth Moore, *The Body in Context: Sex and Catholicism, Contemporary Christian Insights* (New York: Continuum, 2001), 200–201.

13. MLL, 423–424.

14. See Second Vatican Council, "Pastoral Constitution on the Church in the Modern World," (*Gaudium et Spes*), 1965, nos. 48.1 and 49.2; Pope John Paul II's apostolic exhortation "On the Role of the Christian Family in the Modern World" (*Familiaris Consortio*, hereafter FC), 1981, no. 11.

15. Joan Roughgarden, *Evolution's Rainbow: Diversity, Gender, and Sexuality in Nature and People* (Berkeley: University of California Press, 2004). See especially chap. 8.

16. Bruce Bagemihl, *Biological Exuberance: Animal Homosexuality and National Diversity* (New York: St. Martin's Press, 1999).

17. MLL, p. 422.

18. *HV*, no. 17.

19. Cristina L. H. Traina, "Papal Ideals, Marital Realities: One View from the Ground," in *Sexual Diversity and Catholicism: Toward the Development of Moral*

Theology, ed. Patricia Beattie Jung with Joseph Andrew Coray (Collegeville, Minn.: Liturgical Press, 2001), 269–288.

20. William L. Portier et al., "A *Modus Vivendi?* Sex, Marriage, and the Church," *Commonweal* 139, no. 1 (January 13, 2012): 12–19.

21. Rachel K. Jones and Joerg Dreweke, *Countering Conventional Wisdom: New Evidence on Religion and Contraceptive Use* (New York: Guttmacher Institute, 2011).

22. "Sex and the Modern Catholic: A *Tablet* Special on *Humanae Vitae* 40 Years Later," *The Tablet* 28 (July 2008). http://bit.ly/17JfcVP.

23. In its survey of U.S. Catholics published October 28, 2011, the *National Catholic Reporter* indicated that 60 percent indicated they could be highly committed Catholics without adhering to official church teaching on contraception. Only 10 percent thought church leaders alone should have the final say about what is right or wrong in regard to contraception.

24. Pontifical Council for the Family (hereafter PCF), "*Vademecum* for Confessors Concerning Some Aspects of the Morality of Conjugal Life" (1997), no. 37, http://www.vatican.va/roman_curia/pontifical_councils/family/documents /rc_pc_family_doc_20001109_de-facto-unions_en.html.

25. Ibid., no. 40.

26. Ibid., no. 43. Thanks to Cristie Traina for noting that this coheres with the *CCC*'s emphasis on the gradual acquisition of virtue and growth into heterosexual marriage.

27. Complementarity is mentioned by John Paul II in *FC*, no. 19. It is mentioned again in the *CCC*, no. 2357, and resurfaces explicitly as sexual complementarity in the CDF's CRP, no. 7.

28. Salzman and Lawler, *The Sexual Person*, 85.

29. Ibid., 86–87, 141. It certainly outweighs reproductive complementarity, but I would argue this is only so because of its service to—its iconic role in relation to—the reproductive meaning of human sexuality.

30. The U.S. bishops note precisely this point, that is, that the marriage equality movement makes heterogenital complementarity irrelevant to the "communion of persons" that marriage is. MLL, 423.

31. Salzman and Lawler, *The Sexual Person*, 90–91, 152.

32. Rowan Williams, "The Body's Grace," in *Our Selves, Our Souls and Bodies: Sexuality and the Household of God*, ed. Charles Hefling (Boston: Cowley, 1996), 58–68.

33. John M. Gottman, Robert W. Levenson, James Gross, et al., "Correlates of Gay and Lesbian Couples' Relationship Satisfaction and Relationship Dissolution," *Journal of Homosexuality* 45, no. 1 (2003): 450.

34. Salzman and Lawler, *The Sexual Person*, 313. See n. 84 in chap. 7; here they cite several studies in this regard.

35. Ibid., 90–91; 152.

36. Congregation for Catholic Education, "Educational Guidance in Human Love: Outlines for Sex Education," 1983, no. 4.

37. David G. Myers and Letha Dawson Scanzoni, *What God Has Joined Together: The Christian Case for Gay Marriage* (New York: HarperSanFrancisco, 2005), 55. For slightly lower estimates, see the work by Edward O. Laumann et al., *The Social Organization of Sexuality: Sexual Practices in the United States* (Chicago: University of Chicago Press, 1994).

38. Stephen J. Pope, "The Magisterium's Arguments Against 'Same Sex Marriage': An Ethical Analysis and Critique," *Theological Studies* 65 (2004): 550.

39. Code of Canon Law, can. 1061.1, http://www.vatican.va/archive/eng1104/_index.htm.

40. While the church discourages civil divorce, it recognizes that it is sometimes legally necessary for the protection and welfare of spouses and children; in practice, Christians who seek an annulment from the Catholic Church must have a civil divorce before the annulment is granted.

41. "The fundamental human rights of homosexual persons must be defended." U.S. Catholic Bishops, "Always Our Children" (hereafter AOC) (Washington, D.C., United States Catholic Conference, 1997), http://www.usccb.org/issues-and-action/human-life-and-dignity/homosexuality/always-our-children.cfm.

42. CDF, "Some Considerations Concerning the Catholic Response to Legislative Proposals on the Non-Discrimination of Homosexual Persons," 1992, no. 11, http://www.vatican.va/roman_curia/congregations/cfaith/documents/rc_con_cfaith_doc_19920724_homosexual-persons_en.html.

43. AOC.

44. PCF, "Family, Marriage and *De Facto* Unions," 2000.

45. In the past decade, support for marriage equality in the United States has gone from 25 percent to 53 percent. According to a poll published by the Public Religion Research Institute in March 2011, Catholics are more supportive than other Christians in the United States. When asked if they would approve of gay people getting married in city hall, a whopping 73 percent noted their approval. See "Catholic Attitudes on Gay and Lesbian Issues: A Comprehensive Portrait from Recent Research," by Robert P. Jones and Daniel Cox, March 2011, http://publicreligion.org/site/wp-content/uploads/2011/06/Catholics-and-LGBT-Issues-Survey-Report.pdf.

46. Along with the marriage equality movement, the U.S. bishops also identified heterosexual contraception, divorce, and cohabitation as challenges to marriage (MLL). In a letter dated October 4, 2011, Archbishop John Nienstedt of Minneapolis–St. Paul asked all the priests in his diocese to appoint a parish captain to chair ad hoc parish committees to support the proposed amendment

to the Minnesota state constitution that would define marriage as a union of one man and one woman. In Nienstedt's view, this is the church's top priority.

47. Robert Nugent, "The Civil Rights of Homosexual People: Vatican Perspectives," *New Theology Review* 7 (August 1994): 72–86.

48. Richard A. Peddicord OP, *Gay and Lesbian Rights: A Question: Sexual Ethics or Social Justice?* (Kansas City, Mo.: Sheed and Ward, 1996).

49. Daniel C. Maguire, "Morality of Homosexual Marriage," in Robert Nugent's *A Challenge to Love: Catholic Views of Homosexuality* (New York: Crossroads, 1983), 118–134. On April 6, 2006, Maguire self-published a pamphlet entitled "A Catholic Defense of Same-Sex Marriage." Here Maguire both refutes arguments against same-sex marriage and mounts a positive case for it. http://www.religiousconsultation.org/Catholic_defense_of_same_sex_marriage.htm.

50. Patricia Beattie Jung and Ralph F. Smith, *Heterosexism: The Ethical Challenge* (Albany, N.Y.: SUNY Press, 1993). The present author went on to develop this line of reasoning further in "The Call to Wed: A Catholic Case for Same-Sex Marriage," *Liturgy* 20, no. 3 (2005): 31–42.

51. David Matzko McCarthy, "Homosexuality and the Practice of Marriage," *Modern Theology* 13, no. 3 (July 1997): 371–397. The following year McCarthy went on to argue that both heterosexual and homosexual couples can in their nuptial witness signify for the wider community God's constancy and steadfast fidelity. "The Relationship of Bodies: A Nuptial Hermeneutic of Same-Sex Unions," *Theology and Sexuality* 4, no. 8 (March 1998): 96–113.

52. Francis DeBernardo, *Marriage Equality: A Positive Catholic Approach* (Mount Rainer, Md.: New Ways Ministry, 2011). http://newwaysministry.org/Marriage_Equality_Book.html.

53. In the last fifty years the percentage of adult U.S. citizens who were married has dropped from nearly 80 percent to only 52 percent. Catholics in this regard are not far off the national average: only 53 percent of adult U.S. Catholics are married today. The median age for first marriage has risen considerably; in 2010 the median age for U.S. women was 26 and for men 28. For more information, see Mark M. Gray, "Exclusive Analysis: National Catholic Marriage Rate Plummets," *Our Sunday Visitor Newsweekly* (June 26, 2011).

54. William C. Buffie, "Public Health Implications of Same-Sex Marriage," *American Journal of Public Health* 101, no. 6 (June 2011): 986–990. See also Mark L. Hatzenbuehler, Conall O'Cleirigh, Chris Grasso, et al., "Effect of Same-Sex Marriage Laws on Health Care Use and Expenditures in Sexual Minority Men: A Quasi-Natural Experiment," *American Journal of Public Health* 102, no. 2 (February 2012): 285–291.

55. M. V. Lee Badgett, *When Gay People Get Married: What Happens When Societies Legalize Same-Sex Marriage* (New York: New York University Press, 2009).

56. Ibid., 67.

57. "For Women Under 30 Most Births Occur Outside Marriage," *New York Times* (February 17, 2012).

58. It is not clear precisely who these others are, though it is implied that their sense of sexual identity may be "unstable." It is reasonable to presume Rome is referring here to those who are bisexual and/or transgendered, perhaps even to women, whose sexual identities prove to be more "fluid" over time.

59. CDF, CRP, no. 5.

60. Ibid, no. 6.

61. MLL, 424.

62. AOC.

63. CDF, CRP, no. 7.

64. Bridget Fitzgerald, "Children of Lesbian and Gay Parents: A Review of the Literature," *Marriage and Family Review* 29 (1999): 57–75. See Robert Preidt, "Kids Adopted By Same-Sex Couples 'Thriving,'" *HealthDay Consumer News Service* (July 29, 2010). There is no empirical foundation for the claim that children of lesbian and gay parents suffer deficits in personal development. Though no longer new, research remains limited, especially in regard to the children of gay fathers.

65. Nanette Gartrell and Henny Bos, "U.S. National Longitudinal Lesbian Family Study: Psychological Adjustment of 17-Year-Old Adolescents," *Pediatrics* 126, no. 1 (July 2010): 28–36.

66. In a 2005 summary of the research review of "Gay and Lesbian Parenting," authorized and subsequently published by the American Psychological Association, Charlotte J. Patterson concludes that there is no evidence of elevated rates of homosexual or bisexual orientation or unusual gender role behavior among children raised in gay male– or lesbian-headed households. http://www.apa.org/pi/lgbt/resources/parenting.aspx.

67. Subcommittee for the Promotion and Defense of Marriage, U.S. Conference of Catholic Bishops, "Frequently Asked Questions on the Defense of Marriage," http://www.usccb.org/issues-and-action/marriage-and-family/marriage/promotion-and-defense-of-marriage/frequently-asked-questions-on-defense-of-marriage.cfm.

68. Thomas Berg, "Taking Exception," *Christian Century* 126, no. 13 (June 30, 2009): 12–13.

69. Second Vatican Council, "Declaration on Religious Freedom" (*Dignitatis Humanae*), 1965, no. 7.

70. *CCC*, no. 2358.

71. I want to be clear here that this argument does not intend to make either marriage or parenthood compulsory. It does not feed what Bella DePaulo termed "singlism," the tendency in our culture to stigmatize adults who are single.

Rather, without denying notable exceptions to the contrary, it marshals evidence that commends marriage vows to lovers and parents. See Bella DePaulo, *Singled Out: How Singles Are Stereotyped, Stigmatized, and Ignored, and Still Live Happily Ever After* (New York: St. Martin's Press, 2006).

72. Like the American Psychological Association, the American Psychiatric Association, the American Academy of Pediatrics, and the American College of Obstetricians and Gynecologists, the American Medical Association supports marriage equality for same-sex couples. See its policy, H-65.973, Health Care Disparities in Same-Sex Partner Households. This and related AMA policies are to be found at http://www.ama-assn.org/ama/pub/about-ama/our-people/member-groups-sections/glbt-advisory-committee/ama-policy-regarding-sexual-orientation.page.

73. The nurture of children is undoubtedly one very important way married couples can contribute to the well-being of society, but both straight and gay couples do so in a variety of other ways as well. However, their delineation is not possible within the constraints of this brief essay.

74. ABC reporter Susan Donaldson James reported these figures on June 23, 2011. They are confirmed by analyses sponsored by the Pew Research Center in "Flaws in Same-Sex-Couple Data," by D'Vera Cohn. http://www.pewsocialtrends.org/2011/09/27/census-bureau-flaws-in-same-sex-couple-data/?src=prc-newsletter.

75. To some extent the civil privileging of marriage is fair. When people marry, they take on many responsibilities and burdens not routinely carried by those who remain single under the law. For example, married couples are responsible for each other's debts and, as divorce law makes clear, in some cases even for the divorced partner's ongoing economic welfare. Though spouses cannot be criminally prosecuted for their partner's crimes, their (joint) estate can be subject to civil suit. This is not to say that the system that ties many basic human rights to marriage is altogether fair. When access to basic goods is linked to marriage, then marriage is not just civilly promoted. It is made de facto "compulsory," and this is wrong.

76. Pope, "The Magisterium's Arguments," 538.

77. Macky Alston has described his same-sex wedding as functioning like an exorcism, a ritual that cast out the shame he had internalized. http://www.beliefnet.com/News/2003/07/My-Blessed-Gay-Marriage.aspx#.

78. Another study demonstrates improvements in gay men's health after legalization in state of same-sex marriage. See Badgett, *When Gay People Get Married*.

79. On December 10, 2009, the Vatican reiterated its opposition to "all grave violations of human rights against homosexual persons," including their abuse

and execution by the state. Initially this emboldened Archbishop Cyprian Lwanga of Uganda to denounce his country's notorious Anti-Homosexuality Bill. Nevertheless, in June 2012 Lwanga joined other members of the Uganda Joint Christian Council in their endorsement of the "kill-the-gays bill." Presumably, he believes the death penalty will be removed from the bill, which criminalizes homosexuality, while it is "in committee." Those familiar with its legislative history in Uganda, however, suggest this will not happen.

Response to Patricia Beattie Jung
JOAN M. MARTIN

1. The phrase is taken from the *Catechism of the Catholic Church* (New York: Doubleday, 1997): 2357; CRP, 4.

2. Pope Paul VI, *Humanae Vitae*, 1968, no. 11.

3. Kelly Brown Douglass, "Contested Marriage/Loving Rationality," in *Sexuality and the Sacred: Sources for Theological Reflection*, 2nd ed., ed. Marvin M. Ellison and Kelly Brown Douglas (Louisville, Ky.: Westminster/John Knox, 2010), 383.

4. See Richard A. Norris Jr., "Some Notes on the Current Debate Regarding Homosexuality and the Place of Homosexuals in the Church," 437–511, esp. 472–482; and Margaret A. Farley, "Same-Sex Relationships and Issues of Moral Obligation," 541–547, both in *Anglican Theological Review* 90, no. 3 (Summer 2008).

5. Marvin M. Ellison, *Same-Sex Marriage? A Christian Ethical Analysis* (Cleveland, Ohio: Pilgrim, 2004), 154–156. I am grateful to Ellison's work for the development of my thinking over the years and my changing reflections on marriage as an interpersonal and social relationship calling for justice making as the undergirding moral value for both.

6. I have changed their names to protect their identities.

7. Same-Sex Marriage and Catholicism: Dialogue, Learning, and Change
LISA SOWLE CAHILL

1. Connecticut Catholic Conference, Statement on Same-Sex Marriage (October 10, 2008), http://www.ctcatholic.org/Statement of Bishops on Court-Same-sex.php.

2. USCCB News Release, "Attacks on DOMA Threaten Marriage, Church-State Relations, Warns Archbishop Dolan in Letter to President" (September 22, 2011), http://www.usccb.org/news/2011/11-179.cfm.

3. Congregation for the Doctrine of the Faith, "Considerations Regarding Proposals to Give Legal Recognition to Unions Between Homosexual Persons,"

2003, no. 4, http://www.vatican.va/roman_curia/congregations/cfaith/docu ments/rc_con_cfaith_doc_20030731_homosexual-unions_en.html, citing *Catechism of the Catholic Church*, no. 2357.

4. Ibid., no. 7.

5. Tim Muldoon, "Introduction: Catholic Identity and the Laity," in *Catholic Identity and the Laity*, ed. Tim Muldoon, College Theology Society Annual 54 (Maryknoll, N.Y.: Orbis, 2008), 11.

6. "*Lumen Gentium*: Dogmatic Constitution on the Church," *Vatican Archive* (November 21, 1964), no. 37, http://www.vatican.va/archive/hist_councils/ii_vat ican_council/documents/vat-ii_const_19641121_lumen-gentium_en.html.

7. Carolyn Weir Herman, "The *Sensus Fidei* and Lay Authority in the Roman Catholic Church," in *Catholic Identity and the Laity*, 165.

8. Ibid., 160.

9. Public Religion Research Institute, "Report: Catholic Attitudes on Gay and Lesbian Issues: A Comprehensive Portrait from Recent Research" (March 22, 2011), http://publicreligion.org/research/2011/03/for-catholics-open-attitudes-on -gay-issues/.

10. Danielle Kurtzleben, "Divorce Rates Lower in States with Same-Sex Marriage," *US News* (July 6, 2011), http://www.usnews.com/news/articles/2011/07/06 /divorce-rates-lower-in-states-with-same-sex-marriage.

11. Stephanie Pappas, "Why Gay Parents May Be the Best Parents," *Live Science* (January 17, 2012), http://www.livescience.com/17913-advantages-gay- parents.html.

12. It must be noted—though not developed here—that Catholic advocacy for "gay marriage" is itself traditionalist in that it assimilates homosexuals to the traditional heterosexual norm of sex only within a committed, monogamous relationship. A more radical discussion concerns the question whether sex is "naturally" monogamous and whether homosexual persons should aspire to "marriage." See Mark D. Jordan, *Blessing Same-Sex Unions: The Perils of Queer Romance and the Confusions of Christian Marriage* (Chicago: University of Chicago Press, 2005); and Marcella Althaus-Reid, Regina Ammicht Quinn, Erik Borgman, and Norbert Reck, eds., *Homosexualities* (London: SCM, 2008).

13. Henry Davis SJ, *Moral and Pastoral Theology*, vol. 2: *Precepts*, 5th ed. (New York: Sheed and Ward, 1946), 200.

14. Ibid., 209.

15. Thomas Aquinas, *Summa Theologiae*, I–II.94.a4.

16. International Theological Commission, "The Search for Universal Ethics: A New Look at the Natural Law," 2009, nos. 1–2; unofficial English translation by Joseph Bolin (May 25, 2010), http://www.pathsoflove.com/universal-ethics -natural-law.html.

17. Ibid., no. 61.

18. Ibid., no. 80.

19. *Catechism of the Catholic Church* (London: Cassell, 1994), no. 2357.

20. Patrick T. McCormick, "Catholicism and Sexuality: The Sounds of Silence," *Horizons* 30 (2003): 191.

21. Margaret A. Farley, *Just Love: A Framework for Christian Sexual Ethics* (New York: Continuum, 2006), 286.

22. Congregation for the Doctrine of the Faith, "Notification Regarding the Book *Just Love. A Framework for Christian Sexual Ethics* by Sister Margaret A. Farley, R.S.M." (March 30, 2012), http://www.news.va/en/news/cdf-publishes -notification-on-book-just-love.

23. Todd A. Salzman and Michael G. Lawler, *The Sexual Person: Toward a Renewed Catholic Anthropology* (Washington, D.C.: Georgetown University Press, 2008), 124.

24. Ibid., 161.

25. Ibid., 232.

26. Committee on Doctrine of the United States Conference of Catholic Bishops, "Inadequacies in the Theological Methodology and Conclusions of *The Sexual Person: Toward a Renewed Catholic Anthropology* by Todd A. Salzman and Michael G. Lawler" (September 15, 2010), 12, http://www.ewtn.com/library/ BISHOPS/inadsexper.HTM.

27. Ibid., 7.

28. National Conference of Catholic Bishops, Committee on Marriage and Family, "Always Our Children: A Pastoral Message to Parents of Homosexual Children and Suggestions for Pastoral Ministers" (Washington, D.C.: United States Catholic Conference, 1997).

29. Ibid., 2.

30. Ibid., 3.

31. Ibid., 8–9.

32. Barbara Jean Daly Horell, *"Always Our Children?* Young Catholics Consider the Pastoral Message," in *Human Sexuality in the Catholic Tradition*, ed. Kieran Scott and Harold Daly Horell (Lanham, Md.: Rowman and Littlefield, 2007), 152.

33. Marriage of first cousins is prohibited by Canon 1091 of the 1983 Code of Canon Law, although dispensations are possible.

34. Pius XI, *Casti Connubii*, no. 24, http://www.vatican.va/holy_father/pius_xi /encyclicals/documents/hf_p-xi_enc_31121930_casti-connubii_en.html.

35. Second Vatican Council, *Gaudium et Spes*, nos. 47 and 48, http://www.vatican.va/archive/hist_councils/ii_vatican_council/documents/vat-ii_const _19651207_gaudium-et-spes_en.html.

36. Ibid., nos. 48 and 50.

37. Canon 1055.

38. Paul VI, *Humanae Vitae* (*On the Regulation of Birth*), no. 8, http://www.vati can.va/holy_father/paul_vi/encyclicals/documents/hf_p-vi_enc_25071968_ humanae-vitae_en.html.

39. Ibid., no. 9.

40. Ibid., nos. 10–11.

41. Ibid., no. 12.

42. Ibid., nos. 10 and 16.

43. Pew Forum on Religion and Public Life, *U.S. Religious Landscape Survey*, 2007, http://religions.pewforum.org/reports/.

44. This theology was developed especially in the pope's Wednesday audience talks of 1979–1981, and the key themes are recapitulated in *Familiaris Consortio* (Apostolic Exhortation *On the Family*), nos. 11–20, http://www.vatican.va/holy _father/john_paul_ii/apost_exhortations/documents/hf_jp-ii_exh_19811122 _familiaris-consortio_en.html. For the audience talks and other relevant writings, see John Paul II, *The Theology of the Body: Human Love in the Divine Plan*, with a foreword by John S. Grabowski (Boston: Pauline Books, 1997).

45. *Familiaris Consortio*, no. 11.

46. For a critical dialogue about this theology, see Lisa Sowle Cahill, John Garvey, and T. Frank Kennedy SJ, eds., *Sexuality and the U.S. Catholic Church: Crisis and Renewal* (New York: Herder and Herder, 2006), esp. the chapters by David Cloutier and William Mattison.

47. "The marriage breakup rate in America for first marriage is 41% to 50%; the rate after second marriage is from 60% to 67% and the rate in America for 3rd marriage are from 73% to 74%." "Divorce Statistics and Divorce Rate in the U.S.A." (April 5, 2012), http://www.divorcestatistics.info/divorce-statistics-and -divorce-rate-in-the-usa.html.

48. Forum on Child and Family Statistics, *America's Children in Brief: Key National Indicators of Well-Being, 2012*, http://www.childstats.gov/americaschil- dren/fam_fig.asp.

49. See Frederick Hertz, "Divorce and Marriage Rates for Same-Sex Marriage," blog post (November 10, 2011), http://www.huffingtonpost.com/frederick -hertz/divorce-marriage-rates-fo_b_1085024.html.

50. For a discussion of some of these, see Lisa Sowle Cahill, "Marriage: Developments in Catholic Theology and Ethics," *Theological Studies* 64 (2003): 95–103.

51. Julie Hanlon Rubio, *A Christian Theology of Marriage* (New York: Paulist Press, 2004), 239–240. See also Julie Hanlon Rubio, "Family Ethics: Beyond Sex and Controversy," *Theological Studies* 74 (2013): 138–161.

8. Embracing the Stranger: Reflections on the Ambivalent Hospitality of LGBTIQ Catholics

MICHAEL SEPIDOZA CAMPOS

1. The silencing of the moral theologian Charles Curran in 1986, perhaps more than any other, embodies the mechanism of exclusion that the institutional church exerts over dissenting voices. Likewise, the expulsion of DignityUSA—along with the forced withdrawal of Jeannine Gramick and Robert Nugent—from active LGBTIQ Catholic ministry attests to institutional efforts to shape outreach to LGBTIQ Catholics in accordance with Catholic moral teachings.

2. Congregation for the Doctrine of the Faith, "Letter to the Bishops of the Catholic Church on the Pastoral Care of Homosexual Persons," *Vatican Archive* (October 1, 1986), sec. 3, http://www.vatican.va/roman_curia/congregations/cfaith/documents/rc_con_cfaith_doc_19861001_homosexual-persons_en.html.

3. By relocating "queer" *away* from claims about individual subjectivity and toward a phenomenon of space, I rely on Sarah Ahmed's retrieval of "orientation" as a directional metaphor. She claims: "the term 'orientation' is itself a spatial term: it points to how one is placed in relation to objects in the sense of 'the direction' one has and takes toward objects." I suggest that insofar as the Roman Catholic Church maintains an ambivalent welcome to LGBTIQ Catholics, it never really lives up to the heteronormative impulse to expel queerness. Thus the church maintains an implicitly queer orientation. See Sarah Ahmed, *Queer Phenomenology: Orientations, Objects, Others* (Durham, N.C.: Duke University Press, 2006), 69.

4. Marcella Althaus-Reid, *Indecent Theology: Theological Perversions in Sex, Gender, and Politics* (New York: Routledge, 2000), 70–71.

5. I spent a year and a half with the monks of Weston Priory in Weston, Vermont. See further note 7, below.

6. Jacques Derrida, "Jacques Derrida—Hostipitality," *Angelaki: Journal of the Theoretical Humanities* 5, no. 3 (December 2000): 9. Emphasis mine.

7. Leo Rudloff made his monastic vows at St. Joseph's Abbey in Gerleve, Germany. During his tenure as abbot of the Dormition in Jerusalem, Rudloff founded Weston Priory in Vermont, with the initial intention of recruiting American monks to revive the dwindling numbers of the Dormition. As a result, Rudloff spent much of his nearly twenty-year tenure crossing the Atlantic and traversing three continents. For a close reading of Rudloff's life, see John Hammond, *A Benedictine Legacy of Peace: The Life of Abbot Leo A. Rudloff* (Weston, Vt.: The Benedictine Foundation of the State of Vermont, 2005).

8. Introduction to Benedict of Nursia, *The Rule of St. Benedict* (RB), ed. Anthony C. Meisel and M. L. del Mastro, 1st ed. (Garden City, N.Y: Image, 1975), 32.

9. Leo Rudloff OSB, "The Living Rule of Saint Benedict as Lived by the Monks of Weston Priory," unpublished manuscript (early 1970s). Emphasis mine. An aside: during these days of highly contested conversations around appropriate definitions of "marriage," I find Rudloff's claim queerly prophetic.

10. I locate an implicit "biopower" at work in the constitution of monastic community itself. See Michel Foucault, *The History of Sexuality*, trans. Robert Hurley (New York: Vintage, 1990), 1:139. The cultural theorists Talal Asad and M. B. Pranger echo similar strategies at play in the constitution of medieval monastic practices. See Talal Asad, "On Discipline and Humility in Medieval Christian Monasticism," in *Genealogies of Religion: Discipline and Reasons of Power in Christianity and Islam* (Baltimore, Md.: Johns Hopkins University Press, 1993), 125–167; and M. B. Pranger, "Religious Indifference: On the Nature of Medieval Christianity," in *Religion: Beyond a Concept*, ed. Hent de Vries, The Future of the Religious Past (New York: Fordham University Press, 2008), 513–523.

11. Revisiting Aelred of Rievaulx's reflection on monastic love as that which "comes from the will," the Benedictine scholar Michael Casey asserts the necessity of individual agency in the consolidation of community. See Michael Casey, *Strangers to the City: Reflections on the Beliefs and Values of the Rule of Saint Benedict* (Brewster, Mass.: Paraclete, 2005), 171. Martín Hugo Córdova Quero discerns a queer impulse in Aelred's deployment of desire as grounding for monastic friendship. See Córdova Quero, "Friendship with Benefits: A Queer Reading of Aelred of Rievaulx and His Theology of Friendship," in *The Sexual Theologian: Essays on Sex, God, and Politics*, ed. Marcella Althaus-Reid and Lisa Isherwood (London: T&T Clark, 2004), 27–46.

12. In the process of integration, individual impulses are never fully absorbed into the social body. Foucault, in fact, asserts that it "is not that life has been totally integrated into techniques that govern and administer it; it constantly *escapes* them." There prevails therefore a sense that biopower stands in constant vigilance of disruptive elements within the social body. See Foucault, *The History of Sexuality*, 1:43. As an incorporating principle for monastic life, stability evokes the complex, systemic, and all-encompassing corporealization that undergirds Foucault's *biopower*, what he describes as a series of "concrete arrangements (*agencements concrets*) that would go to make up the great technology of power . . ." Ibid., 1:140.

13. In the third chapter of the Rule, Benedict cautions against the domination of individual desires over the common good: "Individual desires have no place in the monastery and neither inside nor outside the walls should anyone presume to argue with the abbot. If he dares do so, he should be punished according to the Rule." RB 3, Benedict of Nursia, *The Rule of St. Benedict*, 51. Córdova Quero locates a corollary dynamic in Aelred's writings. But rather than quell the potency of

(homoerotic) love/desire as a distraction to the common life, Aelred wields desire as basis for friendships that strengthen monastic commitment. See Córdova Quero, "The Sexual Theologian," 44.

14. Schillebeeckx's vision of an expansive church affirms an "ecumene of the world religions and the ecumene of humankind, to which agnostics and atheists also belong." Later, he specifies this belonging as defined by a shared "suffering" (referring to Johannes Baptist Metz). Edward Schillebeeckx, *Church: The Human Story of God* (New York: Crossroad, 1990), 189.

15. Recent conversations on the Roman Catholic approach to sexuality/gender became heated with the investigation of the Leadership Conference of Women Religious (LCWR) by the Congregation for the Doctrine of the Faith. Religious activist Jim Wallis observes that these women—rendered "strangers" in their own church—have been reprimanded "for not sufficiently upholding the bishops' teachings and doctrines and paying much more attention to issues like poverty and health care than to abortion, homosexuality, and male-only priesthood." Indeed, I suggest that these impositions of (patriarchal) power illuminate a fear of the potential disintegration of institutional integrity. See Jim Wallis, "Having the Sisters' Back," in Sojourners, "God's Politics: A Blog by Jim Wallis and Friends" (April 25, 2012), http://huffingtonpost.com/jim-wallis/having-the-sisters-back_b_1451791.html?ref=yahoo&ir-Yahoo.

16. *Lumen Gentium* upholds an ecclesiological framework that *controls* and *disciplines* diversity toward uniformity: "the people of God [is] made up of different peoples but in its inner structure also it is composed of various ranks. This diversity among its members arises either by reason of their duties, as is the case with those who exercise the sacred ministry for the good of their brethren, or by reason of their condition and state of life, as is the case with those many who enter the religious state and, tending toward holiness by a narrower path, stimulate their brethren by their example." "*Lumen Gentium*: Dogmatic Constitution on the Church," *Vatican Archive* (November 21, 1964), http://www.vatican.va/archive/hist_councils/ii_vatican_council/documents/vat-ii_const_19641121_lumen-gentium_en.html, sec. 13.

17. *Gaudium et Spes* (Pastoral Constitution on the Church in the Modern World), *Vatican Archive* (December 7, 1965), sec. 16, http://www.vatican.va/archive/hist_councils/ii_vatican_council/documents/vat-ii_cons_19651207_gaudium-et-spes_en.html.

18. Rivera locates an ethical imperative to one's apprehension of otherness: "The glory of God may be seen as the manifestation of the intrinsic transcendence of creatures. A sign of the luring excess of the Other, as well as of his/her unappropriable otherness, glory 'crosses the divide between aesthetics and ethics.'" Mayra Rivera Rivera, *The Touch of Transcendence: A Postcolonial Theology of God*, 1st ed. (Louisville, Ky.: Westminster John Knox, 2007), 138.

19. *Gaudium et Spes*, no. 16.

20. Ahmed, *Queer Phenomenology*, 160.

21. Jean-Luc Nancy's antidote to the suffocating limits of the enclosure is *dis-enclosure*—a notion that not so much breaks through limits as one that reorients spatiality determined not by limits but by a network of relationships: "In a sense, it is the dissolution or a dissipation of the space of clear topographical distinctions, of the space of territories and boundaries, of domains and enclosures. The space of separations is yielding to the thrust of a spatiality that *separates the separations from themselves*, that seizes the general configuration, in order simultaneously to spread it out in a continuum and to contort it into an interlacing of networks." See Jean-Luc Nancy, *Dis-Enclosure: The Deconstruction of Christianity* (New York: Fordham University Press, 2008), 161. In the same spirit, I suggest that Rudloff's ambivalent hospitality reorients the boundaries of the monastic enclosure toward a *network* of relationships that upholds both familiarity and mystery.

9. *Domine, Non Sum Dignus*: Theological Bullying and the Roman Catholic Church

PATRICK S. CHENG

1. Patrick S. Cheng, "Faith, Hope, and Love: Ending LGBT Teen Suicide," *Huffington Post* (October 6, 2010), http://huff.to/9oe2ku.

2. Dan Savage and Terry Miller, eds., *It Gets Better: Coming Out, Overcoming Bullying, and Creating a Life Worth Living* (New York: Dutton, 2011), 1–8.

3. "Kenneth Weishuhn Suicide: Details In Gay Iowa Teen's Death After Allegedly Enduring Threats Emerge," *Huffington Post* (April 18, 2012), http://huff.to/J3hUdr.

4. Andy Towle, "Seventeen-Year-Old Jack Reese Committed Suicide Near Ogden, Utah: Rally Planned," *Towleroad* (April 29, 2012), http://bit.ly/IfikLu.

5. "Jay 'Corey' Jones, Gay Minnesota Teen, Commits Suicide After Allegedly Being Bullied," *Huffington Post* (May 11, 2012), http://huff.to/LxtSM7.

6. Laura Hibbard, "Brandon Elizares, Gay Teen, Commits Suicide, Writing 'I Couldn't Make It. I Love You Guys,'" *Huffington Post* (June 14, 2012), http://huff.to/L8ytqo.

7. In this essay, I use the term "theological bullying" to refer to the bullying of theologians who dissent from the official teaching of the Roman Catholic Church with respect to the sinfulness of same-sex acts. By contrast, I use the term "classroom bullying" to refer to the bullying of LGBT students by their classmates and/or teachers at school.

8. *Catechism of the Catholic Church*, no. 2357.

9. Jim Wright, *Preventing Classroom Bullying: What Teachers Can Do* (February 2004), 3. http://bit.ly/RuxKTR.

10. Barbara Coloroso, *The Bully, the Bullied, and the Bystander* (New York: Collins Living, 2003).

11. Ibid., 13–14, 20–22.

12. Congregation for the Doctrine of the Faith, "Letter to the Bishops of the Catholic Church on the Pastoral Care of Homosexual Persons" (October 31, 1986), no. 3, http://bit.ly/4CFwuO.

13. Congregation for the Doctrine of the Faith, "Doctrinal Assessment of the Leadership Conference of Women Religious" (April 18, 2012), II, http://bit.ly/QdXFec.

14. For example, the bishops of the Roman Catholic dioceses of Raleigh and Charlotte mailed postcards to Roman Catholics in the state urging them to vote in favor of North Carolina Amendment 1. See Patrick O'Neill, "N. Carolina Dioceses Mail Postcards Supporting 'Traditional Marriage,'" *National Catholic Reporter* (May 4, 2012), http://bit.ly/KAe34V. See also *NOM Exposed*, http://www.hrc.org/nomexposed.

15. Byrne Fone, *Homophobia: A History* (New York: Picador USA, 2000).

16. See John J. McNeill, *The Church and the Homosexual*, 4th ed. (Boston, Mass.: Beacon, 1993), 217–241.

17. An overview of their work may be found on the New Ways Ministry website, http://newwaysministry.org/co-founders.html. Theological works authored and/or edited by Gramick and Nugent include Jeannine Gramick and Pat Furcy, eds., *The Vatican and Homosexuality: Reactions to the "Letter to the Bishops of the Catholic Church on the Pastoral Care of Homosexual Persons"* (New York: Crossroad, 1988); Jeannine Gramick and Robert Nugent, eds., *Voices of Hope: A Collection of Positive Catholic Writings on Gay and Lesbian Issues* (New York: Center for Homophobia Education, 1995); Robert Nugent, ed., *A Challenge to Love: Gay and Lesbian Catholics in the Church* (New York: Crossroad, 1983); Robert Nugent and Jeannine Gramick, *Building Bridges: Gay and Lesbian Reality and the Catholic Church* (Mystic, Conn.: Twenty-Third, 1992). For a documentary film about Gramick, see *In Good Conscience: Sister Jeannine Gramick's Journey of Faith*, directed by Barbara Rick (Out of the Blue Films, 2006).

18. Letter from Timothy M. Dolan to Barack Obama (September 20, 2011), http://bit.ly/p8Lk95.

19. Statement of Timothy Dolan (May 9, 2012), http://bit.ly/J1MxvO. The United States Conference of Catholic Bishops has stated that it is a "requirement of our faith" to exercise "political responsibility" that opposes "intrinsic evils which can never be justified." United States Conference of Catholic Bishops, *Forming Consciences for Faithful Citizenship: A Call to Political Responsibility from*

the Catholic Bishops of the United States, rev. ed. (Washington, D.C.: United States Conference of Catholic Bishops, 2011), vi–viii.

20. Gareth Moore, *A Question of Truth: Christianity and Homosexuality* (London: Continuum, 2003), 282.

21. Ibid.

22. As Mark Jordan has noted, although the Roman Catholic hierarchy purports to use natural law reasoning in its arguments against homosexuality, the rhetorical structure of its arguments effectively forecloses any debate on the subject. That is, any dissent is "now silenced with blunt claims of authority." Mark Jordan, *The Silence of Sodom: Homosexuality in Modern Catholicism* (Chicago: University of Chicago Press, 2000), 49.

23. David Crary, "Catholic Bishops Challenge Girl Scouts USA for Conflict with Church Teaching," *Huffington Post* (May 10, 2012), http://huff.to/ITwVzo.

24. Mary E. Hunt, "Bishops Search for Condoms in Cookie Boxes," *Religion Dispatches* (May 21, 2012), http://bit.ly/J99Apm.

25. Laura Hibbard, "Dominic Sheahan-Stahl Denied Michigan High School Keynote Speaker for Being Gay," *Huffington Post* (April 26, 2012), http://huff.to/JHba7i.

26. Verena Dobnik, "Joseph Amodeo Quits Catholic Charities Board Over Cardinal Dolan's Stance on LGBT Youth," *Huffington Post* (April 7, 2012), http://huff.to/IoE5Te.

27. Coloroso, *The Bully*, 78–84. Not surprisingly, many of these same characteristics are present in the formation process of Roman Catholic seminarians. See Jordan, *The Silence of Sodom*, 167–171 (noting how seminarians are required to "spy on one another" and "report any infractions of discipline immediately").

28. Patrick S. Cheng, *Radical Love: An Introduction to Queer Theology* (New York: Seabury, 2011).

29. Patrick S. Cheng, "Radical Love: Why Christianity Is a Queer Religion," *Huffington Post* (March 29, 2011), http://huff.to/hdWOVv.

30. Catholic League for Religious and Civil Rights, "Religious Reality Check" (March 30, 2011), http://bit.ly/IQMPGD.

31. See Lev 20:13, NRSV ("If a man lies with a male as with a woman, both of them have committed an abomination; they shall be put to death; their blood is upon them").

32. Josh Nathan-Kazis, "Catholic League's E-Feud with Rabbi Waskow," *Jewish Daily Forward* (June 20, 2012), http://bit.ly/OyRlO8.

33. Coloroso, *The Bully*, 62–72.

34. See New Ways Ministry, http://newwaysministry.org.

35. See Women's Alliance for Theology, Ethics, and Ritual, http://waterwomensalliance.org.

36. See Gen 1:27.

37. The title of this subsection alludes to Gramick and Nugent, *Voices of Hope*.

38. In addition to *The Church and the Homosexual*, McNeill's works include *Both Feet Firmly Planted in Midair: My Spiritual Journey* (Louisville, Ky.: Westminster John Knox, 1998); *Freedom, Glorious Freedom: The Spiritual Journey to the Fullness of Life for Gays, Lesbians, and Everybody Else* (Boston: Beacon, 1995); *Taking a Chance on God: Liberating Theology for Gays, Lesbians, and Their Lovers, Families, and Friends* (Boston: Beacon, 1988).

39. Robert Goss, *Jesus Acted Up: A Gay and Lesbian Manifesto* (New York: HarperSanFrancisco, 1993); *Queering Christ: Beyond Jesus Acted Up* (Cleveland, Ohio: Pilgrim, 2002).

40. Elizabeth Stuart, *Just Good Friends: Towards a Lesbian and Gay Theology of Relationships* (London: Mowbray, 1995); *Gay and Lesbian Theologies: Repetitions with Critical Difference* (Aldershot: Ashgate, 2003).

41. Jordan, *The Silence of Sodom*.

42. Donald L. Boisvert, *Out on Holy Ground: Meditations on Gay Men's Spirituality* (Cleveland, Ohio: Pilgrim, 2000); *Sanctity and Male Desire: A Gay Reading of Saints* (Cleveland, Ohio: Pilgrim, 2004).

43. Cheng, *Radical Love*; Patrick S. Cheng, *From Sin to Amazing Grace: Discovering the Queer Christ* (New York: Seabury, 2012). *Rainbow Theology: Bridging Race, Sexuality, and Spirit* (New York: Seabury, 2013).

44. Mary E. Hunt, *Fierce Tenderness: A Feminist Theology of Friendship* (New York: Crossroad, 1991); Mary E. Hunt and Diann L. Neu, eds., *New Feminist Christianity: Many Voices, Many Views* (Woodstock, Vt.: Skylight Paths, 2010).

45. Hunt's online essay about the Vatican's crackdown on women religious, "We Are All Nuns," has been widely circulated and was quoted by the *New York Times*. See Mary E. Hunt, "We Are All Nuns," *Religion Dispatches* (April 25, 2012), http://bit.ly/I6bruB. For Hunt's online essay about the CDF's censure of *Just Love*, see Mary E. Hunt, "Notify This! Vatican Bungles Response to Sexual Ethics Book," *Religion Dispatches* (June 9, 2012), http://bit.ly/LJO6iS.

46. James Alison, *Broken Hearts and New Creations: Intimations of a Great Reversal* (London: Continuum, 2010), 183.

47. James Alison, *Faith Beyond Resentment: Fragments Catholic and Gay* (New York: Crossroad, 2001); Alison, *Broken Hearts and New Creations*.

48. Alison, *Broken Hearts and New Creations*, 182, 185.

49. Orlando O. Espín, *Grace and Humanness: Theological Reflections Because of Culture* (Maryknoll, N.Y.: Orbis, 2007), 51–79; CLGS Latino/a Roundtable, http://bit.ly/gKAxfp.

50. Espín, *Grace and Humanness*, 63.

51. M. Shawn Copeland, *Enfleshing Freedom: Body, Race, and Being* (Minneapolis, Minn.: Fortress, 2010), 82–83.

52. Michael Sepidoza Campos, "The *Baklâ*: Gendered Religious Performance in Filipino Cultural Spaces," in *Queer Religion: LGBT Movements and Queering Religion*, ed. Donald L. Boisvert and Jay Emerson Johnson (Santa Barbara, Calif.: Praeger, 2012), 2:167–191.

53. Lai-shan Yip, "Listening to the Passion of Catholic nu-tongzhi: Developing a Catholic Lesbian Feminist Theology in Hong Kong," in Boisvert and Johnson, *Queer Religion*, 2:63–80.

54. Joseph N. Goh, "*Mak Nyah* Mariology," *Communion* 3 no. 3 (March 2012): 4–7, http://bit.ly/NUSAvt.

55. For the EQARS website, see http://www.eqars.org.

56. For an audio interview of Duddy-Burke challenging Pope Benedict XVI's assertion that same-sex marriage would threaten human dignity and the future of humanity itself, see http://bit.ly/Ai3BQG.

57. http://waterwomensalliance.org. See also Hunt and Neu, *New Feminist Christianity*.

58. For Rue's story, see http://bit.ly/IsotRn.

59. For Manson's blog posts, see http://bit.ly/KmxweS.

60. Amie M. Evans and Trebor Healey, eds., *Queer and Catholic* (New York: Routledge, 2008).

61. Dugan McGinley, *Acts of Faith, Acts of Love: Gay Catholic Autobiographies as Sacred Texts* (New York: Continuum, 2004); Richard Giannone, *Hidden: Reflections on Gay Life, AIDS, and Spiritual Desire* (New York: Fordham University Press, 2012).

62. Rembert G. Weakland, *A Pilgrim in a Pilgrim Church: Memoirs of a Catholic Archbishop* (Grand Rapids, Mich.: Eerdmans, 2009); Paul Murray, *Life in Paradox: The Story of a Gay Catholic Priest* (Winchester: O Books, 2008).

63. Donal Godfrey, *Gays and Grays: The Story of the Gay Community at Most Holy Redeemer Catholic Church* (Lanham, Md.: Lexington, 2007).

64. Edward F. Gabriele, *Cloud Days and Fire Nights: Canticles for a Pilgrimage out of Exile* (Winona, Minn.: Saint Mary's Press, 1997).

65. Lowell Gallagher, Frederick S. Roden, and Patricia Juliana Smith, eds., *Catholic Figures, Queer Narratives* (New York: Palgrave Macmillan, 2007).

66. Mary Ellen Lopata and Casey Lopata, *Fortunate Families: Catholic Families with Lesbian Daughters and Gay Sons* (Victoria, Canada: Trafford, 2003).

67. See *Star Wars: A New Hope*, directed by George Lucas (1977; Los Angeles: Lucasfilm, Twentieth Century Fox Corporation), Princess Leia Organa speaking to Grand Moff Tarkin, http://imdb.to/JsweLv.

68. Matt 8:8; Luke 7:6.

69. L. William Countryman, *Dirt, Greed, and Sex: Sexual Ethics in the New Testament and Their Implications for Today*, rev. ed. (Minneapolis, Minn.: Fortress, 2007), 246. See also Tom Horner, *Jonathan Loved David: Homosexuality in*

Biblical Times (Philadelphia: Westminster, 1978), 122; Nancy Wilson, *Our Tribe: Queer Folks, God, Jesus, and the Bible* (New York: HarperSanFrancisco, 1995), 162.

70. See, for example, Michael Bernard Kelly, *Seduced by Grace: Contemporary Spirituality, Gay Experience, and Christian Faith* (Melbourne, Australia: Clouds of Magellan, 2007), 59–62 (describing the rainbow sash movement in which people wearing rainbow sashes to Mass are denied communion).

71. Second Vatican Council, *Lumen Gentium*, Dogmatic Constitution on the Church, no. 28 (November 21, 1964), http://bit.ly/MEkem.

10. Wild(e) Theology: On Choosing Love

FREDERICK S. RODEN

1. Oscar Wilde, *De Profundis and Other Writings*, ed. Hesketh Pearson (New York: Penguin, 1986), 175.

2. On Raffalovich's Jewishness, see Frederick S. Roden, "Marc-André Raffalovich: A Russian-French-Jewish-Catholic Homosexual in Oscar Wilde's London," in *Jewish/Christian/Queer: Crossroads and Identities*, ed. Frederick S. Roden (Burlington, Vt.: Ashgate, 2009), 127–137.

3. See Frederick S. Roden, *Same-Sex Desire in Victorian Religious Culture* (New York: Palgrave Macmillan, 2003), chap. 6, a discussion of Raffalovich's *Uranisme et Unisexualité* (1896).

4. Marc-André Raffalovich, *Uranisme et Unisexualité* (Lyons: Storck, 1896), 32. My translation.

5. For further on Raffalovich and Gray, see Frederick S. Roden, "Michael Field, John Gray, and Marc-André Raffalovich: Re-Inventing Romantic Friendship in Modernity," in *Catholic Figures, Queer Narratives*, ed. Lowell Gallagher, Frederick S. Roden, and Patricia Juliana Smith (New York: Palgrave Macmillan, 2007), 57–68.

6. E. E. Bradford, "Is Boy-Love Greek?" in *The New Chivalry and Other Poems* (London: Kegan Paul, 1918), p. 31, line 6.

7. See Frederick S. Roden, "The Catholic Modernist Crisis, Queer Modern Catholicisms," in *Catholic Figures, Queer Narratives*, ed. Lowell Gallagher, Frederick S. Roden, and Patricia Juliana Smith (New York: Palgrave Macmillan, 2007), 1–18. My gratitude goes to Philip Healy, Raffalovichian *par excellence*, for his many suggestions and pioneering work on this subject.

8. Thomas Michael Loome, "Tyrrell's Letters to André Raffalovich II," *The Month* 229 (1970): 140.

9. Ibid.

10. Ibid.

11. Ibid., 142.

12. Ibid., 144.

13. See Roden, *Same-Sex Desire*, chap. 5; Patrick R. O'Malley, "Religion," in *Palgrave Advances in Oscar Wilde Studies*, ed. Frederick S. Roden (New York: Palgrave Macmillan, 2004).

14. Oscar Wilde, *The Soul of Man Under Socialism & Selected Critical Prose*, ed. Linda Dowling (New York: Penguin, 2001), 135.

15. Ibid., 137.

16. See Roden, *Same-Sex Desire*, chap. 5, for a detailed discussion of Wilde as theologian.

17. Psalm 130:1–2, 5, KJV.

18. Wilde, "De Profundis," in *De Profundis and Other Writings*, 165.

19. Ibid., 171.

20. Ibid., 175.

21. Ibid., 176.

22. Ibid., 179.

23. John 10:10, NRSV.

Afterword

PAUL LAKELAND

1. *Lumen Gentium*, nos. 13–16.

2. Bernard Lonergan, *A Second Collection* (Philadelphia: Westminster, 1974).

3. Ibid., 1–9.

4. Ibid., 67.

5. For an extraordinary and extended reflection on this and many other matters, see Margaret Farley, *Just Love: A Framework for Christian Sexual Ethics* (New York: Continuum International, 2006).

Contributors

LISA SOWLE CAHILL is the J. Donald Monan Professor of Theology at Boston College.

MICHAEL SEPIDOZA CAMPOS is a Catholic high school teacher and a member of Emerging Queer Asian / Pacific Island Religion Scholars.

PATRICK S. CHENG is associate professor of historical and systematic theology at Episcopal Divinity School.

ELIZABETH A. DREYER is a professor emerita of religious studies at Fairfield University and adjunct professor of historical theology at Hartford Seminary, Connecticut.

JEANNINE GRAMICK is a co-founder of New Ways Ministry.

KELBY HARRISON is an ordained minister in the Universal Fellowship of Metropolitan Community Churches, an independent scholar, and an academic consultant.

J. PATRICK HORNBECK II is chair and associate professor of theology at Fordham University.

GERARD JACOBITZ is assistant professor of theology at St. Joseph's University.

MARK D. JORDAN is the Reverend Priscilla Wood Neaves Distinguished Professor of Religion and Politics at the John C. Danforth Center at Washington University in St. Louis.

PATRICIA BEATTIE JUNG is professor of Christian ethics and the Oubri A. Poppele Professor of Health and Welfare Ministries, Saint Paul School of Theology.

PAUL F. LAKELAND is the Rev. Aloysius P. Kelley SJ Professor of Catholic Studies and director of the Center for Catholic Studies at Fairfield University.

JAMIE L. MANSON is a journalist and columnist for the *National Catholic Reporter*.

JOAN M. MARTIN is associate professor at Episcopal Divinity School.

MICHAEL A. NORKO is associate professor of psychiatry at Yale University School of Medicine.

MICHAEL JOHN PERRY is the Robert W. Woodruff Professor of Law at Emory University School of Law.

FREDERICK RODEN is associate professor of English at the University of Connecticut.

Index

Congregation for Catholic Education,
7, 48, 89, 100, 208n23, 223n36
Congregation for the Doctrine of the
Faith, 7, 34, 46–47, 48, 77, 83, 88,
92–94, 95–96, 97, 112, 113, 124, 141,
146–47, 165
Congregation for Religious, 66
conscience, 120, 130, 144, 161
Copeland, Sister M. Shawn, 171
Coriden, James A., 199n56
Cozzens, Donald, 101, 103–4, 210n2
Curb, Rosemary, 63
Curran, Charles, 7, 115, 231n1

DeBernardo, Francis, 126
Declaration on Certain Questions
Concerning Sexual Ethics, 195n20,
195n21, 196n23, 196n27, 205n13,
210n5, 220n2
Declaration on Religious Freedom,
129
Decree on Ecumenism, 87
de la Huerta, Christian, 80
Derrida, Jacques, 158, 162
Dignity (ministry), 48, 57, 61, 72
Dillon, Michelle, 57
discourses: in conflict with one
another, 27, 33, 54, 146; as modes of
organizing identity, 26, 35, 201n4;
as socially constructed, 26, 31
discrimination, 17, 124, 130
Dogmatic Constitution on the Church,
142, 183, 233n16
Dolan, Archbishop Timothy Cardinal,
166, 167
"don't ask, don't tell," 102, 214n48
Douglas, Kelly Brown, 135

Ellison, Marvin, 138
Emerging Queer Asian Religion
Scholars, 171
Employment Non-Discrimination
Act, 17
Episcopal Church, The, 48, 49

epistemology, 148
Espín, Orlando O., 170–71
exclusion policy, 110–13
experience, as theological locus,
147, 148

Farley, Margaret, 10, 116, 138, 146–47,
170, 209n3
Farrell, Pat, 83
friendship, 67
Foucault, Michel, 27, 39, 44, 53, 55; on
the Christian pastorate, 31–32, 53;
on docile bodies, 32–33, 53; History
of Sexuality, 28–32; on the
production of truth, 30

Gallup studies, 16
Gaudium et Spes. See Pastoral
Constitution on the Church in the
Modern World
George, Robert P., 10, 11
gender: identity, 11; roles, 8, 136
Giampietro, Anthony, 9
God: human person made in the
image of, 25, 88, 89, 188; Spirit of
(Holy Spirit), 58, 59
Goh, Joseph, 171
Gramick, Jeannine, 48, 166
Gregory, Bishop Wilton, 206n6
Griffin, James, 110–11
Gumbleton, Bishop Thomas, 13

Habermas, Jürgen, 38
Hanigan, James, 9, 117
Herman, Carolyn Weir, 142
Himes, Michael and Kenneth,
89–90, 91
Hollenbach, David, 8, 218n25
homophobia, 41, 50, 58
homosexual acts. See sexual activity:
same-sex activity
Humanae Vitae, 115, 116, 151,
222n22
Hunt, Mary, 14, 41, 167, 170

CATHOLIC PRACTICE IN NORTH AMERICA